MW01060147

MAVERICK
TRADING

MAVERICK TRADING

PROFESSIONAL TECHNIQUES TO CREATE GENERATIONAL WEALTH

DARREN FISCHER

JON FROHLICH

ROBB REINHOLD

New York   Chicago   San Francisco   Lisbon   London
Madrid   Mexico City   Milan   New Delhi   San Juan
Seoul   Singapore   Sydney   Toronto

The **McGraw·Hill** Companies

1 2 3 4 5 6 7 8 9 0   DOC/DOC   1 6 5 4 3 2 1

ISBN   978-0-07-178431-3
MHID   0-07-178431-4

e-ISBN   978-0-07-178434-4
e-MHID   0-07-178434-9

This publication is designed to provide accurate and authoritative information in regard to the subject matter covered. It is sold with the understanding that neither the authors nor the publisher are engaged in rendering legal, accounting, securities trading, or other professional service. If legal advice or other expert assistance is required, the services of a competent professional person should be sought.

—From a Declaration of Principles Jointly Adopted by a Committee of the
American Bar Association and a Committee of Publishers and Associations

Charts of stocks generated courtesy of www.StockCharts.com

Concepts and material in Chapter 9 courtesy of Darren Miller, Ph.D. For more information, please visit www.PsychTrader.com.

McGraw-Hill books are available at special quantity discounts to use as premiums and sales promotions or for use in corporate training programs. To contact a representative, please e-mail us at bulksales@mcgraw-hill.com.

This book is printed on acid-free paper.

CONTENTS

INTRODUCTION

For the average retail investor, the only person who has a truly vested interest in seeing that investor's portfolio grow is the investor himself. Yet Wall Street would have the masses believe that investing and trading are dangerous, that these endeavors are best left to so-called professional money managers, that the theory and practice behind managing money is too complicated for the average person, and that you can't beat the game, so just go along for the ride.

These ideas are as patently false as they are deeply ingrained in the psyche of the retail investor.

If the benchmark of the game is to match the returns of the broad markets, you can beat the game consistently and soundly with proper risk controls and some methodical doctrine.

As we were developing this book in late 2010 and early 2011, we looked back at what has transpired since the last market top in late 2007. During that period, staid American (and international) institutions were reduced to ashes—Bear Stearns: acquired at pennies on the dollar while in a shambles; Lehman Brothers: bankrupt, with people still sorting through the mess; AIG: bailed out by the U.S. government, with the taxpayers being unlikely to see a full return on their largesse; General Motors: bankrupted and nationalized.

Pension plans are grossly underfunded and are likely to remain so as a result of poor risk management and outsourcing of due diligence by the plan administrators.

Individual 401(k) plans and IRAs have lost more than half their value and are struggling to regain their former levels.

Since the market began tumbling in earnest in early 2008 alongside the U.S. housing market, people have felt poor and have had a deep distrust of the markets, and they are only now beginning to raise their heads and investing again.

This new investment and trading activity may well be short lived, as market volatility in late July and early August 2011 sent many retail traders running for cover, not knowing whom or what to trust.

In contrast, 2008 to 2010 were some of Maverick Trading's best years, with gains of more than 100 percent in 2008 as the markets plummeted, more than 50 percent in 2009, and again more than 50 percent in 2010 as the broad market returned 14 percent and change. So how did we do it?

We've seen quite a bit in our careers across a number of asset classes, both at the retail level and at the level of the institutional investor (the people who move the markets). We've consulted, counseled, and coached retail, semipro, and professional traders and fund managers on structure, strategy, and risk management techniques. We've been involved personally and/or professionally in stocks, options, bonds, foreign exchange, commodities, real estate, multistrategy hedge funds, funds of funds, private equity, and venture capital, but we have always gravitated back to trading.

We love trading. No, we really love trading. Each of us has been trading for between 10 and 15 years. Get us together around a table, and sooner rather than later the talk turns to trades that we've done. Good trades, bad trades, spectacularly wrong calls, other traders who have blown up their portfolios, traders who took three months off to travel through some distant country, traders who retired before they were 50, or 40, or 35—we talk about it all. It reminds outsiders of hunters on safari, sitting around a campfire reminiscing about their great stalks, successful but grueling hunts, and the trophies that got away.

Trading is the way we've decided to make our livings. For each of us, the adage that finding a job you love means never "working" a day in your life rings true. Because of the profession we've chosen, we have more time to spend with our families, the time and wherewithal to travel, the freedom to work nearly anywhere, and control of our financial futures.

One page in and you're thinking, "Well, yes, all well and good, but so what? I want that life, too. What's in the secret sauce?"

The secret sauce is simple in theory, and we've already given it to you: *we treat trading as a profession.* We don't dabble in the markets; this isn't a hobby, and we don't wing it. Nor do we sit hunched over in front of a massive array of computer screens, bug-eyed and sallow-faced, watching every move tick by tick.

Every trade we make has a plan *before* we execute it: we identify the setup, calculate our risk and potential reward, stick to the plan, cut our losses quickly, and take profits when our positions reach their anticipated targets.

In 2010 and 2011, we had more than 1,000 people inquire about joining Maverick Trading, from people with no trading experience to people with more than 20 years in the industry. One of the most common questions we received was, "What do you look for in a trader?" Really, the question is, "What does it take to make a good trader? What does it take to turn someone who is interested in trading into a professional trader?"

In short, we look for people who are open to learning, are disciplined or willing to learn discipline, and are willing to operate in a collegial environment. We can teach someone to trade, but only if she is willing to learn. We can lay out risk controls down to the penny, but they don't do any good if they're not implemented every time. We don't want people with delusions of grandeur or an overdeveloped ego; these are the people who implode their portfolios without taking responsibility for their own actions.

Each of us, at various times, has been humbled by the markets, performing such miracles as turning $50,000 into $25,000.

"Nice trick," you say. "Why on earth should I give up some of my hard-earned disposable income to a bunch of yahoos who have lost their own money in the past? Why don't I just answer that e-mail from that nice young man in Nigeria?"

Because we've learned from our mistakes, and you can learn from them as well without making them. The trading system contained in this book took more than a decade to develop, the lessons were hard-won, and the road was painful. More important, the system works, as our firm's performance has proven.

This is a book about trading and how to become a professional trader. It is not a book about long-term investing, nor is it a book about day trading, although you can certainly use some of the techniques and strategies in it to help you improve your performance in those endeavors. Our positions are predominantly swing trades and position trades, holding positions from a few days to a few months.

The trading system in this book relies on pattern recognition (chart reading), impeccable risk management, understanding yourself . . . and fifth-grade math. As a matter of opinion, fifth-graders would probably do fairly well because they don't overthink things and tend to follow instructions. So if you have a fifth-grader available, by all means, put her to work early and often. Our head trader, Robb Reinhold, had his son trading the e-mini futures as young as third grade, simply by explaining trends, support/resistance lines (he explained them as trampolines), and loss prevention.

If you've looked at books on technical trading and either fallen asleep or gotten ill, fear not. We don't use a laundry list of technical indicators like stochastics, Bollinger bands, Williams %R, and other such measures. We use price and volume, supply and demand, and fear and greed, with a dash of simple moving averages for flavor.

So, on to the crux of the matter: is this book for you? If you can answer yes to the following questions, then this book may be able to help you improve your trading performance.

1. Do you want a simple system with the proven ability to produce remarkable gains, year-in and year-out, regardless of market direction?
2. Do you want the opportunity to grow your portfolio with predefined risk parameters and have an opportunity to build generational wealth?
3. Are you willing to invest a few hours each week planning your trades prior to entering the orders and executing them?
4. Are you willing to establish and follow stringent risk controls and not give a bad trade "just one more day"?
5. Are you willing to take responsibility for your portfolio's performance?
6. Do you want to free up some time to spend with your family, travel, and generally enjoy life?

In all honesty, if you can't answer yes to these questions, it would be best if you found another system.

However, if you can take a moment to reflect on the answers, and you find that you can say yes to each of the questions with a clear conscience, then we welcome you to our world with open arms.

Let the journey begin.

Don't Put It All on Black: Risk Management

We don't care if you ignore every other chapter in this book and get your trading ideas by sacrificing a goat under the light of a full moon. If you don't make a commitment, right here and right now, to developing and following a comprehensive and methodical risk management strategy, please put this book down, walk over a few aisles, pick up *Roulette for Idiots*, and plan your next trip to Las Vegas. There are a multitude of casinos that would like to develop a lifelong relationship with you.

Trading without a risk management system is gambling. Gambling relies on hope. When you gamble, in the long run, the house always wins. The balance of this book will lay out in minute detail a proven system for making money in the markets, but if you don't master risk management from the beginning, we guarantee that you will lose money, regardless of the trading or investing system you decide on in the end.

INEFFECTIVE RISK CONTROL

Ineffective risk control is, if anything, more dangerous than a lack of risk controls. At least with a lack of risk controls, your emotions will let you know when the pain becomes too great, and you will liquidate your position. Adherents of ineffective risk controls spout watchwords like an oracle and will often follow their creed straight to a 55-gallon drum of Kool-Aid and an imploded portfolio.

This book is not a rehash of Warren Buffett's investment philosophy. Buffett's strategy, while successful, does not fit with our investment style. Additionally, a multitude of authors have covered and tried to emulate Buffett.

However, Buffett does have two rules that we follow:

Rule 1: Don't lose money.
Rule 2: Never forget rule 1.

Keeping this bit of wisdom in mind, we've found that we need to convince people who are new to Maverick's system to break some bad (money-losing) habits.

Dollar Cost Averaging

This is also known as DCA. Should someone suggest with a straight face that this concept is either an investment strategy or a method of risk control, run, do not walk, out of his office. Such people should not be entrusted with a piggy bank, much less with substantial amounts of capital.

In this misguided concept, you establish a position and then continue to add to that position if it begins to decline in value, thereby lowering the average unit cost of the position. The basic tenet of DCA is that you get to buy more of something with less money. We would rather buy more of something with more money.

DCA makes a very large and dangerous assumption: what goes *down, must* come *up*. Wrong, no, *nyet, nein, non*. Just take a look at Lehman Brothers (bankrupt), old General Motors (bankrupt), Citibank (down 90 percent from its all-time high), and any of a myriad of stocks that either have gone the way of the dodo bird or have failed to exceed their previous highs of several years ago.

From an objective viewpoint, every dollar that your portfolio declines in value today is one less dollar that you can use to trade tomorrow. Most amateur traders don't understand the mathematics of dollar cost averaging on losing positions. Imagine a trader who sells his winning trades after a $500 profit but lets a losing trade go against him, doubling and tripling down as the stock moves lower. When he finally has to sell the position, he will take a loss of several thousand dollars, erasing 5 to 10 of his positive trades. The negative mathematics of doubling down on losing positions ensures that the trader will have an abysmal reward/risk ratio in the end. At Maverick, we teach pyramiding in winning trades to get the mathematics working in our favor, adding to a trader's reward/risk ratio.

The arguments made by financial advisors who advocate DCA as a method of risk control have several implications that we disagree with philosophically. (1) These advisors tell you that you can't time the market, so don't worry about short-term swings. (2) These same advisors illustrate the supposed benefits of this strategy by showing examples where the stock or mutual fund is higher than your entry price when you exit the position, with the implication that you *can* time the market when you get out. If this isn't an example of talking out of both sides of your mouth, we don't know what is.

Darren: In a previous firm, I consulted with alternative asset funds seeking to raise capital from institutional investors. In 2008, I was speaking with a long-only fund manager to determine if it would be worthwhile for his firm and mine to enter into a relationship. As any fund manager would be, he was extremely excited at the prospect of gaining access to institutional capital. He gave an elaborate presentation focusing on the fact that he was a stock picker par excellence and went over his entire methodology regarding how his bottom-up approach was certain to pick winners "over the long run." For his cornerstone example, he highlighted an office supply company that was already in an established downtrend.

After listening to his presentation, I said, "Well, this looks interesting, but what do you do if you're wrong?"

His reply: "What do you mean?" A little red LED in my brain started blinking at the rapid rate.

"When would you exit the position? What would you do if this stock dropped 50 percent?"

"I'd buy more." Not with my money, I thought. I ended the call shortly afterward and politely declined interest in working with his fund in the future. That stock did, in fact, go on to fall 50 percent from where it was when the manager recommended it and has yet to recover.

Even professional managers who control millions and even billions in pension funds, endowments, and trusts can fall victim to the dangers of dollar cost averaging.

Efficient Market Theory

Proponents of the efficient market theory (EMT) hold that you can't time the market, that the price action reflects all that is known about the stock at the time, and that trying to time the market is ultimately detrimental to a portfolio. These people believe that the best investment philosophy is to systematically invest in a broad-market index fund.

Ah, the world of academia. Viewed strictly at a single point in time, from a strictly economic point of view, this idea has a certain appeal, especially immediately after significant events (such as earnings surprises, natural disasters, or management changes).

However, viewed over time and with some simple psychology, we have found that you can time the market, with remarkable accuracy. EMT fails to adequately take into account fear and greed among the market drivers (institutional investors).

Systematic Investing

Whoever first came up with the term *systematic investing* should be applauded for her marketing genius (notice that we don't say her investing acumen). This concept conditions people to think that it's acceptable to lose money. The implication is that the money manager to whom you are writing the check every month is smarter than you are. What crap.

This doesn't mean that you shouldn't put aside some income every month to increase your trading capital. It just means that we don't feel it is prudent to blindly send a check to a mutual fund every month, regardless of its performance.

Systematic investing is an offshoot of dollar cost averaging. Think of it as DCA on a much broader scale with a marketing spin. In plain language, the mutual fund people are saying, "Send us a portion of your money on a regular basis, regardless of our performance, because we know better. Investing is dangerous for you, but easy for us, and you'll just screw it up if you try to go it alone. Don't pay any attention to the man behind the curtain. Short-term losses are to be expected; don't ask about underperformance, outright losses, window dressing, our modest management fee, the marketing fees we charge to let you and others know how great we are, or any of the other fees we use to bleed you dry and then tell you that losses aren't our fault."

The cold reality is that 75 to 80 percent (depending on the year) of so-called professional mutual fund managers *underperform* their benchmark indices. To add insult to injury, the fund managers get to pick which index they benchmark to.

"But what about peer rankings?" you say. That's like putting a bunch of underperformers in the room and ranking them by how little they underperformed.

Mutual fund charters often stipulate that the fund will be fully invested (less than 5 percent in cash) at all times. That's like saying, "You *will* stay on that ship at all times, even if it is sinking."

Blind Diversification

This theory holds that if you pick individual stocks, you should have some exposure to a variety of sectors (for example, having five technology companies in your portfolio is not diversification, but having one company each from the technology, consumer staples, financial, energy, and industrial sectors is diversification) because various sectors come into and out of favor in the market, and as a few stocks lose value, the others will gain value. This practice offers some protection in a bull market, but what happens in a massive bear market where *everything* loses value?

You will see shortly that we trade our portfolio using a basket of positions. That is not the same as diversification. We are actively picking strong sectors and weak sectors and taking positions accordingly.

Hope

Hope is the first form of risk control for many new retail investors. The hope method involves blindly buying a stock, often taking too large a position, and then hoping the value increases. The hope method usually results in a new investor watching a position decline in value day after day. Occasional up days are met with maniacal glee; the down days are met with increasing gloom and stress.

When the position moves substantially against them, such as a 10 percent correction or, even worse, a significant gap down, adherents of the hope method say, "OK, I can weather this. I'll just wait until it gets back to the price I bought it at and then get out with a breakeven. I can live with that."

Unfortunately, these investors have just become part of the herd. All the other investors, including institutions, who bought at an unsustainable high are thinking the same thing and acting the same way.

Often a stock will approach its previous high, probably where the investors bought it, and then fail to break through to a new high. Then the mantra among the hope investors becomes, "Just one more day."

"Just one more day" turns into a week with further losses. The week becomes a month. The trade becomes an "investment for the long term." Dollar cost averaging starts to look like a good option. The losing position becomes a substantial portion of the portfolio. The pain mounts, and these investors are checking the position every 30 minutes. Finally, the pain becomes unbearable, and they capitulate and wind up selling at the bottom.

All of these are ineffective risk controls. They do nothing to actually control risk and actually contribute to and reinforce losses.

WHAT CAN YOU CONTROL?

To clarify a few things:

1. You are a retail investor/trader. Your purchase or sale of a few hundred or a few thousand shares of a stock will not appreciably move the market, either igniting a bull run or precipitating a catastrophic sell-off.
2. Institutional investors (pension funds, market makers, endowments, long-only funds, mutual funds, and hedge funds) are not actively out to make you lose money. Their primary concern is making money for their funds and their clients. Quite simply, they don't care if you come along for the ride or get run over by the bus.
3. You cannot anticipate every piece of information that will affect the markets, so don't try. You don't control what goes on in another country, what a company's earnings announcement will be, what an analyst will say about said earnings, or how the institutional investors will react to any piece of news.
4. The only things that you can control are which positions you take and how much capital you are willing to risk on each position. That's it.

Of the two things that you can control, position selection and the amount of capital you are willing to risk, the amount of capital you are willing to risk is more important. You will never be correct in 100 percent of your trades or investments. When you are starting out, you will be doing well if 50 percent of your trades are profitable. As you gain more experience, a good year will be 60 percent correct trades. Any year you bat over .700 will be a year to remember. The sooner you accept these statistics and move on, the sooner you will be profitable.

To make trading a long-term, profitable career, you need to adopt the mantra, "I would rather be profitable than right."

NOT ALL LOSSES ARE CREATED EQUAL

A loss is a loss is a loss, isn't it? No. There are many factors that can cause a loss. Price, timing, direction, momentum, volatility, and external factors can all cause losses. In the following chapters, we will be discussing strategies primarily involving options. You will find situations where you may ultimately be correct on direction, but you are off on timing, and the decay in time value makes the position lose value. Likewise, volatility in a position may make certain strategies and tactics prohibitively expensive, so that the reward/risk ratio doesn't make sense. In other instances, you may find an outperforming stock with an excellent setup, but a broad-market move may move the position against you.

As mentioned previously, an experienced trader, using established guidelines and entry points, should expect 60 percent correct trades. Put another way, even when you do everything correctly, four out of every ten trades will lose money. The losing percentage is even higher for a trader who trades by the seat of his pants and bases his decisions on emotion rather than rules.

A trade that moves against you and is exited at a predetermined loss after being properly selected with a high-probability setup and with the appropriate strategy is an acceptable loss. Letting a trade move against you when you have no predefined loss limit is not an acceptable loss.

TRADING AS A BASKET

No trader enters a trade expecting to lose money. Ask a trader right before or right after she enters a trade what she expects to happen, and you will universally hear that the trade will be spectacularly profitable. Unfortunately, for a significant percentage of trades, this is not the case.

Trading as a long-term career is a game of statistics. Some trades will be profitable, and some trades will generate losses. The common cliché is to let your winners run and to limit your losses. This is easier said than done, especially for traders who have never been taught risk control.

A common and career-shortening practice of new and/or undisciplined traders is to devote all their available capital to a single trade at a time. Additionally, maintenance margin requirements typically allow traders to increase their position after an overnight holding period.

Increasing a position in this manner can produce spectacular gains, but more often it produces spectacular losses, unnecessary stress, and interference with a trader's objectivity.

For example, using some system (which one is immaterial at this point), a trader identifies what looks like a good trade in XYZ Corporation. Let's say he has $10,000 in a margin account, the overnight margin requirement is 50 percent, and the maintenance margin requirement is 25 percent.

Absolutely convinced that this trade will produce a profit, the trader buys $20,000 of XYZ (half of which is his $10,000 and half is the broker's money). The next day, the stock hasn't moved appreciably. As he looks at his trading power, the brokerage says he has another $10,000 in buying power at his disposal [his $10,000 account less $5,000 (25 percent maintenance margin on

$20,000 in XYZ stock) divided by 50 percent (the overnight margin requirement)]. He buys another $10,000 of XYZ.

On Day 3, he finds that he has another $5,000 in buying power, so he adds to his position again, ending up with $35,000 in XYZ.

After the bell on Day 3, an event occurs—let's say an earnings announcement—and XYZ gaps down 5 percent. The value of his XYZ position is now $33,250, a loss of $1,750. A 5 percent drop in XYZ decimated his account by 17.5 percent. Additionally, because of the volatility, the brokerage may increase the maintenance margin requirements on XYZ, and the trader may face a margin call or forced liquidation. This series of actions is summarized in Table 1-1.

Additionally, the trader now needs to make trades equal to a 21 percent gain just to get back to his starting position.

Typically, one of three things will happen: the trader will make more all-or-nothing bets (often incurring even greater losses), he will throw in the towel and not trade anymore, or he will learn risk controls and methodically work his way back to profitability.

It can't be stressed enough that at least 40 percent of your trades will generate losses. It may be the first 40 percent, the last

Table 1-1   Results of Over-Leveraged Trading Actions

Day	Trading Cash	Initial Margin	Buying Power	Value of Shares Purchased	Maintenance Margin	Position Value
1	$10,000	50%	$20,000	$20,000	25%	$20,000
2	$10,000	50%	$10,000	$10,000	25%	$30,000
3	$10,000	50%	$5,000	$5,000	25%	$35,000
4	$8,250	50%	$250	$0	25%	$33,250
Profit/Loss	−$1,750					−$1,750
	(−17.5%)					(−5.0%)

40 percent, or interspersed throughout the trading activity of a year. Despite all the preparation that you will do prior to a trade, you never know whether the trade will be a winner or a loser until it is done.

The key is to not incur a loss in any single trade that is so catastrophic that it knocks you out of your trading career.

Rather than devoting all your preparation and effort to finding a single trade at a time and then committing all your capital to that trade, the better, safer, and less stressful method is to find and make multiple trades at the same time, ending up with a basket of positions.

At Maverick Trading, we will typically look at three to six setups per week, of which one to four will trigger (we will discuss trade triggers at a later time), and we will commonly have between four and ten open positions at any one time. Over the course of a year, we will make between 150 and 200 trades.

This practice forces traders to continually refresh their portfolios, eliminating languishing and unprofitable positions to free up capital for new, potentially profitable setups.

Figure 1-1 is a fairly common statistical distribution of trades for a trader who does everything correctly.

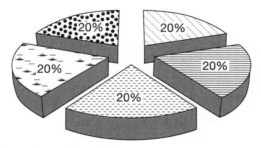

◻ Gain of more than 2:1
◫ Gain of between 1:1 and 2:1
◻ Gain of between breakeven and 1:1
▬ Loss of up to 50% of risk capital
▪ Loss of between 50% and 100% of allocated risk capital

Figure 1-1   Typical Trade Distribution

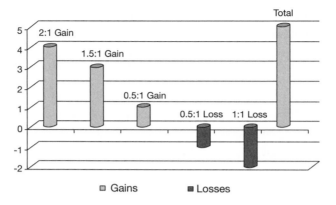

Figure 1-2   Portfolio Impact from Expected Trade Distribution

How does this win-loss distribution affect a portfolio? We'll cover the actual allocation of risk capital shortly, but for the sake of illustration, let's say that a trader was willing to risk $1 on each of 10 trades with the expected win-loss distribution. The outcome is shown in Figure 1-2.

So, of 10 trades, we have 6 winners and 4 losers. On $10 risked, we have $8 in gains and $3 in losses, for a net of $5 in gains: in all, a 50 percent return.

Not possible, not sustainable, not realistic, too risky, you say. Well, Maverick's system has done this, consistently.

REWARD, RISK, AND POSITION SIZE

We'll cover how to identify setups with favorable reward/risk parameters in the following chapters, but the important concept to grasp right now is that we look for situations where our anticipated reward is two to three times what we're willing to risk.

This doesn't mean that we're going to buy a $10 stock and expect that it will run to $30 or $40. One, looking for a 300 to 400 percent move in a stock is a fool's errand; two, it will take too much time; and three, it will tie up too much capital.

What we're looking for are setups where it appears that there is $1 of downside and the potential for $3 or more of upside.

We're far more likely to find a position where the stock is trading at $50 and has strong support at $49, but has the potential to make a $3 move to the upside. A 6 percent move in a stock over a few days to a few weeks is infinitely more likely than a 300 percent move in the same period.

Think of risk control as a Las Vegas game where you get to write the rules of the game. Here are the rules:

1. The house doesn't care if you count the cards and identify setups where the odds are in your favor. If the odds aren't in your favor, you don't have to play. This is the pattern recognition (chart reading) portion of Maverick's system.
2. You can bet small amounts of capital, let's say $1. This is the benefit of relying on options.
3. You're looking for a setup where it is likely that if you bet $1, you can make $3 or more.
4. The winning hand plays out over several cards. If it looks like you're starting to lose, you can choose to pay the dealer only 30 cents.

You couldn't pry us away from the table if we could play this game in Las Vegas. This is our idea of risk control.

What happens when the position moves against you and your position has declined to the maximum you are willing to risk?

You exercise your stop and walk away. You don't hang in there. You don't give it "just one more day." You exit, take the small loss up front, and go find another opportunity.

Retail traders often develop emotional attachments to positions. This happens for a variety of reasons, but it all boils down to the natural inclination to want to be right about a trade. Forget about being right all the time; concentrate on being consistently profitable each week, month, and year, and over your whole career.

As a word of warning, you will have positions move back to profitability as soon as you have exited. It happens; it's infuriating, and you will regret exiting the position.

But far more often, the position will continue to move against your original thesis, and you will be happy that you exited it.

Although we will go into far greater depth later in this book on how to set stops and contingent orders, it is imperative to ingrain in your mind that you must identify your maximum risk before you enter a trade, and when your stop is reached, the trade is done.

Hand in hand with defining your risk is determining your position size. We've already discussed the importance of trading in a basket. There is no set number of trades that you need to have active at any one time. We have had as many as 15 active trades at once and as few as 1, depending on market conditions and our outlook.

Your position size is determined by your risk tolerance. A more conservative trader will risk less per trade; a more aggressive trader will risk more per trade. So what is the magic number for you?

You must determine your own style of trading and what your risk tolerance is. We have found that a good rule of thumb is between 1 and 3 percent of total portfolio value per trade.

As an example, say you have a $10,000 portfolio and your risk tolerance is medium. The recommendation would be to risk 2 percent of your portfolio value per trade, or $200 per trade.

So let's say you identify a stock that is trading at $20, with $1 of downside and $3 of upside. You are willing to risk $200 per trade, so your maximum position size would be 200 shares ($200 maximum risk divided by $1 per share downside risk). Your expected reward is $600 (200 shares multiplied by $3 potential upside).

If you identified a $20 stock with $1.50 of downside and $4.50 of upside, your maximum position size would be 133 shares ($200 maximum risk divided by $1.50 per share downside risk).

The amount you are willing to risk should and will fluctuate with the value of your portfolio. If, for example, you have a good month and your portfolio grows from $10,000 to $11,000 and your risk tolerance has not changed from 2 percent of total portfolio value, then on the next set of trades you make, you would be willing to risk $220 per trade, up from $200. Likewise, if you have a bad month and the value of your portfolio falls to $9,000, then you would then be willing to risk only $180 per trade, down from $200.

Another precept of risk control to keep in mind is to start small. This is a new system for you, and you will have some kinks to work out once you put it into practice. No matter how many times you read the guidelines, there will be some things that are not completely clear until you've used them a few times on your actual trading platform, using real money.

There is nothing wrong with sizing your positions so that you risk only 0.5 to 1.0 percent per trade when you are first starting out, or until you determine what your true risk appetite is.

The final rule to keep in mind is: if you are worried about a position, it is too big. Reduce the position or liquidate it.

In periods of market uncertainty, like greatly overextended markets, tops, and bottoms, we will routinely cut our position sizing in half until the market asserts or reasserts the direction in which it wants to go.

Strict, methodical risk control will reduce the stress that is common in trading, especially for beginning traders. Leaving the emotion and the human factor out of the decision to liquidate a position will help ensure that you don't get carried away and let a small loss become a large loss.

This will let you regroup and trade another day.

2

PLAYGROUND ECONOMICS: DETERMINING MARKET DIRECTION

THE LONG AND THE SHORT OF IT

Long and *short* are industry terms for buy and sell. When you enter a long position, you buy something with the idea that its price will rise and then you will sell it at some time in the future, making a profit. When you enter a short position, you sell something with the idea that its price will fall and then you will buy it back for less than you sold it for, also making a profit.

Since you'll be trading your portfolio as a basket of positions, the usual case will be that you have some long positions (which you bought to open them) and some short positions (which you sold to open them).

Depending on the conditions of the broad market at any given time, your portfolio will also have a long bias, meaning that your portfolio is skewed to benefit from a rising market, a short bias, where your portfolio will benefit from a falling market, or a neutral bias, where your portfolio is equally weighted in both long and short positions.

Trading and investing systems themselves have biases. Most are biased toward the long side, meaning that they work best in a rising (bull) market. We term ourselves *Market Agnostic*, meaning that we don't care if the market is rising, falling, or moving sideways. We seek to make money in any market and will adjust our portfolios accordingly to take advantage of the conditions at hand.

Later on, when we discuss specific options techniques, you'll see that each complete position has a long side (called a *leg*), where you've bought something in the anticipation that it will rise in value, and a short side (leg), where you've sold something in the anticipation that the value will fall so that it will be worth less when you buy it back.

Do you have to short? What if you're used to and comfortable with going long?

Markets go up and markets go down. Never to short anything, whether it be stocks themselves or options related to stock, is like sitting down at a grand piano and playing every other note of a sonata. The individual notes may sound nice, but the whole piece is disjointed and doesn't sound very attractive.

When it is done correctly (and we'll give you the guidelines you need to do it correctly), shorting allows you to profit on both sides of the market, allows you to fully define both your risk and your reward, and allows you to decrease your risk in individual positions.

For any trader who wishes to make a consistent return from the market, shorting stock (or making bearish trades) is essential, as the markets can have periods of time lasting weeks and months in which the majority of stocks decline. One prospective trader who was seeking to join our firm told our head trader that he could not short stock or enter any bearish positions for religious reasons. Our head trader advised him to get into another business, as long-term trading success will be very difficult without the ability to be bearish on the market at appropriate times.

DEMAND AND SUPPLY SEESAW

For a minute, forget everything you know, were taught, or thought you knew about economics. We're going to cut through most of the esoteric fluff and get right to the heart of the matter. All we need is a schoolyard playground (if there are any around anymore).

In this playground, you have one seesaw and two children, Demand and Supply. Demand always sits on the left; Supply always sits on the right. Time moves from left to right. The direction in which price moves is always to the right, indicated by the arrow on the right side of the seesaw.

Today, Demand and Supply both weigh about the same, so the seesaw looks like Figure 2-1.

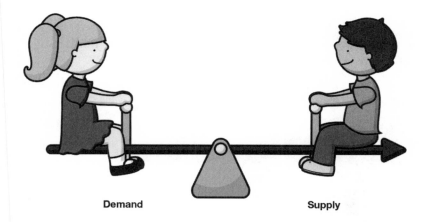

Demand   **Supply**

Figure 2-1

You can see that since Demand and Supply both weigh the same, the seesaw is level, and price remains constant and level.

The next day, Demand grabs a cookie on her way out the door, so now she weighs more than Supply, as in Figure 2-2.

Since Demand weighs more than Supply, price will rise as well.

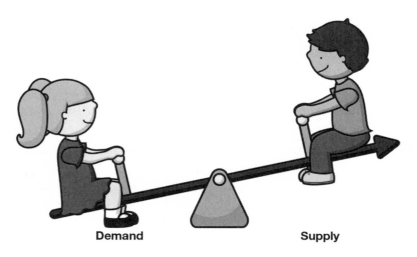

Demand   **Supply**

Figure 2-2

Supply got tired of being stuck in the air all day, so the next day, he grabbed two extra cookies on his way out the door (see Figure 2-3).

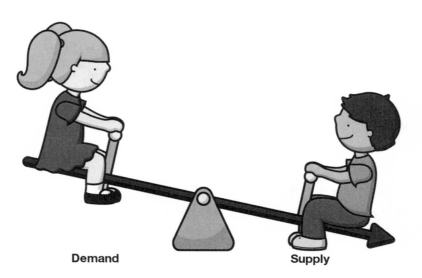

Demand   **Supply**

Figure 2-3

Now, since Supply weighs more than Demand, price will decline.

Occasionally, Demand will jump on the seesaw, totally surprising Supply. When that happens, Supply will sometimes get thrown into the air, which is called a gap up in price (see Figure 2-4).

Demand   **Supply**

Figure 2-4

Likewise, Supply will sometimes surprise Demand by jumping on the seesaw, causing a gap down in price (see Figure 2-5).

Now let's expand the concept from two children called Demand and Supply to an entire schoolyard of kids with just two names, Demand and Supply. Some will be fairly small kindergarteners and some will be some fairly beefy fifth-graders, with a whole spectrum in between.

The combined weight of all the children who are on the seesaw at once is the same thing as volume in a stock.

Demand   Supply

Figure 2-5

You see this all the time in the market. Two roughly equal-sized children are quietly and happily playing on the seesaw, with not much movement in price either way. Then suddenly one of the larger children becomes attracted to the seesaw and jumps on one side, spiking volume and causing a price movement.

This concept holds true for stocks, the sectors those stocks are in, and the broad market as a whole. When the weight of demand is greater than the weight of supply day after day, prices rise. Conversely, when the weight of supply is greater than the weight of demand over time, prices fall.

THREE ESCALATORS

Elementary school children make great investing teachers. Take a couple of them to a multistory mall or department store and turn them loose. Sooner or later they will find the escalators. The next logical activity is, of course, escalator races.

In the course of an afternoon, children learn that when you run up an escalator that is moving up, you get to the next level more quickly than if you stand still for the ride. They also learn that when you run down an escalator that is going down, you get to the lower level faster than if you stand still.

The next lesson is that when you walk up an escalator that is going down, you can go nowhere for quite a long time until you finally get tired and end up back at the bottom. The final lesson is that if you run up an escalator that is going down, you can get to the top, but you'll be expending a lot of energy for not much gain.

The same lessons that apply in escalator races apply in trading: 'tis much easier to go with the flow than to fight the escalator. The mall cops don't hassle you as much, either.

Imagine that there are three escalators side by side. One is labeled Broad Market, the next is labeled Sector, and the last is labeled Stock (see Figure 2-6).

When all three escalators are going the way you want to go, you can get there much more quickly than if one or more of the escalators are working against you.

The general rule is that when you are looking for a trade, at least two of the three escalators must be going the way you want to go. If one escalator is working against you, you don't want to be as aggressive as when all three are with you.

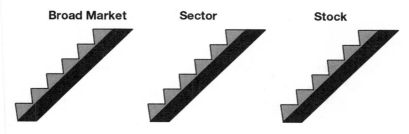

Figure 2-6

Here are some examples.

In Figure 2-7, all three escalators are moving upward. You could safely take a long position in the stock with a high probability that the stock price will move upward.

Broad Market   **Sector**   **Stock**

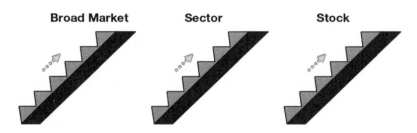

Figure 2-7

In Figure 2-8, the broad market is moving down, but the sector and the stock itself are in uptrends. This commonly happens when investors seek to become defensive in the early stages of a broad-market pullback or bear market. You could safely enter a long position in the stock.

Broad Market   **Sector**   **Stock**

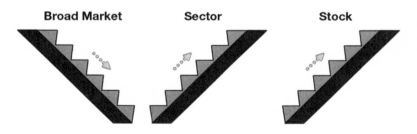

Figure 2-8

In Figure 2-9, the broad market is in an uptrend, and the particular stock is in an uptrend as well, but the sector is in a downtrend. Money is flowing into the market, out of the sector, but into the stock. This usually happens when there is a best-in-show stock that is dominating its industry. Money will flow out of

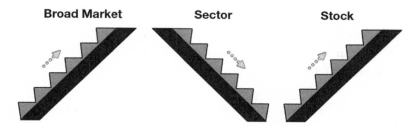

Figure 2-9

its competitors and into the outperforming stock in the sector. You could establish a long position in the stock in this scenario, but there are probably hundreds of other stocks out there in other sectors that are attracting a lot of capital. If you do enter the trade, you should be less aggressive and be prepared to exit the position if the stock itself begins to show signs of weakness. Even in an outperforming company, money flow out of a particular sector can taint even the best performers.

You generally would not enter a position in the setup in Figure 2-10. Money is flowing into the broad market and the sector, but the individual stock is in a downtrend, with money flowing out of it. This situation occurs in chronically underperforming companies. You don't want to take a long position in the stock because it is in a downtrend, but you don't necessarily want to take a short position because of the money flowing into the broad market and the sector. A better option would be to enter a long position in the ETF (exchange-traded fund) of the particular sector.

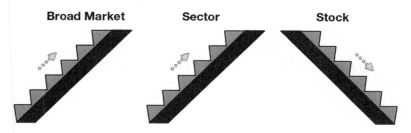

Figure 2-10

Figure 2-11 shows the perfect situation in which to short a stock. Money is flowing out everywhere. In a situation like this, you can continue to short for a long time until one of the escalators reverses.

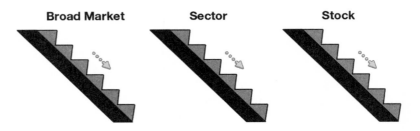

Figure 2-11

Scenarios like the one in Figure 2-12 occur frequently in bull markets, where the overall market continues to trend upward, but sectors within the broad market rotate into and out of favor. You can take a short position in the stock with a high probability that the stock will continue downward in the near future.

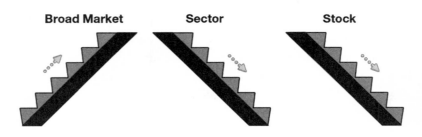

Figure 2-12

In Figure 2-13, we see a broad-market downtrend, but an outperforming sector with a downtrending stock. This is often a shortable position, but you need to be aware that the money flowing into the sector may eventually reach the stock, halting its decline.

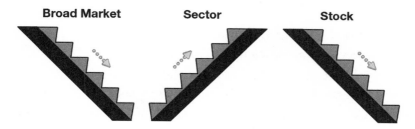

Figure 2-13

Finally, in Figure 2-14, we have a downtrending market, a downtrending sector, and an uptrending stock. As tempting as it might be, you most likely would not want to short the stock. Even in bear markets, selected stocks still garner interest and demand, often for long and irrational periods of time. The better position would be to short the sector ETF.

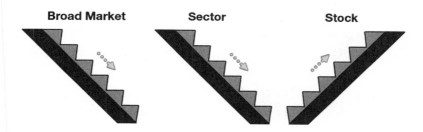

Figure 2-14

PURE ENERGY

For the next concept, you'll need a school-age child (between 5 and 12); a medium-size hill with trees, bushes, gopher holes, and other interesting things; and a can of caffeinated soda with a large amount of high-fructose corn syrup (we use Coke, symbol KO).

Hand the child the can of Coke and tell him to go to the top of the hill, then watch what he does.

Most likely, he'll run partway up the hill until something catches his attention, and then he'll stop and investigate. He might backtrack down the hill a short way if he passed something that caught his attention. After a short while, he'll race up the hill a little more until he gets a little winded.

He's a little hot and a little tired, and he wants to take a short break. He stops running and investigates something else that catches his attention. Then he cracks open the Coke and drinks it down. That little metabolism needs fuel.

Rest, investigate, poke around, drink some more Coke, and then . . . BAM. Sugar rush, and it's off to the races again, straight to the top of the hill. Mission accomplished.

Once he gets to the top of the hill, call him back down. One of two things will happen.

He will either race straight back down the hill, hell-bent for leather, or he will walk down steadily, not pausing much because he saw everything of interest on the way up. If it's been a long day, he may take a few short breaks. Either way, he gets down much more quickly than he went up.

Markets, sectors, and stocks act the same way. As much as we would like them to, they never get to where we want them to go as quickly or in as straight a line as we would like.

Like the boy on the hill, stocks build energy and expend energy. They need time to rest in order to build more energy to continue their travels. They will go a little way up (or down), get tired, meander, explore, take a break, and then continue their journeys.

This concept of energy in stocks plays an important role as we explore Maverick's system and put it into practice. Just remember, a pause in a narrow range is a building of energy, and movement either way is an expending of energy.

THE VIEW FROM ON HIGH: MAVERICK'S TOP-DOWN APPROACH

In order to be successful, you need to trade the market that's in front of you, not the market that you would like to see. Remember the mantra: "I would rather be profitable than right."

Another item to remember is, "Markets can remain irrational longer than you can remain solvent."

In short, don't fight the trend. There are traders out there who consistently make money in countertrend trading. However, they are few and far between, and they buy quart bottles of Maalox. We would rather forgo the peptic ulcers and sleepless nights and capitalize on the trends.

As we discussed in the previous section, on the Three Escalators, having a stock that is in an uptrend or a downtrend is not enough in and of itself to take a position, either long or short. You want to have as many factors working for you as possible. Remember Chapter 1 and the rules for risk control that we wrote for our imaginary Las Vegas game: you get to count the cards.

Why Top-Down and Not Bottom-Up?

Simply, over the years, we've found top-down investing to be easier and more profitable. We've found that the macro picture informs the micro picture more consistently than looking at it from the other end of the telescope.

The large institutional investors determine the direction of the markets, the sectors, and the individual stocks that make up those sectors. These institutional investors employ armies of analysts and invest billions of dollars in economic and stock-centric research. These analysts are the ones who pore over earnings reports, conference calls, economic reports, legal proceedings, news, and rumors. There is no reason for us to invest time and money to repeat this same research when the actions of the institutions will let us know what all their research showed. We're not in the game to move the markets; we're just along for the ride, hopping on whatever bus is fastest at the time.

There are some traders out there who wait with bated breath for every scrap of news that emerges concerning their positions. The natural reaction for these traders is to view every bit of news they see as being complimentary to the position they've taken, long or short. After all, everyone wants to be right, right?

For these traders, each bit of news translates into a piece of the puzzle that becomes, in their minds, a self-fulfilling prophecy or, better yet, a self-licking ice cream cone. There is a strong tendency to become emotionally attached to your positions when you are using a bottom-up approach. Traders begin to think and say such things as: "This is a great company; why doesn't it attract institutional sponsorship?" or "This is such a dog. I can't believe it keeps going up."

At Maverick, we don't care what the news is; we care only about the reaction to it. We often bring up the concept that every investor or trader out there is looking at essentially the same information (unless your name is Martha Stewart), but they're coming up with two completely different decisions on whether to buy or sell the stock. After you conclude your research, you decide that it is a great company and a great time to buy. We, on the other hand, after our research, have concluded that the company is garbage and is a great short. Which one of us is right? Easy. The market will show us who is right. If the market goes up, you were right. If the market goes down, we were right. You could write a 55-page essay giving all the reasons that you should have been right. But remember, we would rather be profitable than right. That's why we look at things from the top down.

The first step in our Top-Down Approach is to look at the broad market as a whole. To do this, you'll pull up charts of the S&P 500 Index, the Nasdaq Composite, and the Dow Jones Industrial Average. All you're looking for is whether money is flowing into the markets or out of the markets—who is bigger on the demand-supply seesaw. The question you want to answer is: in the past three months, has the broad market gone up or down?

Here is an example. In Figure 2-15, we can see that from December 1 to February 1, the broad market has been moving up. Demand has been greater than supply, and money is flowing into the market.

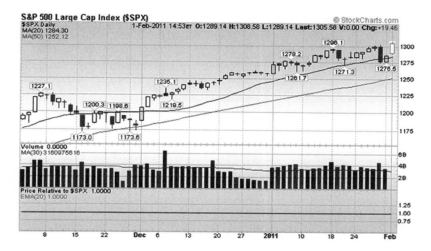

Figure 2-15   The Broad Market

If the market has been going up, your portfolio will have a bias to the long side. If the market has been going down, your portfolio will have a bias to the short side. Notice that we don't say that you'll be completely long or completely short. We'll explain why shortly.

The next step in the Top-Down Approach is to identify strengths and weaknesses within the broad market. The method for accomplishing this is to view the individual sectors.

The next activity is to pull up charts of S&P 500 sector ETFs. You need to determine what each sector is doing: moving up, moving down, or moving sideways. Additionally, you need to determine which sectors are the best performers and which sectors are the worst performers.

In Figure 2-16, we can see that for the past 68 trading days (about three months), the top-performing sector has been energy, gaining just over 15 percent during that time. Also, we can see that the worst-performing sectors have been utilities and consumer staples, with both being down about 7.5 percent during the same period.

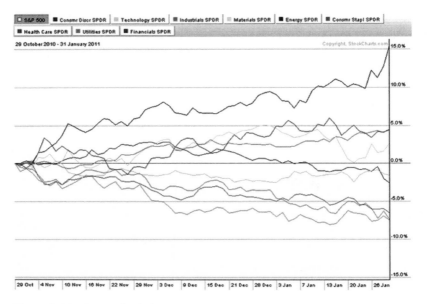

Figure 2-16   Sector Analysis

From this simple analysis, we now have three sectors that we can look to for some candidates. We're going to look for an opportunity to enter some long positions in the energy sector and to enter some short positions in consumer staples.

Before we do that, you probably have a few questions or objections. Most likely, these objections are along the lines of:

"But energy can't keep going up. Energy is too expensive here. Don't I want something cheaper?"

"Surely consumer staples and utilities have bottomed. Doesn't this represent a buying opportunity?"

The answers are no and no.

One thing we've learned, and the market has proven correct, is that money will keep flowing into a sector, or out of a sector, until it stops doing so.

The reasons behind this are simple. Traders working for institutional investors make their bonuses, and, more important, keep their jobs, based on how well they perform (that is, how much money they make for their firm).

Remember that these institutions, as a whole, pay billions of dollars for bottom-up market research, and they want to get a return on this investment, so they have to put it to use.

The way it works at institutions is that the analysts present their reports and make their cases for certain sectors or stocks to an investment committee at the institution.

The committee then makes the decision on what to buy and how large a position the firm wants to take. These aren't small positions, either. There is so much capital in these institutions that they can't afford to buy issues in 100-share lots, or even 1,000-share blocks. An order for 100,000 shares of a stock trading around $50 would not be out of the norm. That's $5 million just for one order.

After the decision is made on what to buy and how much to buy, the order then goes to the traders at the institution.

Where we can be surgical in our decisions, because we're wielding a scalpel, these institutional traders are wielding two-handed claymores. They can't get into or out of a position quickly without disrupting the market. They just have too much capital. If the trader puts the whole order out in the market at once, she'll spike the price, increasing the cost to her firm, decreasing the potential profit, lowering her bonus, and upsetting her family and her firm. She could even lose her job, get a divorce, and end up out on the street, homeless and unemployed.

Now go back up one level to the investment committee. The people on the investment committee have equal incentives to perform better than their peers and/or against a benchmark. If the investment committee picks a bad sector or a bad stock, the firm can't get out of it quickly, either, unless the committee members want to ram the order through, drop the price dramatically, and lose even more money, bonus, family, job, and so on.

Traders often have some discretionary funds that they can put to work in something they like, and the investment committee, especially in mutual funds, is usually getting more money to work with on a monthly basis.

The net result of all this is that when an institution finds an investment that is working, it continues to throw money at that investment until it no longer works. If it ain't broke, don't fix it. Likewise, when it has a losing position, it will often be loath to put more money into it and will try to liquidate the position as quickly as possible.

Traders and investment committees throughout the industry will pick up on one another's trades and ride one another's coattails, which is why you see the same stocks mentioned repeatedly in the news.

Money attracts money in the market, up until the point where it just doesn't anymore. Losses attract losses in the market, up until the point where the institutions feel that they just can't let a deal go past.

This brings us to a recurring theme within Maverick Trading: trade the market that's in front of you, not the one you think it should be.

That said, the third and final part of Maverick's Top-Down Approach is to select specific positions to take. As our market and sector analysis showed, we are looking for some long positions in the energy sector and some short positions in the consumer staples sector.

This is the point where a good stock screener is helpful. A screener that gives you access to thumbnail charts is also helpful in sorting through a large number of stocks in a short period of time. In addition to screening for sector and industry, there are a few other criteria that you want to screen for as well.

- **Price.** Except in rare instances, you should set your screener to show only stocks with prices above $20. First, the majority of lower-priced stocks don't garner institutional attention, and this will be important, as we will see shortly. Second, since we will primarily be using options, you want the strike price of the options to work for you, not against you. Nearly all $10 stocks have options strike prices in $2.50 increments, but so will $25 stocks and usually $50 stocks. This means that the same $2.50 move represents a 25 percent move for a $10 stock, a 10 percent move for a $25 stock, and a 5 percent move for a $50 stock. Taking this even further, even at the larger strike intervals of higher-priced stocks, like the $10 intervals in strike prices in $300 and $600 stocks (think Apple and Google), each strike then represents only a 3 percent move (Apple) or even a 1.66 percent move (Google). Your chances of correctly anticipating a move of 5 percent or less are exponentially better than your chances of anticipating a 25 percent move.

- **Volume.** Look only at stocks that have an average volume of more than 500,000 shares per day. Below that level, the market for the stock is so thin that you will have a wide range between the bid (what market makers are willing to pay for the stock) and the ask (what market makers are willing to take for the stock). In very liquid stocks, the spread between the bid and the ask is often as low as $0.01. In extremely illiquid stocks, the bid-ask spread could be as large as $0.25 to $0.50. That's $25 to $50 for a lot of 100 shares. Likewise, the bid-ask spread in the corresponding options will be proportionally as wide. You want to make money as soon as possible, not $25 to $50 after you enter the position.

- **Optionable and shortable**. We use options, and we use both sides of the market. You don't want to spend time researching a potential position, only to find out that there are no options available or that you can't play the short side of the trade.

To continue our example, we are searching for a company in the energy sector that looks like it will rise in price. We input our criteria into our stock screener and get about 30 different stocks that meet those criteria.

One stock that meets our criteria is Petrohawk Energy (symbol HK), shown in Figure 2-17.

Here we can see that Petrohawk has followed its sector nicely, gaining 23 percent from its low in November to its last close and outperforming the energy sector as a whole. This would be a good candidate because it is breaking through to new highs. Remember that institutions continue to pour money into what works until it doesn't work anymore.

The process is essentially the same on the short side, except that on the short side, we are looking for pronounced weakness. We've already identified the two weakest sectors in the past three months: utilities and consumer staples. For our example, we'll look in consumer staples for a stock that seems to be in an established downtrend.

Figure 2-17

We go back to the stock screener we're using and input our screening criteria: consumer staples for the sector, average volume over 500,000, price over $20, and stocks that are both optionable and shortable.

After our screen, we come up with about 50 candidates that meet the criteria we searched for. That may sound like quite a few, and you may be intimidated at first, but remember that you're just glancing at the chart of the stock to find the weakest examples. If you use a screener that allows you to view a thumbnail of the chart, this process goes much more quickly.

In identifying candidates, practice makes perfect and speeds up the process. This will also be easier after you've read the upcoming chapter on chart reading. In the beginning, your tendency will be to pore over each chart. After some practice, you'll be able to spend about a second on each chart, picking some candidates and discarding others.

After looking at the candidates that met our criteria, we've identified General Mills (symbol GIS) as a likely candidate to become a profitable short position. Figure 2-18 shows the chart.

Figure 2-18

Right here, General Mills is a fairly good candidate to watch for a few days to see if it develops into a situation where it would be highly probable that we could make some money on the short side. GIS is sitting right near its lows for the past three months. Over that time period, it has consistently underperformed compared to the broad market.

Here is a secret that will save you a lot of money in the future: you won't always find a clear setup to make a case for a long position, a short position, or even a neutral position. Sometimes you will have a market that is trending one way and a sector that is trending the same way, but none of the candidates that your stock screener produces will show a clearly defined trend or pattern. Price action at the tops and bottoms of a market can become disjointed and erratic. When this happens, don't worry. Move on to a different sector or don't trade. The key is to not force a bad position. There will be plenty of candidates throughout the year.

Maverick's Top-Down Approach forms the basis for the rest of Maverick's system. Each week you should look at how the markets have developed over the previous week. Even if you don't intend on trading in the next few days, you should take a look at the charts and learn what the broad market has been doing, what sectors have been strong and what sectors have been weak, and what were the top performers in the strong sectors and the weak performers in the weak sectors. You're always looking for relative strength and weakness.

This technique gives you a free ride on the backs of the institutional investors, who, if you remember, have paid a lot of money for an army of analysts to conduct research. Let the institutions do the heavy lifting for you and use every edge you can get.

3

Reading the Tea Leaves: An Introduction to Chart Reading

TRIBES OF TRADING

We are chartists. This is not a political organization or a religious sect (although some of our differently inclined colleagues would beg to differ). All it means is that we look at charts to determine the most probable course of action for a stock. It is the basis of technical investing. It is also the basis of Maverick's Top-Down Approach. We don't care about the news about a stock; we care only about the reaction to the news. If a poorly run company posts bad earnings, but keeps climbing in price, we don't care; we're looking for the fastest bus in the city, not the prettiest one, and it doesn't matter if it's heading uptown or downtown.

Now, we'll be the first to point out some of the rough spots in our approach, our particular tribe of trading. The first thing we need to get out in the open is that some adherents of and converts to technical investing are, well, odd and take things to an extreme.

It's OK. We can still get along with them, but they're like that weird branch of the family that you talk to only during family reunions. You're related to them, and there is nothing you can do about it; you politely inquire as to their well-being while you're dishing up the potato salad, but you're quite happy that they live in a different part of the country for the rest of the year. That's fine; they feel the same way about you.

To explain what we mean, at Maverick we concentrate on chart patterns (as we'll see shortly) and volume. We also rely on simple moving averages. Price Relative (to an index) and Average True Range are also tools that we use. When it comes down to it, we're very much bread-and-butter members of the tribe of technicians. Frankly, the other families in our tribe of technicians usually have 40-lb brains. What's worse is that they know it. What's even worse is that they continually like to prove it.

We've got a bunch of different families within our tribe of technicians. There are the Bollingers, the Stochastics, the Williams, the Elliot Wavers, the Fibonaccis, and the MACDs, just to name a few. They are all offshoots of the original two clans: Price and Volume.

These clans are vociferous in their defense of the honor and effectiveness of their individual clans. At the family reunions, there will often be shouting matches at the smorgasbord. We're just trying to get some fried chicken, and all of a sudden Basil Bollinger and Frank Fibonacci will start screaming at each other over the deviled eggs. Stan Stochastic decides to get into the mix, and the chicken leg we were about to grab goes flying into Wanda Williams's lemonade.

We used to try to be conciliatory and bring peace by reminding everyone that we're all part of the same tribe. That stopped the arguments for about three seconds, up until the other clans realized that we didn't specialize and we didn't need a slide rule or a supercomputer to make our calculations, and hence we didn't have 40-lb brains and thus had no standing in the argument.

At this point, we usually just pack up the kids and the cooler and spend the rest of our vacation at Disney World (symbol DIS).

It's gotten to the point where we just send our regrets to the family reunion organizers, along with our trading performance for the past year. Needless to say, we're rarely on anyone's Christmas card list.

Occasionally, some clans will try to interbreed in an attempt to combine the best traits of the respective clans, but since they are coming from the same gene pool, the results are as expected: an even more esoteric and socially misanthropic offshoot family that would make a geneticist balk at the prospect of a second generation.

At Maverick, we respect the contributions that each clan of our tribe of technicians has made. In some cases they are effective and, therefore, profitable. However, to borrow an analogy, technical indicators are like horseradish in a roast beef sandwich. A little bit is good. After a while, you think more might be better. Pretty soon, if you're not careful, you're eating a horseradish sandwich because you don't realize that the beef fell out from between the slices of bread. You can get caught up in analysis paralysis or, worse yet, come to feel that a particular technical indicator is infallible. Technical indicators are used to *help* you make a decision on a trade, not to *make* the decision for you.

Now that we've aired our family linen for all to see (we know we've just met, but we already feel close to you), what are the other tribes of trading, and how is Maverick different?

The other major camp in stock selection is the fundamental traders (who do, in our opinion, make up both a political organization and a religious sect, at least in the world of finance). Fundamental traders do care about the way the bus looks, often regardless of whether the bus is heading uptown or downtown. Fundamental traders look at earnings reports, monitor insider buying and selling, listen to conference calls, keep track of lawsuits, monitor new product pipelines, and take a look at management changes, proxy fights, and changes in boards of directors. Fundamental traders can, and often do, know more about the issues and events affecting a company than its top management.

And bless their little hearts for it. We have nothing against fundamental investors and traders. Sometimes they are right. There have been many people and famous investors who have made money strictly by investing from a fundamental perspective.

But that's not our style. We have seen hundreds of examples of well-run companies with excellent earnings and products that absolutely get crushed in the market. Likewise, we have seen poorly run companies with no earnings to speak of get vaulted to stratospheric levels for no discernible reason. Psychologically, a fundamental investor can become married to a position, even to the detriment of a real-world marriage. The thing is, no one likes to be wrong. In the end, the fundamental trader is often right, but in the meantime, his portfolio can be decimated until the market comes around to his way of thinking.

You can place a fundamental trader next to a technical trader and have the fundamental trader shorting a stock while the technical trader is buying like crazy. The fundamental trader is going to look over at the trader and ask why the technical trader is buying such a poorly run company. The trader can agree wholeheartedly that the company is poorly run, but for some reasons the institutions are buying, and so is she.

Likewise, you can have a technical trader shorting a well-run company at the same time the fundamental trader is buying. The fundamental trader can't understand why the technical trader is selling such a good company, with excellent earnings and management. The reason is the same: because the institutions are selling.

The fundamental investor cares about being right. The technical trader cares about being profitable. We would rather be profitable than right.

The third tribe in investing/trading is the fundamental technical analyst. You've probably guessed the demographic of this tribe simply from the name, but for the sake of completeness, a fundamental technical analyst (FTA approach) looks for companies that have both good fundamentals and good technical characteristics.

This tribe is generally respected by the other two. The problem with this outlook is that it is primarily biased to the long side. Systems employing this approach do well in bull markets, but stagnate or remain in cash during corrections and bear markets. Again, there is nothing wrong with this, but we prefer to make money on both sides of the market.

Now that you know the demography of the land of finance, welcome to the tribe of technicians. Here's your uniform. Step forward briskly; the orientation is about to begin.

FINDING THE RIGHT MAP: TYPES OF CHARTS

There are several types of charts that technical investors use. The object of a chart is to give you an easy-to-understand map of where a particular market, sector, or stock has been in order to give you an idea of its probable next move: up, down, or sideways.

The first type of chart that most people see is a simple line chart. A line chart plots the closing prices over whatever period (time frame) you are looking at. You could have a chart that plots the weekly closing prices over a period of a year, the daily prices over a month, or the prices every five minutes for a day. A line then connects the closing prices in sequence.

Figure 3-1 is a three-month chart showing the daily closing prices of Boeing (symbol BA).

In our opinion, line charts are pretty useless. You could have a wild price swing during a period, but if the security closed at a level that was substantially the same as the previous period's closing price, a line chart wouldn't show that. We want to be able to get a glimpse of what the institutional investors are thinking and doing, and a line chart just doesn't provide that type of detail. Broad swings and the trading range of a particular issue can signify events to watch.

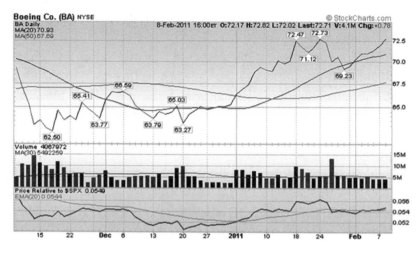

Figure 3-1   Line Chart

The next type of chart is the Open-High-Low-Close (OHLC) bar chart. This type of chart provides more of the information we are looking for because it lets us know where the market, sector, or stock opened; what it did throughout the day, week, or month; and where it closed. This type of chart lets us know who was in control of the demand-supply seesaw during a specific period of time.

Figure 3-2 shows the same chart of Boeing in an OHLC format.

On the surface, it looks as if we have all the information we need, so why go to a different chart style? The simple answer is that you can go blind looking at an OHLC chart. The lines are too small to see clearly after a few charts, and it takes longer to grasp the price movement. This may be fine when you're 18 years old and have the visual acuity of an eagle, but once you get above 30, you tend to like things in a little larger format.

Additionally, we may search through 150 charts at a time looking for a few trades. In our introduction to Maverick's Top-Down Approach, we looked at more than 60 charts to find two

Figure 3-2   OHLC Chart

trades. Using an OHLC chart can turn a $2^1/_2$-minute task into a 10-minute task. This may not sound like a big deal, but over time, it adds up. It's like using a flathead screwdriver on a Phillips head screw. You will get the job done, but it will take you longer than if you had the right tool.

So, what type of chart do we recommend?

Japanese Candlesticks

Much has been written about the mythical and awesome power of Japanese candlestick charting techniques. If you've had any exposure to charting before, you're probably expecting us to break out a nice haiku:

> *Candlestick lights the*
> *Way to understanding cash*
> *Flows to good profits*

Sorry to disappoint you. We use candlestick charts because they are the best tool out there for gathering and synthesizing a good deal of information in a short period of time. We can see everything we want to see quickly to separate the wheat from the chaff, discarding unsuitable trading candidates quickly so that we can get down to the detailed evaluation of the remaining candidates.

Candlesticks give the same information as an OHLC chart—where the stock opened that day, what its high and low for the day were, and where it closed for the day—but they are much easier on the eyes and allow you to visualize the actual movement at a glance.

Figure 3-3 shows the Boeing chart one last time in a candlestick format.

You can see that the chart is simply easier to read. Your eye is naturally drawn to large up and down moves.

So, no Zen meditation is required to read candlesticks (unless Zen meditation is your thing), no knowledge of the Japanese language is required to unlock their meanings, and you don't need to eat sushi to use candlesticks (although we're fond of sushi anyway). Candlesticks are simply the best tool

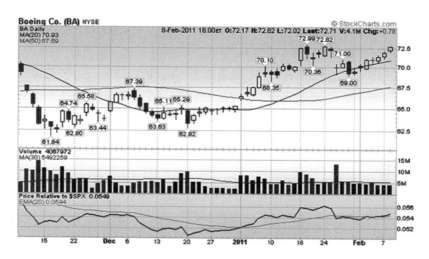

Figure 3-3   Candlestick Chart

out there. If someone comes up with a better charting technique that can give us the same or better data more quickly than candlesticks, we'll drop candlesticks like a hot rock in favor of the new technique. Until then, we're sticking with candlesticks.

CANDLESTICK BASICS

There are two parts to a candlestick: the body and the shadows, or wicks. The body shows the difference between the opening price and the closing price. The shadows show any price movement above or below the opening price or the closing price.

Figure 3-4 shows a stock where the price closes higher than the opening price. In the figure the body is hollow. This is the convention that lets you know that the closing price was higher than the opening price. The shadows show that at some time during the day, the price of the stock was higher than the closing price and lower than the opening price.

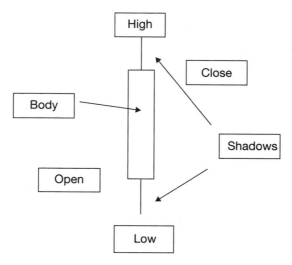

Figure 3-4   Rising Candle

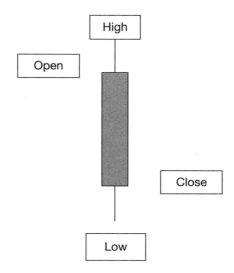

Figure 3-5   Falling Candle

Figure 3-5 shows a stock where the price closes lower than the opening price.

The difference is that the body of this candle has been filled in. This is the convention that lets us know that the stock price closed lower than the opening price. Again in this example, at some point during the day, the price rose above the opening price and fell below the closing price, which is indicated by the shadows.

It is the body of the candle that lets us see the true direction and magnitude of the price movement.

Figures 3-6 and 3-7 give some additional examples.

When you are reading charts, you will often see moments of indecision or exhaustion. This is indicated by movement of the stock throughout the day, but little to no difference between the opening and closing prices. The candle is almost completely shadow with no body. Examples of these candlesticks, called dojis, are shown in Figure 3-8.

Running of the Bulls

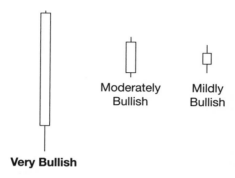

Figure 3-6   Bullish Patterns

Da Bears!

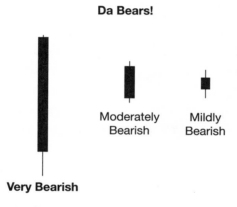

Figure 3-7   Bearish Patterns

Dojis

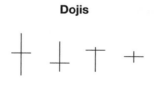

Indecision or Exhaustion

Figure 3-8   Dojis

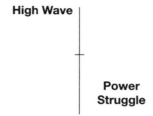

Figure 3-9   High Wave

A particular type of doji that indicates a power struggle between buyers and sellers is called the High Wave (see Figure 3-9). Neither buyers nor sellers can gain control throughout the day.

Prices don't always march up or down in an orderly fashion. Sometimes there will be a gap between the previous day's closing price and the next day's opening price. These gaps can foretell either the beginning of a price movement or the end of a price movement.

Breakaway gaps and breakdown gaps often indicate the beginning of a significant and extended move in price. Such gaps often occur after a period of consolidation, during which the stock price doesn't move significantly one way or another. During the consolidation period, the demand-supply seesaw is roughly equal, and volume decreases. The stock is building energy during this period, and when that energy is released, the move is often explosive. It is akin to a playground bully coming up to the seesaw and stomping on it, sending the price wildly up or down.

In Figure 3-10, we see that the stock essentially went nowhere for an extended period of time and then gapped up sharply from the previous day's close. This type of price movement is usually triggered by unexpected news. Some piece of information, and it doesn't matter what it is, has changed the outlook of the institutional investors and their analysts, making the stock more attractive and greatly increasing demand.

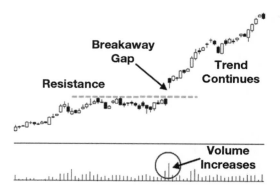

Figure 3-10   Breakaway Gap

As tempting as it is to blindly buy during this period, it is often better to wait at least one day to see whether the breakout is backed by continued demand or if it is simply a one-day over-reaction to the news.

The key is to remember that we're interested in what the institutions are doing and that collectively they cannot enter or exit a position in a single day. The day after a large move will often indicate continued increased demand, and this will signify the beginning of a significant march upward.

Conversely, breakdown gaps often indicate the beginning of an extended downtrend in a stock. Breakdown gaps are most often triggered by completely unanticipated news. The situation usually develops in the following manner.

As soon as the surprise news event breaks, the portfolio managers and chief investment officers are on the phones to their traders telling (read yelling at) them to exit their positions in the stock as quickly as possible (now). If the traders have been granted any discretionary abilities, they are probably already clicking SELL in substantial blocks as quickly as they can. The playground bully has just jumped onto the supply side of the demand-supply seesaw.

As a whole, the institutions can't exit their positions quickly (that is, in a single day). The portfolio managers and the investment officers realize that the damage has been done and that the best course of action is to limit the damage as much as possible. After the day of the breakdown gap, the order will come down to the traders from on high that they should exit the position at a more orderly pace, selling into any strength. The actual conversation is usually something akin to, "Sell this dog at the best price you can get, but get completely out before the end of the month or you're fired."

Here is where the retail investor helps the institutions, much to her personal detriment. The retail investor looks at the gap down and says, "Wow! What a buying opportunity!" Admit it; we've all done it at some point. The buying pressure from retail investors actually produces some price support for the stock.

During this period, the institutional traders are looking for any strength and dumping 5,000 shares here and 10,000 shares there until they've liquidated their positions in the stock. Once they are out, they turn their backs on the stock completely. The stock has lost institutional sponsorship and interest, leaving just the retail investors holding the stock.

When this happens, it can be years before institutions regain interest in the stock. Traders and portfolio managers have better memories than elephants and don't want to risk getting burned again anytime soon.

Figure 3-11 shows a stock with a catastrophic breakdown followed by a long downtrend.

Gaps up and down can also signify the end of a trend. These are called blowoff gaps or exhaustion gaps. The difference between an exhaustion gap and the breakaway and breakdown gaps is that the exhaustion gap is not usually news-related, but represents the last available money going into or coming out of the stock. To put this situation into perspective, no one wants to be the last person to arrive at a good party, and no one wants to be the last to leave a bad party.

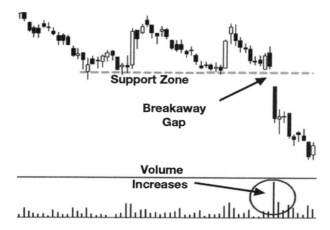

Figure 3-11   Breakdown Gap

A great analogy for a blowoff top is going to a party on the weekend. When you are one of the first to arrive, you groan as you are put to work by the host, wondering when other people will show up and whether this party will be any good. As time goes on, more and more people begin to show up. The music gets a little better and a little louder. The food gets better, and the next thing you know the party is cranking. Everyone is packed shoulder to shoulder, having a great time. Some guy is swinging on the chandelier, and you think to yourself, "This is great. This is the best a party can possibly get!" And you know what? You're right . . . and you should leave immediately. Because if you stay, the next thing you know is that the guy is falling off the chandelier, someone will throw up all over you, and the cops will bust down the door from a disturbing the peace call. You had your chance to leave gracefully, but now you are leaving covered in someone else's vomit (and maybe your own too) and escorted by the police.

An exhaustion gap in an uptrend usually follows a long march upward in the stock. The stock has gotten the attention of the institutions and the retail investors alike. The institutions have told their traders to get positions in this stock, and they've been steadily driving up the price (putting more weight on the demand side of the seesaw). Remember, the institutions will keep throwing money at a position that is working, and the institutions all piggyback on one another's trades.

This type of activity draws attention; financial reporters need something to talk about. This is the point where the common retail investors start to get interested. For days, the retail investors watch the stock, waiting, hoping for a pullback so that they can get in. The portfolio managers at the institutions are now aggravated because their positions in the stock are not as large as they would like, and now the word is out that there is interest in the stock, and also aggravated because the institutions down the street are riding their coattails. Can't those guys do their own research and find a different stock to get into? (Never mind that they've also piggybacked on other people's trades, probably just last week.)

At this point, the portfolio managers get on the phone to their traders and tell them to hurry up and get the position fully filled before there is no room left for a profit. This thing can't run forever. Hurry up or you're fired.

This activity all builds to a crescendo, and the next day the traders are lining up their orders before the open. The retail investors finally decide that they can't wait anymore and they just have to get to the party. Everyone is lining up orders before the opening of the market.

Because everyone has just stomped on the demand side of the seesaw, the market makers have to go pretty far up the list to find people who are willing to sell to all the people who want to buy. Finally they find enough sellers, and the stock opens far above the price at which it closed at the day before. The stock trades massive volume that day. Everyone is happy because they finally have a position in this hot stock.

Then the orders dry up. There's nothing on the buy side. Everyone who wanted to buy has bought.

Now a few people want to sell, but no one is buying at the price they were buying at yesterday. Yesterday, people were saying, "We just have to get into this great stock. This will make us all rich"; today they are saying, "This is crazy; no one will buy this dog at these prices. It's time to lock in profits and/or preserve capital." Demand has left the playground, and prices fall back down.

That's an exhaustion gap. Figure 3-12 shows an example.

Notice the strong uptrend, the massive volume on the day of the gap up, and then the gap back down in price the next day.

You can also see exhaustion gaps on the downside, as well. The situation is completely reversed. A stock will be in a pronounced downtrend, and finally everyone feels that they just absolutely have to get out, gapping the price down in capitulation. The pain is too great, and the portfolio managers are all telling their traders, "Just get out! I don't care what the price is! Get out!"

Half the institutions (the half that don't currently have positions in the stock) look at the price and say, "This is still a good company. I can't let a price like this go by. Let's get a position in this."

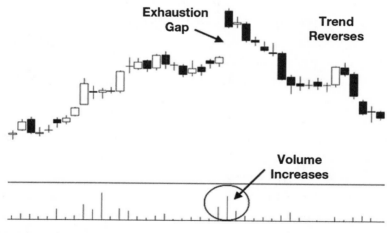

Figure 3-12   Bullish Exhaustion Gap

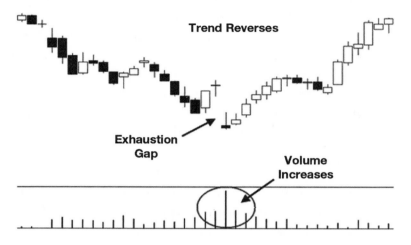

Figure 3-13   Bearish Exhaustion Gap

By now, everyone who wants to sell has sold, and the next day the price gaps back up as demand is restored. Figure 3-13 is an example of an exhaustion gap that signaled the end of a downtrend.

Extended-range candles represent massive but orderly changes in price, and expenditures of energy. Unlike gaps, extended-range candles start at an orderly opening price and move in one direction the entire day. These candles often signal the beginning of a trend as well.

After an extended-range candle (a very large one-day move), the next day often has a harami candle. *Harami* is Japanese for "pregnant woman" or "expecting." It is a short-term pause as the institutional managers and traders collectively look at one another and say, "What now, guys?" . . . or when your girlfriend tells you that she is unexpectedly pregnant and you say, "What now, guys?"

After a bullish extended-range candle, short-term traders who bought the stock just previous to the run want to lock in a profit, so they sell. Other institutions that may have missed the move or didn't get their entire position filled want to get in at a lower price. They're just as cheap as everyone else, and they don't want to pay top dollar for something that they can get at a discount.

After a bearish extended-range candle, the short-term traders who shorted the stock also want their profits and will buy back their shorts to cover their positions, driving the price up. The institutions that are in the process of liquidating their positions view this day as a reprieve and will happily sell to the people who are seeking to cover their short positions or initiate a long position.

A typical harami will retrace between one-third and one-half of the previous day's extended-range candle. When this occurs, there is a high probability that the new trend, initiated by the extended-range candle, will continue in the direction of the extended-range candle.

If what initially looks like a harami candle retraces more than half of the extended-range candle, it is likely that the move is over and the stock will either consolidate or reverse the direction of the initial move (see Figures 3-14 and 3-15).

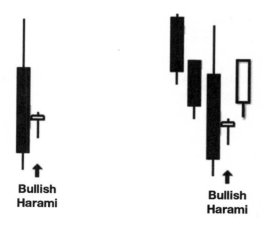

Bullish Harami

Bullish Harami

Figure 3-14   Bullish Harami

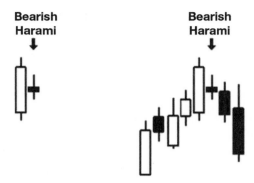

Figure 3-15   Bearish Harami

More often than not, stocks display patterns that clearly foretell a change in direction. You can actually pinpoint the day when equilibrium was reached and the opposing side took over the show. These candlestick patterns commonly come in three flavors: dojis, shooting stars, and hammers.

We've already discussed the doji a bit, but it is the point where the activity of both demand and supply are equal; neither party can gain the upper hand, and the stock closes at or very near the point where it opened, with movement both up and down during the day. The activity on the day following a doji is normally confirmation that the direction has changed. If the direction continues its previous course, then the doji is considered a point of indecision, where the institutional decision makers are taking a break to reevaluate the situation and determine what course is correct. Going back to our analogy of the seesaw for supply and demand, the doji is typically the first candle you see that will tell you when enough people have jumped on the other side of the trade to swing the balance back to a neutral area (see Figure 3-16).

The shooting star is a bearish reversal pattern. The stock opens in an orderly manner and then rises significantly in price for a portion of the day. At some point during the day, sellers come in and push the price of the stock back down, retracing all

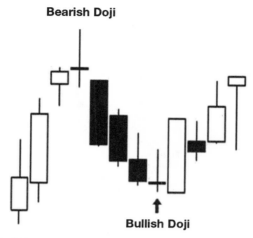

Figure 3-16   Bullish and Bearish Doji

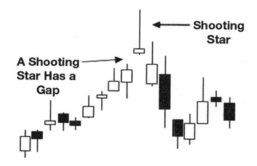

Figure 3-17   Shooting Star

the gains made previously during the day and often closing lower than the open (see Figure 3-17).

Hammer patterns are exactly the opposite of shooting stars and are bullish reversal patterns. The stock opens normally and is driven down significantly during the day. Usually near the end of the day, buyers will decide that the price represents an opportunity and will come in strength. With the majority of the sellers already out of the market, the buyers will cause the price to retrace its fall earlier in the day and cause the stock to close at a price higher than its open (see Figure 3-18).

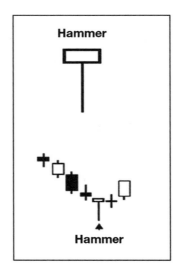

Figure 3-18   Hammer

FLOORS AND CEILINGS: SUPPORT AND RESISTANCE

Examining the concept of support and resistance is an exercise in the study of group psychology.

How does that make you feeeeel? Just kidding. It all boils down to three things: greed, fear, and memory. These traits are present in every institutional decision maker, institutional trader, and retail trader. All we are doing when we study support and resistance is looking at these traits as they exist in the market as a whole.

- **Greed.** Remember, investment committees, portfolio managers, and institutional traders receive their personal compensation and bonuses based on their ability to make money for their fund and their partners (in the case of hedge funds). They all want the family mansion, the elegant car, the private school for their kids, the lavish vacation at the exclusive tropical resort. They get these things by making money for their firms.

In their minds, they think, "If I do A (make money for my firm), then I get B (house, car, school, and so on)." It's positive reinforcement at its best. You see the same behavior in a group of monkeys that have been trained to press a button to get a banana.

- **Fear.** Conversely, those same institutional players are also motivated by fear. As we discussed previously, their compensation, home life, and so on are negatively affected if they lose money for their firms. If they do C (lose money), then D happens (loss of bonus, job, family, and house; begging on the street for spare change in a $2,000 suit; and so on). That's just like the monkey who gets an electric shock rather than a banana when he presses the wrong button.
Fear and greed each have two faces that have to be taken into account to understand support and resistance. Fear encompasses not only an aversion to losing money, but also a phobia of not extracting the greatest possible profit. Greed covers the desire to make a profit, but also a desire to want to lose less on a bad position. In short, profit is good, a larger profit is better, and a small loss is better than a big loss.
- **Memory.** Each of the institutional players remembers both the bananas she's received and the jolts of electricity she's gotten. Additionally, she remembers where she bought or sold a stock. Actually, she can see it on her Profit and Loss Statement, which is often updated in real time.

The next concept will seem self-evident at first blush, but please bear with us. There is a buyer and a seller in every transaction. Every time you buy something, someone has to be willing to sell it to you. Every time you sell something, someone has to be willing to buy if from you.

Each buyer and each seller has his own motivations. If you're buying, you may be buying from someone who has been long in the position for five minutes or from someone who got a piece of the initial public offering back in the last millennium, or you may be buying from someone who is shorting the stock. Likewise, when you are selling, you may be selling to someone who is establishing a long position in the stock or you may be selling to someone who is covering a short position. Whatever motivates whoever is on the other side of the trade from you is immaterial. Just remember that someone had a motivation to take the other side of the trade.

Now, the more trusting and dangerous readers will raise their hands politely and point out that of course someone is taking the other side of the trade: it is the market maker, and he is taking the other side because it's his job. That's nice in theory, but it doesn't float, much like a concrete dinghy.

Market makers and floor specialists are motivated by fear and greed to the same extent as the institutional players are and to the same extent as retail traders are, despite regulations to the contrary. It's difficult to change millions of years of evolutionary behavior.

- **Evolutionary greed:** Must get meat to feed family or wife kick out of cave.
- **Evolutionary fear:** No roast meat in hand. Hurt much. Use stick.

Two things to keep in mind: (1) market makers and floor specialists are pocketing the difference between the bid and the ask (if you ever wondered where that nickel went), so of course they are going to facilitate trades, but (2) they get to see the whole institutional order book as it comes in, before everyone else. They will always keep some inventory on hand in the issues they cover, but if, for instance, they see a freight train of institutional sell orders queuing up, they will fill the bids (the buy orders) with their own inventory to get ahead of the herd. Likewise, when they can see selling pressure lightening up and buying interest building, they will hit the ask (the sell orders) to build their inventory back up and ride the wave higher.

No, we're not cynical conspiracy theorists committing libel. There have been actual studies that indicate that this happens up to 80 percent of the time. Now, that's not to say that the practice is legal. It's specifically prohibited by law and exchange regulations, and if people get caught doing it, they face some pretty stiff penalties, both monetary and of the "I Can Call You Betty and You Can Call Me Al" variety.

The key point we're illustrating with this side trip is that no matter who is in between the buyer and seller facilitating the transaction, there is a buyer and seller for every transaction, and it is their individual motivations that make a transaction happen at any given price.

Now let's go back to the psychology of transactions. There are two institutions, A and B. Institution A bought 100,000 shares of XYZ stock two years ago when it was trading at $25. It now trades at $50, a pretty nice gain for Institution A. Institution A's research (in which the firm has invested quite a bit of money) says that while XYZ might have some more juice left in it, ABC stock looks like it's getting ready to take off, and Institution A should free up some capital to initiate a position in ABC.

Institution B looks at its own research, which says that XYZ company could run to $60 in the next few months, and Institution B should ride the wave for a quick gain.

Institution A is happy to sell its shares of XYZ at $50 so that it can free up capital to start a position in ABC. Institution B is happy to buy those shares because its research says that they have 20 percent upside in the near future. The transaction is made on the exchange, and Institution A has its cash and Institution B has 100,000 shares of XYZ.

The price of XYZ goes up to $55, and then another seller, Institution C, comes into the market and sells its holdings in XYZ, driving the price back down to $50. Institution B still thinks that XYZ will run to $60 and still thinks that $50 is an attractive price. It will buy all it can at $50. Institution B has now established support for XYZ at $50.

Over the next month, XYZ trades up to $60. Institution B now begins to unload its shares into the market, but it can't dump everything into the market at once, or else it will upset the demand-supply seesaw, so it sells a little bit at a time.

In comes Institution D, which is a hedge fund. Hedge funds aren't constrained the way mutual funds and other long-only institutions are and can short the market. Institution D thinks that XYZ is incredibly overvalued at $60 and thinks it can drop to $50 very quickly. So Institution D sells XYZ short at $60 and will continue to do so as long as its thesis remains the same.

Institutions B and D have now created overhead supply in XYZ, which causes resistance to the stock. XYZ can't move past $60 until that overhead supply has been worked through and eliminated.

Now we have a chart that looks like Figure 3-19.

Multiply each position taken in the previous scenario by 100 or even 1,000 institutional players and you get a picture of the workings of the market. There are thousands of institutional actors arriving at a series of similar conclusions, some motivated to buy and some motivated to sell, but all of them making up the demand-supply seesaw and establishing support and resistance levels for a stock, a sector, or a broad market.

Support and resistance also follow trendlines. Two axioms cause this: (1) buy at wholesale prices and sell at retail prices, and (2) the trend is your friend.

Once a stock or a market establishes a clear trend, you have groups of institutions making collections of similar decisions, even though they may have arrived at those decisions through

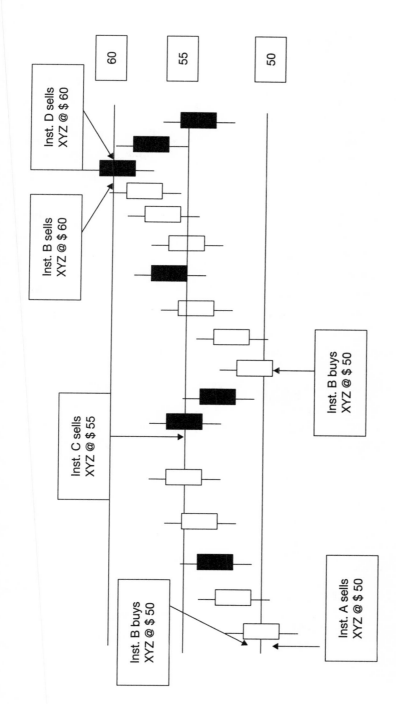

Figure 3-19 Support and Resistance

vastly different paths. It doesn't matter how each of them arrived at its destination—only that they showed up at the party.

Everyone wants to buy something for less than what she sells it for. This is true on the long side as well as for short sellers. On the long side, you are buying first and selling later (hopefully at a higher price). On the short side, you are selling first and buying later (this time, hopefully at a lower price). Each group of actors is contributing to a collective decision as to what the wholesale price of an issue is and what the retail price of the same issue is.

Astonishingly often, these series of collective decisions create visible trends that can be connected by a straight line showing support and resistance in an issue.

An uptrend will often look like Figure 3-20.

When prices approach retail levels, it is an indication that those institutions that are looking to buy the stock are collectively saying that there is no more room to make a profit in the trade. Consequently, the sellers begin to outnumber the buyers, and prices head back down.

As prices approach wholesale levels, it is an indication that sellers feel that the stock is worth more in the short-term future than what they can get for it now. At that point, buyers outnumber sellers, and prices head back up.

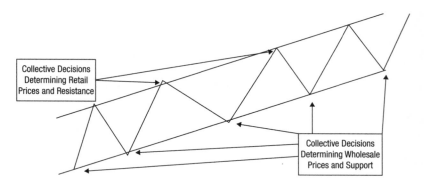

Figure 3-20   Uptrend

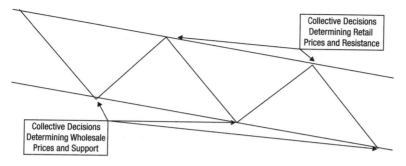

Figure 3-21   Downtrend

The same collective decisions also occur in a downtrend, as shown in Figure 3-21.

The high points in the trend occur when sellers, which include both institutions with long positions who want to sell to exit their positions and short sellers who want to sell to open their positions, determine that the price won't climb any higher in the short term and that this is the best deal that they will get.

The low points in the trend, the points of support, occur when buyers whose analysis indicates that the stock is attractive at this level and want to establish a long position and short sellers who don't feel the stock will decline any lower and want to buy to exit their short positions decide to act.

Simple Moving Averages will also form their own trendlines. A Simple Moving Average (SMA) takes the last X number of closing prices, adds them together, and then divides by X. A 20-period SMA takes the last 20 closing prices of a stock, adds them together, and divides by 20. A 50-period SMA takes the last 50 closing prices of a stock, adds them together, and divides by 50.

It is important that you know what you're looking at and what the period represents when you're using SMAs. If you're looking at a daily chart, a 20-period SMA will show the SMA for the last 20 trading days (four weeks). If you're looking at a chart with weekly periods, a 20-period SMA will be for the last 20 weeks (about 4¹/₂ months, or 100 trading days). Likewise, a 50-period SMA on a weekly chart will show weekly closing prices for nearly a year.

Most charting programs let you set the period length for several different SMAs. At Maverick, we recommend and use the 20-day SMA and the 50-day SMA. We generally look at daily charts that are three to six months in duration, and we want to know where short-term and medium-term support and resistance are in a particular stock.

The shorter the period of an SMA is, the more responsive it will be to the movement in a stock, and the support and resistance that it represents are shorter-term and more easily broken through. The longer the period of an SMA, the less responsive it will be to the movement of a stock, and the support and resistance that it represents are correspondingly stronger.

We have to explore a side road here for a little bit. Why do we recommend and use the 20-day and 50-day SMAs to find support and resistance? Answer: because those SMAs are what the majority of institutional traders are looking at. We want to go along for the ride, not blaze our own trail.

An activity that is common among new technical traders is to find a stock and then adjust the period of the SMAs to give a best-fit line to the stock movement. A chart with a 20- and 50-day SMA might not show consistent support and resistance, but the trader will find something with, let's say, a 25-day SMA and a 42-day SMA and then trade on it.

Don't. Please.

The trader is creating artificial support and resistance in his own mind, not objectively looking at where support and resistance really are with industry-common metrics. If a stock you are looking at doesn't show support and resistance on the 20- and 50-day SMAs, find another stock. If you don't, you'll be like the Lone Ranger surrounded by hostile Indians and frantically searching for Tonto, who has decided that now is a good time to reconnect with his roots.

There are too many highly liquid stocks with institutional interest out there that do closely adhere to the 20- and 50-day SMAs for support and resistance for you to be trying to start your own weird clan of the tribe of technical traders.

Darren: My dad was a machinist for over 30 years. When he was first learning his trade, he started out as a tool and die maker. Tool and die makers work with maddeningly tight tolerances, and there is no room for mistakes. My dad spoke with a few tool and die makers and learned that they generally burned out after a few years and went into general machinery. Very few people could successfully spend their entire careers as tool and die makers, and they often had a haunted look and shortened lives from the stress. The same holds true for technical traders who seek to create their own tools from scratch. It is a laborious process involving a great deal of trial and error to come up with a tool that may work only in highly specialized situations.

If I need something to tighten a bolt, I'm not going to buy a forge and cast my own wrenches; I'm going to drive down to the local home improvement store and buy a wrench or socket that someone has already made and tested that I know will do the job.

Here are several examples of stocks that closely followed their 20- and 50-day SMAs for support and resistance.

In Figure 3-22, you can see how the stock would find support at its 20- and 50-day SMAs, often bouncing off the SMAs to new highs within the trend.

In Figure 3-23, you can see that this stock was clearly in a downtrend, and every time it touched either the 20- or the 50-day SMA, it was knocked back down to new lows as sellers took the opportunity to unload their shares at or near the trendline made by the SMA.

Figure 3-22   Uptrend Adhering to Moving Averages

Figure 3-23   Downtrend Adhering to Moving Averages

Sometimes stocks may be trending, but not adhering to support or resistance made by either the 20- or the 50-day SMA. Support and resistance represent the safest places to buy and sell.

Why walk down a dark alley in a bad neighborhood to get to the store when you could stay on the main street, which is safer and well lighted? You might not get mugged in the alley, but you're more likely to get mugged there than on the well-traveled street.

When a stock, sector, or market breaks through support or resistance, that is a signal that either a new stage of a trend has begun or the old trend has reversed. Both situations occur for one of two reasons: either all the overhead supply has been sold off and there is no one who is willing to sell until the price rises (supply is less than demand), or all the buyers at a particular level have bought and there is no one left to buy until the price gets lower (demand is less than supply).

A break through support or resistance is an excellent opportunity to establish a position, either long or short, depending on the direction of the breakthrough. A new stage in an established trend is just beginning, and you are able to get in at the start of the move; once a breakthrough is made, there is a high probability that what used to be resistance will become support and what used to be support will become resistance.

In a stock that breaks through resistance to the upside, that level of resistance becomes support for the new trend because the institutions that bought at the level of the previous resistance will continue to buy at that level, and they will also hold because they can see that most of the institutions that wanted to sell have done so already, so that the overhead supply is probably exhausted. Breakouts to the upside will often retrace themselves to that previous level of resistance, which is now support, and then take off to the upside (see Figure 3-24).

Conversely, when a stock breaks through support to the downside, the previous support level becomes resistance. Institutions that bought at the previous level of support want to get out of the position with as small a loss as possible, and any time the price approaches that level, they will sell until they can exit the position. Again, you will often see a retracement in a stock that

Figure 3-24   Resistance Becoming Support

has broken down back to the new level of resistance, followed by a quick slide down until a new level of support can be established (see Figure 3-25).

Figure 3-25   Support Becoming Resistance

When stocks break through trendlines and SMAs that previously provided support or resistance, it is a signal that the trend has reversed. If you established a position at support or resistance as indicated by the trendline or SMA, a breakthrough of that trendline means that it is time to liquidate the position for a small loss.

For whatever reason, the collective decisions of the institutional investors have determined that the previous trend is no longer valid. Wait until the new trend asserts itself and then look for a safe place to enter the trade.

Support and resistance are key concepts in Maverick's trading system. We buy at support and we sell at resistance because they provide safety.

CHART PATTERNS

Uh-oh, we caught you. Yep, red-handed, too.

You picked up this book, looked in the table of contents, and then turned to this section without reading anything before it. Shame on you. Go back to the front of the book and read it from the beginning. Cheater.

Back already? Boy, that was quick.

Before we get started on bullish chart patterns, we need to establish a few ground rules.

Rule 1. All the chart patterns in this book give a good *probability* of being either bullish or bearish, depending on which chart pattern it is. Quantum physicists will grasp this right away. These chart patterns are the same thing as Schrödinger's cat before you open the box.

For everyone else who has clicked on a Web ad promising the key to stock market greatness through the power of never-fail charting, we have to say with all honesty that these chart patterns can sometimes fail to develop. Unanticipated news might come out, a buyer or seller might come to the table late, action in another stock in the sector could influence the stock in question, a trader could misread volume cues, or a trader could misread the entire chart. However, if we had to put money on it, and we do so every day, the charts by themselves, with no other input, when properly read, are going to be right 50 percent of the time.

Rule 2. Never use only the charts of a stock to make a trade decision. We have absolutely no doubt that we could teach you the chart patterns and you would be able to randomly call up ticker symbols and find some names whose charts would mimic what we teach. We can also guarantee that if you did that, you would lose money in the long run because you would be totally neglecting what the broad market and the stock's sector are doing. Use Maverick's Top-Down Approach. We took years to get it right; don't reinvent the wheel. Some studies have shown that up to 80 percent of a stock's movement, up or down, is directly related to what the broad market and the stock's sector are doing. That is what makes a good chart pattern in a bad market setup a bad trade.

Remember that you get to count the cards and make the odds; use the *probability* of a successful trade as much to your advantage as possible. Don't give the house an edge.

Rule 3. Use your risk controls and position sizing guidelines. Too many times we've seen traders see a great-looking chart setup and sit there clicking BUY . . . BUY . . . BUY . . . BUY with a grin of utter delight on their faces, only to have that grin turn to tears when the setup fails and they realize that their position size was too large.

As much as we would all like to retire to our own privately owned islands tomorrow (where we would trade from the beach), this isn't a Get-Rich-Quick Scheme. This is a Get-Wealthy-Much-Faster-Than-Blindly-Stumbling-About System. One of the keys to that system is to live to trade another day and not let a bad trade wipe you out, forcing you to spend your golden years asking teenagers if they would like fries with that.

Rule 4. Do not enter the trade until you see the trade trigger. Trade trigger? What's a trade trigger? We don't need no stinking trade trigger! What do you think the BUY and SELL buttons are for?

Yes, you do need to wait until the stock reaches a predetermined point before entering the trade. We will cover this in greater detail in Chapter 5, when we illustrate all the steps that we go through in entering and exiting a trade, but suffice it to say that new traders, and many experienced traders, lose money by getting into trades too early.

Remember, a good chart pattern is only a probability that a trade will be profitable. We want, need, have to, must, are compelled to increase the odds in our favor as much as possible, so in all cases we will wait until the trade is triggered by price and volume before we enter the trade.

Based on our experience at Maverick, about one-third of the setups you identify will fail to trigger, and that is perfectly fine. Sometimes the best trades you make are the ones you don't do. If a trade doesn't trigger, then you haven't tied up your capital and you haven't lost any money.

Lean close; we're going to let you in on a little secret. Ready—we very rarely press the BUY or SELL button. That's right, we said that we very rarely press the BUY or SELL button. We set up our trades to trigger automatically, and then, as soon as they are triggered, we enter our orders for protective stops and profit taking.

If we identify a chart pattern a little later, like the day after it's triggered, then, if we think the trade is still safe and viable, we will press the BUY or SELL button manually.

The important concept right now is that each trade has a trigger to enter it and two different triggers to exit it.

There are reasons that we ordered the chapters in this book the way we did. We want people to think about limiting their losses first, thereby preserving their portfolios and their trading careers during the lean times, especially during times when the market is meandering and at the tops and bottoms of market trends. Next, we want people to get into the habit of knowing what the market is doing and what the different sectors are doing before they start picking their own stocks, because, as we said, up to 80 percent of a stock's move up or down is dependent on the direction of the broad market and the direction of the sector.

Only after people understand these concepts do we want them to take a look at individual stocks. It is at this point, after they understand the demand-supply seesaw, the Three Escalators, and the concept of building energy and releasing energy in a stock, that we've seen people succeed in identifying and evaluating good trades, regardless of market direction.

Notice that we don't say that we train good stock pickers. If someone, professional or retail, tells you that she is a good stock picker, all that means is that she can make a profit in a bull market. We train traders who can make a profit regardless of market direction.

The last reason we structured the book the way we did is that we want to wean traders away from the mouse. The work you put into a trade before you make the trade is much more important than the work you do to execute the trade.

BULLISH CHART PATTERNS

The High Base

The high base is a classic example of a bullish breakout through resistance and to new highs. The stock has expended energy moving to a new high in its trend and then consolidates, building energy for the next leg up in its trend. During the consolidation, the energy-building period, the overhead supply is gradually absorbed by the underlying demand, and once the overhead supply is absorbed, the stock breaks out in a new uptrend. Figure 3-26 shows the chart pattern.

Trade Setup You can enter this position in either an uptrending or a downtrending market, as long as the stock's sector or industry group not only is one of the two top-performing

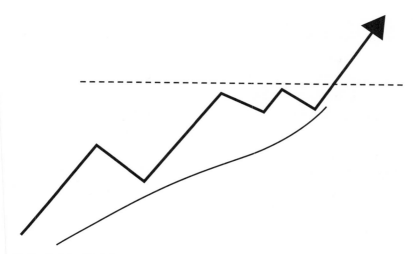

Figure 3-26 High Base

sectors, but is actually making positive gains. Do not enter this trade if your sector analysis (Step 2 in the Top-Down Approach) tells you that all sectors have been making negative returns over the past two to three months. You're looking for best of, not least bad.

If the sector is in a downtrend, don't enter the trade. All you've found is a highflier in a bad sector, and its squadron mates will probably take it down in a ball of flame sooner or later.

When the broad market is in an uptrend and the stock sector is in an uptrend, you're looking good for a normal position size based on your risk tolerance. When the broad market is in a downtrend but the sector is in an uptrend, seriously consider reducing your position size by as much as half. A broad-market downtrend can turn on you like a feral dog, causing even the strongest sectors to turn negative.

With regard to the specifics of the setup, the stock needs to have made a recent swing high. What's a swing high? Despite our reliance on children as teaching tools, a swing high is not what a kid does on a playground swing before jumping off.

Nor is a swing high a 52-week high or a historic high. A swing high is a new high in an *established* uptrend within the past two to three months. We don't buy at the bottom and sell at the top; we take the meat out of the middle and let other people get caught in the reversals.

The point we are making is that you should not buy directly after a stock breaks through a trendline in a reversal. Often stocks will briefly break through a trendline and show promise, only to fall back down into a downtrend. Think of Punxsutawney Phil poking his head up briefly and then deciding that it's too damn cold to come out until spring. He'll head back down, way back down below the frost line, and wait until things are a little warmer before venturing out.

Once the stock has hit its new swing high, it trades sideways in a narrow range with relatively equal highs and lows. This is consolidation; this is the stock building energy after it expended energy to make the new swing high.

At this point, we're waiting for price to catch up with time. This sounds odd, but we're waiting for time to bring the stock back to

1. The lower trendline (the wholesale price in a trending stock)
2. The 20-day SMA (short-term support)
3. The 50-day SMA (medium-term support)
4. Any reasonable wholesale price point

We view this activity as reversion to *a* mean. At Maverick Trading, we are big adherents of the time-tested theory of *reversion to the mean*. Reversion to the mean simply states that short-term fluctuations in prices will eventually return to longer-term, established average rates of growth. For example, let's take the recent real estate bubble that formed in the United States from 2003 to 2007. For more than 70 years, the long-term average appreciation of home prices was around 3.4 percent. During the period from 2003 to 2007, many real estate prices increased by 10, 15, or even 25 percent per year, taking prices substantially above their average or mean levels. Reversion to the mean theory states that the growth rates in prices will eventually return to their long-term, statistical averages over time, regardless of short-term fluctuations. Many people in 2006 and 2007 pointed to this as a reason to avoid real estate, expecting the real estate market to correct in prices while other people were caught up in the greed and fear of a market bubble.

We're trading off of the psychology of the institutional fund managers and traders. They know that this stock has recently performed well. It's on all their watch lists. But they won't buy it until they see a modicum of safety—as indicated by the stock's touching the lower trendline, the 20-day SMA, the 50-day SMA, or any other reasonable wholesale price. At that point, if the trend is to continue, the institutional traders will continue to buy in volume.

The consolidation period should last for a minimum of 5 days and will often last much longer, sometimes as much as 15 trading days. During this period, volume should taper off, but (as part of your stock screen in the Top-Down Approach) average daily volume should still be at least 500,000 shares.

Volume tapering off shows that underlying demand is gradually eating away at overhead supply. Think of your child's pet guppy eating fish food after you feed it. If there is too much food (supply), the fish will get full, the water will sour, and the poor bugger dies (the trend reverses). If there is too little food, the fish will jump out of the tank, morph into an air-breathing monster, and be perpetually out of your grasp (runaway stock), and you will catch it only in its last gasps (trend reversal). During this period of consolidation, there are very few active new sellers in the market, and the guppies are just chewing through the overhead resistance before moving higher.

Check for significant pending news in the near term. While we are not fundamentalist investors, neither are we idiots. If the company you are looking at is in litigation and the case has gone to the jury, wait. Better yet, pick another stock.

Check for earnings. If the earnings announcement surprises on the upside, so be it. Find another stock. In the long run, you'll be better off not holding through earnings. Let the other guy hold. If the announcement surprises on the upside, you can still get in on the move. If it surprises on the downside, you haven't lost anything.

Never, never, never enter a long position if the company has scheduled an earnings release within the next 10 trading days. More than one fortune (or a million) has been vaporized by entering a long stock position prior to an earnings announcement and then having the company botch the earnings. We have specific tactics that we use close to earnings announcements, and this isn't one of them. When do you pull the trigger on the trade? The trigger for a high base is when the stock breaks the high of consolidation or a recent group of relatively equal highs.

If you put the trigger too close to the suspected breaking of the high, you'll get filled on a lot of false breakouts. Our recommendation is that your trigger should be $0.15 above the consolidation high for highly liquid stocks (more than 1 million average daily volume) and $0.25 above the consolidation high for less liquid stocks (500,000 to 1 million average daily volume).

What about volume? On the breakout, you want to see volume of at least twice the daily volume during the consolidation period. You can look at this graphically, or you can set it as a parameter in your buy order. Less volume than that can mean that the underlying demand is not really there or that the institutions are no longer interested in the stock.

But what if the move happens early in the trading day, when volume is low? That's where experience comes into play, and this is one of the few situations where it could pay to be in front of your computer at market close. If volume is anemic or not much more than the daily volume during the consolidation period, you may want to liquidate the position at the market close and wait for another breakout on higher volume. The alternatives are to keep your position with your established loss limit or to tighten up your stop loss to $0.10 to $0.25 below the lowest consolidation low.

The high base is one of the most consistent chart patterns in an uptrending market with an uptrending sector. If you naturally have a long bias to your personality, you would be well served looking for high base patterns in uptrending sectors.

Ascending Triangles

Ascending triangles are like high bases, except that they indicate that at the beginning of the chart pattern, there was significant overhead supply or a motivated short seller in the market. Like the high base, the ascending triangle is a consolidation pattern in which the stock is building energy and buyers are eating away at overhead supply.

Ascending triangles fail more often than high bases. It is a question of who will run out of capital and/or stock first. If the buyers run out of capital before the sellers run out of stock (or run out of capital as well, in the case of a motivated short seller), the pattern will fail and the price will fall back down.

However, the ascending triangle sets up the possibility of a short squeeze. A short seller borrows stock from his broker and sells it in the market, with the idea that the stock will go down in price and he will be able to buy it back at a later time for less than he sold it for, creating a profit. If the price of the stock rises, then the short seller has to buy it back at a higher price than that at which he sold it, creating a loss. A short squeeze occurs when the pain of loss is more than the short seller is willing to bear, so that what was artificial supply (the stock the short seller sold into the market) now has to be bought back to cover and exit the position, adding to the demand already generated from the bona fide buyers.

So, in an ascending triangle pattern, when the overhead supply runs out before the capital supply of the buyers runs out, the price will break to the upside, often beginning a new leg of the uptrend. Figure 3-27 shows the chart pattern.

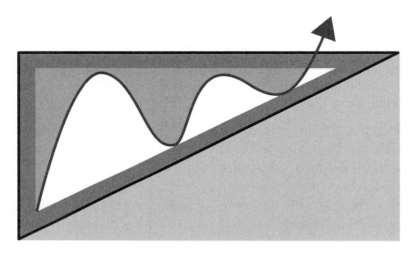

Figure 3-27   Ascending Triangle

Trade Setup As with the high base, you can enter an ascending triangle setup in either an uptrending market or a downtrending market. If the market as a whole is downtrending, the sector the stock is in should again be in the two top-performing sectors, and the sectors themselves should have been making positive gains and not just be the lepers with the most fingers.

As with the high base, the stock needs to have recently made a new swing high. The new swing high should form the roof of the triangle and appear to be a barrier to the stock's moving higher. The stock trades sideways in a narrow range with relatively equal highs and ascending lows, so that the price action looks as if it is being pinched from below. This consolidation period should last a minimum of five days and often lasts much longer.

As with the high base, the stock has expended a great deal of energy and needs some time to recharge, bringing it back to one of the following support areas:

1. The lower trendline (the wholesale price in a trending stock)
2. The 20-day SMA (short-term support)
3. The 50-day SMA (medium-term support)
4. Any reasonable wholesale price point

Again, we're looking for reversion to a mean and some time for the overhead supply to be absorbed by underlying demand. Use your screening tools to ensure that average daily volume is at least 500,000 shares. Check for news and ensure that there are no earnings announcements scheduled in the next 10 trading days.

Volume in an ascending triangle will often taper during consolidation, with volume being larger as consolidation begins and decreasing as the stock approaches one of the support areas. This shows that the overhead supply is being consumed in an orderly manner. As supply dries up, traders on the buy side will wait until time causes the stock to catch up with a support level. At that point, several institutions will make a decision to commit, eliminating the overhead supply at the resistance level and driving the price higher.

The trade trigger for an ascending triangle is the same as that for a high base: when the stock breaks the high of consolidation or a recent group of relatively equal highs. Triggers should be $0.15 to $0.25 above the high, depending on the liquidity of the stock, with lower triggers for more liquid stocks. Volume during the breakout should be at least twice the average daily volume.

In any bullish setup, there is the possibility that the price will gap up on a breakout. The ideal entry occurs during an orderly breakout. Orderly price movement above resistance usually indicates continued demand. As we discussed earlier in this chapter, gaps up in price can mean the beginning of a new leg of an uptrend, but they can also signify a final blowoff in demand.

You will be trading with a plan, not on emotion. Part of that plan is to determine what is the maximum price that you are willing to pay for the stock. You don't want to chase a stock that has gapped up significantly because that erodes your margin of safety. The natural inclination will be to rapidly click BUY if the stock gaps up at the open during a breakout. No one wants to be late to the party.

Don't do it. Stick with the plan. The method we use (when we're buying the stock itself) is to use a buy stop–limit order. The buy stop portion of the order is contingent on the price breaking through the overhead resistance of the consolidation. The limit portion ensures that we don't chase a stock. The buy stop order tells your broker to buy when the price trades above your stop (the breakout). The limit order tells your broker to buy only if you can get the stock for the limit price or less. This creates a window in which your trading plan will be executed. If the stock opens above your window, you won't be filled. We usually set our limit prices $0.10 to $0.20 above our buy stops.

If the stock gaps up during the breakout, wait at least a day to see whether the gap up was an exhaustion gap or whether it represented genuine continued demand for the stock.

Bull Pullback

The bull pullback is a continuation pattern rather than a breakout pattern. A bull pullback represents a safe entry point into a strongly trending stock. Bull pullbacks occur in stocks, in their sectors, and in the broad market. They show orderly profit taking in a healthy market.

Pullbacks are usually driven by shorter-term traders with smaller positions who want to book their profits and move on to the next trading opportunity. Markets and stocks that don't show pullbacks after an extended period of time offer no safe place for entry. The longer a stock or a market expends energy moving in a single direction, the longer and more pronounced the pullback or consolidation will be. Think of stock and market movement in this context as a steady exhalation.

Go ahead and take a deep breath, then slowly and steadily exhale. Now keep going past the natural point where you would normally breathe. Keep going, slow and steady. Getting harder, isn't it? Keep going. Whoa . . . better breathe in now. You were turning blue.

That massive breath you just took is a pullback from an overextended market. You needed oxygen. Your lungs just didn't have anything left to give. The result was that you took a much deeper breath than you normally would, and you inhaled much more quickly than your normal respiration rate. If you really expended some effort exhaling, you're probably coughing in fits and spurts right now, as well. It will also take you a little while to get back to a normal breathing cycle.

Markets and stocks often act the same way when they don't have periodic pullbacks. After that last bit of exhalation, there is nothing left to give. Demand is totally out of energy. The stock or market pulls back quickly and violently as it takes a breath to get some more energy, and the activity afterward is full of volatile movement as the market coughs its way back to a normal routine.

You want to enter a trending market or stock immediately after it's taken that breath during normal respiration. Institutions that want to sell do so in an orderly manner, bringing the stock back down to support and making the stock attractive to new buyers, continuing the trend.

The chart looks like Figure 3-28.

Use the top-down approach to identify a strong sector in a strong market, use the screening criteria to ensure that average daily volume is at least 500,000 shares, and check to make sure that there are no earnings announcements scheduled in the next 10 trading days and there is no pending news.

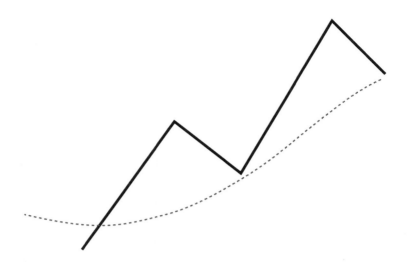

Figure 3-28   Bull Pullback

If you sense a repetitive nature in the way we do things, that's good. This is a system that produces a trading plan. In order to be consistent, we conduct the same analysis every time.

Trade Setup The stock is in an uptrend and has recently made a new swing high. There is a uniform pullback of at least two to three days, meaning consecutive lower daily highs. One-day pullbacks don't count, and you don't want to see any extended-range down candles. You're looking for uniform and orderly selling as traders take their profits.

Volume during the pullback should be less than or equal to the relative volume on the prior swing up. Volume on the pullback that is greater than the volume on the upswing often indicates that the trend has exhausted itself and the pullback is actually the first stage of a downtrend.

The pullback will bring the stock back to any of the following:

1. The lower trendline (the wholesale price in a trending stock)

2. The 20-day SMA (short-term support)
3. The 50-day SMA (medium-term support)
4. Any reasonable wholesale price point

As you can see, we are waiting for a strongly trending stock to return to the mean and give us an opportunity to enter the position at a wholesale level. By adhering to reversion to the mean, we will ensure that we never "chase" a stock and end up overpaying for the trade. It is tempting to buy stocks when they are running to new highs, but reversion to the mean will keep you safer in your trading.

So when is the pullback finished and when can you enter your position? Price will give you an indication. The trade trigger is when the stock breaks the prior day's high. It is also helpful, but not necessary, to see a reversal candle pattern at the area of support, either a doji or a hammer candle. This is a clear indication either that demand has equaled supply or that demand overcame supply at the area of support. When price action breaks the prior day's high, that is the signal that the short-term selling is over and the stock has resumed its uptrend.

We use a buy stop–limit order for a controlled entry into the position. The buy stop is placed directly above the previous day's high, usually $0.05 above. The limit is $0.10 to $0.20 above the stop, creating our window of entry.

The buy order is almost always a day order, meaning that the order will be canceled if it is not triggered that day. In the high base and the ascending triangle, we were waiting for a clear move above resistance. We didn't know when it was going to come, so those buy orders were usually Good Till Canceled (GTC). With a bull pullback, we look at the price action every day to see where the area of support actually occurs. The stock could pull back through its 20-day SMA and find support at the 50-day SMA, for example. We're waiting for price action to tell us that buyers have reentered the stock.

There is a tendency among new traders (and experienced traders) to want to be early to the game and try to call the bottom. There is something galling about having to wait until the price breaks above the previous day's high. Traders start to think that they could have called the bottom of the pullback successfully and that they would be up that much more if they'd actually been there to click the BUY button.

Please don't. Use a buy stop–limit order, and adjust it every day until the stock finds its level of support. You don't know at what level the support will establish itself. Don't guess; let the market tell you where support is. Whatever gains you thought you could make by calling the bottom will not even come close to the losses you will incur when the stock continues down past your buy point to the next level of support, or blows through that as well because the trend is actually over. Trade the market that's in front of you, not the one you wish for.

We would rather be profitable and let the market tell us when to enter than be right about calling a bottom before the market told us to come back in.

Symmetrical Triangle Breakout

The symmetrical triangle breakout is a more complex chart pattern that is useful to traders with some experience under their belts. Symmetrical triangles are difficult to identify early in their formation; what initially looks like noise and an erratically performing stock slowly resolves into a coherent pattern that can break to the upside with little warning. Additionally, symmetrical triangles are prone to failure more often than other bullish chart formations, and what initially looked promising can stagnate or continue erratic performance.

We recommend that you view symmetrical triangles as targets of opportunity. When you find them, great; look at the setup and confirm that it is tradable, but don't go searching for them just to trade a symmetrical triangle.

Trade Setup A symmetrical triangle is formed when a stock has recently made a new swing high and generally trades sideways from that swing high. During the sideways (consolidation) period, the stock displays descending highs and ascending lows, so that it looks as if the price is being pinched from both the top and the bottom. If you draw trendlines on both the descending highs and the ascending lows, you should see a clearly defined triangle pattern emerging, and the slope should be roughly the same on the top and the bottom (hence the term *symmetrical triangle*). If the triangle is skewed to the bottom trendline, it is likely that the trend has finished and the stock is consolidating before moving downward.

Consolidation and formation of the triangle should last for a minimum of 5 days and could take place over 10 to 15 trading days. During this consolidation, volume will often taper, mirroring the formation of the triangle itself, with heavier volume on the left side of the triangle and minuscule volume on the right side immediately prior to the breakout.

To spot symmetrical triangles, use of the Top-Down Approach and daily screening of stocks and charts is necessary. Because of the volatility associated with the symmetrical triangle, we recommend that all three escalators—market, sector, and stock—be in uptrends to maximize the possibility of success. When you find a symmetrical triangle, you will probably have already screened the stock previously and set it on your watch list as a possible candidate for a bull pullback.

This chart formation takes a longer time to develop because some event caused price action to significantly move away from the mean it was following, and now it takes more time for the mean to catch up to the price of the stock. Symmetrical triangles graphically illustrate a situation where there are two equally motivated camps at work. After the stock has made its new swing high, sellers come into the market because they feel that the price has become unsustainably extended from its mean of support, whether it be a trendline, a moving average, or a previous support or resistance level. Once the sellers have moved the price down partway, buyers come back in, halting the selling pressure and moving the price back up, but the buyers don't currently have the strength to completely overcome the sellers. The sellers then come back in, but in smaller number; they halt the advance and drive the price back down, but not in enough force to bring the price down below the mini-swing low. The action looks like a small earthquake on a seismograph, with the tracings centering on a price point and oscillating to either side of the price point, which is exactly what is playing out in the market. The chart pattern is shown in Figure 3-29.

Be sure to use proper screening criteria for volume (more than 500,000 shares average daily volume) and check to make sure there are no earnings announcements scheduled in the next 10 trading days and there is no significant pending news.

Figure 3-29   Symmetrical Triangle

Immediately prior to breakout, volume and price movement should both be in very discrete ranges. Both the buyers, who supported the price and created the bottom leg of the triangle, and the sellers, who created resistance to the price and formed the top of the triangle, have committed all the capital they are willing to commit to their positions. The time it took to form the triangle, the consolidation period, should bring the price back to one of the following support levels:

1. The lower trendline (the wholesale price in a trending stock) if the stock has been trading in an upwardly sloped trend channel
2. The 20-day SMA (short-term support)
3. The 50-day SMA (medium-term support)
4. Any reasonable wholesale price point

A symmetrical triangle offers two trade triggers. For the more conservative trader, the trade trigger will be when the stock price breaks the last mini-swing high, signaling a breakout in force as other institutions that sat out the consolidation have determined that the upward trend is intact and the price is at a support level come into the market in force.

The more aggressive trader will enter the trade when the stock price breaks the upper boundary line as drawn on a chart to illustrate the upper portion of the triangle. In either case, we recommend a buy stop–limit order for a controlled entry, with the limit $0.10 to $0.20 above the stop.

For traders using the more aggressive entry point of the upper boundary of the triangle, it is important to realize that, depending on how you draw the boundary, the price may briefly poke its head above the boundary, filling your order, and then revert to the midpoint of the triangle or below. This may tie up your capital in the position for an extended period of time before the price makes a genuine move one way or the other.

The four basic bullish chart patterns that we've covered—high base, ascending triangle, bull pullback, and symmetrical triangle breakout—and minor variations of these patterns will cover 80 percent of the bullish setups you will encounter as a trader.

By using the Top-Down Approach and identifying the correct chart pattern, you will be entering bullish positions in a safer manner than blindly clicking the BUY button on something that "looks good."

If you've never traded technically before, the best way to identify chart patterns is through practice. You should already be applying the Top-Down Approach on a daily basis to get a feel for what the market is doing and what sectors are strongest and weakest. Go through the stocks in your screen and briefly look at the charts. You will learn to identify the chart patterns quickly.

At Maverick Trading we conduct a Charting Lab for our traders each week. Even though we look at charts on a daily basis, we still see the need to practice in a group setting and refine our skills.

As a trader, you will need to find the balance between over-analyzing a chart, on the one hand, and forcing a bad chart into a preconceived notion of the formation, on the other.

What about the situations where there is an uptrending stock that you want to get into? Just buy it then, right?

To do so is to revert to trading by the seat of your pants. We trade with a plan, and the plan on each trade is designed to provide us with the safest entry point to capitalize on a highly probable follow-through.

We see stocks all the time that exhibit remarkable gains, but that trade erratically and offer no safe entry points. We just let those go by. We may miss out on a few gains throughout the year, but we are consistently profitable, and we'd rather be profitable than right.

BEARISH CHART PATTERNS

At Maverick, we trade both sides of the market, bullish and bearish. Depending on what the broad market and individual sectors are doing, we will often have both bullish and bearish positions. We describe this stance as market agnostic; we don't care which way the market is going; we're going to make money on either side.

If you've studied any other established and tested investment or trading systems, it should be apparent that these systems are biased toward the bullish side. There's nothing wrong with some of these systems when the market is bullish, but your options are extremely limited during a significant correction or an outright bear market: you can either sit on the sidelines in cash (which is sometimes the best strategy regardless of the trading system) or attempt to eke out marginal gains in those few sectors that show strength.

When market, sector, and stock conditions give the signal to do so, it makes sense to take a bearish position. Don't fight the trend; you'll just lose money and a lot of sleep. Remember, we don't care if the bus is going uptown or downtown; we just want to find the fastest bus and ride it for a while.

The investment systems that we're comparing are biased toward the bullish side because conventional wisdom says that the bullish side is safer. This is a carryover from the buy-and-hold mentality of yesteryear coupled with the marketing genius of mutual funds and investment advisors. Few authors and publishers want to deal with the media coverage when someone shorts a rising market, doesn't use risk controls, never checks positions, and then blames the system for massive losses.

Bearish positions can be entered with the same probabilities of success as bullish positions. Likewise, when we enter bearish positions, we use the same sorts of risk controls that we do for bullish positions.

The Top-Down Approach is still used in establishing bearish positions. In fact, the Top-Down Approach is what tells us when to enter bearish positions.

Bearish chart setups effectively mirror bullish chart setups. At Maverick, we predominantly use the low base, descending triangle, bear rally, and symmetrical triangle breakdown.

The Low Base

The low base is a classic example of a stock falling to an established level of support, followed by overhead supply eating through the underlying support, and then falling to new lows.

Trade Setup Use the Top-Down Approach to establish that the broad market is in a downtrend and to establish which sectors are the weakest. The best possible scenario when entering a bearish position is to have the broad market in a downtrend and then to select candidates from the two weakest sectors. In an uptrending or sideways market, you can still find shortable candidates in the two weakest sectors, but be prepared to reduce your position size.

As part of your screening criteria, the price of the stock should be above $15 minimum. Many institutions and mutual funds have precluded themselves from investing in stocks below a minimum share price, usually $5 to $10. You want to have institutional interest in the stock because you want the institutions to have continued motivation to sell. Average daily volume should still be above 500,000 because you want the liquidity and the narrow bid-ask spreads that liquidity provides.

Always check for earnings announcements scheduled in the next 10 trading days and significant pending news. You will often see an underperforming stock hit a level of support in what looks like a low base, only to surprise to the upside on the earnings announcement, reversing the trend. An upside surprise when you are short a stock is not a pleasant position to be in.

The price action will be the stock making a new swing low and finding support. As in the high base, the stock has traded away from a mean and needs time to revert to a mean. From the new swing low, the stock will trade sideways and consolidate in a narrow range with relatively equal highs and lows. The consolidation period should bring the stock price back to one of the following resistance levels:

1. The upper trendline in a stock trading in a trend channel. Remember from earlier in this chapter that upper trendlines represent retail prices and lower trendlines represent wholesale prices. We sell at retail and buy at wholesale, even when we're short and selling first and buying back second.
2. The 20-day SMA (short-term resistance). Downtrending stocks will trade below their SMAs, making the SMAs a level of resistance.
3. The 50-day SMA (medium-term resistance).
4. Any reasonable retail price point.

Institutions that have long positions in the stock want to sell at the best price possible, even in a downtrending stock. If they established the position when the stock was at a higher price, they want to exit with as small a loss as possible.

Providing support are both buyers who feel that the price of the stock has fallen too far, too fast, so that it represents a buying opportunity, and institutions whose fundamental analysis indicates that the stock is a good value at current levels.

Volume will taper during the consolidation period. Sellers don't want to swamp the market with all their shares at once. Not only would that rapidly depress the price, increasing their losses, but they cling to the hope that the stock will rebound, and they don't want to be in the position of having liquidated their entire position just as the stock moves back up.

Once the stock catches up with one of the given levels of resistance, any motivated sellers, including short sellers, will often sell in strength. If the few institutions that were supporting the stock price have committed all the capital they are willing to commit to the stock, there is really no more support for the stock left at the level of consolidation. This causes an imbalance on the demand-supply seesaw, resulting in a decline in price through the consolidation level. The chart looks like Figure 3-30.

The trade trigger for entering a short position from a low base is when the stock price breaks the low of consolidation or a recent group of relatively equal lows. Support on the buy side has been exhausted, and those institutions that were recently buying and providing support are now looking to sell to minimize their own losses. This is added to the supply from the institutions that were liquidating their positions already and the short sellers establishing positions.

We generally enter our short positions using a sell stop–limit. As in a high base, we don't want to let the price get away from us when we're establishing a short position. The stop is placed $0.10 to $0.25 below the consolidation low, depending on the liquidity

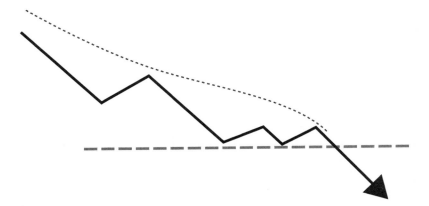

Figure 3-30   Low Base

of the stock. The more liquid the stock, the less the amount of the stop. We don't put the stop directly at the consolidation low or just a penny below it because we don't want to enter a position on a false signal; we want to enter only on a genuine breakdown.

While volume tapered during consolidation, we like to see at least twice the average daily volume on a breakdown. If your order was triggered, but at the end of the day you see that volume was still below the daily average, you may have been triggered on a false signal. You can either keep the position but tighten your risk controls or exit the position and wait for the true breakdown to occur.

The limit portion of the order is usually $0.10 to $0.20 below the stop we established. We treat gaps down in a low base the same way we treat gaps up in a high base. We don't want to chase a stock either way, and we don't want to establish a position in an exhaustion gap. If the stock gaps down on the breakdown below your limit price, wait a day or two to see whether the gap was a true breakdown gap or an exhaustion gap, with the last sellers liquidating their positions in a frenzy of activity and leaving nothing but buyers.

Descending Triangle

Descending triangles are like low bases, except that they show the existence of motivated buyers at the beginning of the chart pattern. Like the low base, the descending triangle is a consolidation pattern in which the stock is building energy and sellers are eating away at the underlying demand.

Like ascending triangles, descending triangles fail more often than low bases. Again, it is a question of who will run out of capital and/or stock first. When the sellers and short sellers run out of stock and capital before the underlying buyers do so, the pattern fails and often reverses. When the buyers providing the underlying support run out of capital first, the pattern triggers as the stock breaks down to new lows. The chart pattern looks like Figure 3-31.

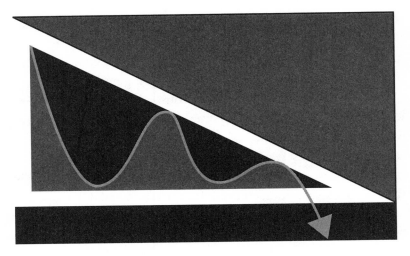

Figure 3-31   Descending Triangle

Trade Setup As with a low base, you can enter a descending tri-angle setup in either an uptrending market or a downtrending market. If the broad market is uptrending, then the stock should be downtrending and the stock's sector should come from one of the two worst-performing sectors of the market. The sectors should actually have been making losses, not just be underper-forming the broad market.

You should have executed your screening criteria for price (above $15), volume, and sector, and checked for earnings (no scheduled announcements in the next 10 trading days) and pending significant news, and the stock should have recently made a new swing low.

From the new swing low, the stock will trade sideways in consolidation with the swing low, establishing a clear support level for the stock. The consolidation lasts a minimum of 5 trading days and could extend to as many as 15 in the case of a volatile stock or significant underlying support. In addition to a clearly estab-lished support level, you should see a series of descending highs forming the upper portion of the triangle. This consolidation should bring the stock price back to:

1. The upper trendline (the retail price in a trending stock)
2. The 20-day SMA (short-term resistance)
3. The 50-day SMA (medium-term resistance)
4. Any reasonable retail price point

During consolidation, the volume will taper off, often proportionally to the height of the triangle that is being formed. The declining volume illustrates that there are three camps with an interest in the stock.

The first camp consists of the motivated sellers who want to get out in the near future. Their analysis says that the stock is likely to continue downward, and they want to exit their positions in the near future to preserve their capital to the greatest extent possible. This accounts for the descending highs and partially accounts for the decreasing volume as the number of institutions decreasing their positions decreases as time moves forward.

The second camp consists of the buyers who are providing the support for the stock forming the base of the triangle. Their analysis indicates that the stock is a value buy at the level they have established, and the stock will continue to be attractive to them at that level. These buyers account for the other half of the volume picture, as they established the bulk of their position early in the formation of the pattern and are adding to the position only when the stock approaches their buy point.

The third camp is made up of the institutions that decided not to sell for whatever reason when the buyers showed up and provided support for the stock. They are in wait-and-see mode. If other buyers become attracted to the stock, those in the wait-and-see crowd look will like steely-eyed geniuses. If other buyers don't come in and those buyers that provided support run out of capital before the sellers run out of stock, the wait-and-see crowd will look like blithering idiots who should have sold when they had the chance.

What triggers the follow-through of the pattern is just a few institutions in the wait-and-see crowd looking at a chart and seeing that the stock price has come back to one of the resistance levels previously discussed. A few of the wait-and-see crowd decide that discretion is the better part of valor and that it is time to get out at present levels while they have the chance. It's better to be the first person out the door in a burning building than the poor guy left to turn off the lights.

Up until this point, the buyers have been able to absorb the volume from the sellers, but the new volume from the first defectors from the wait-and-see crowd has overwhelmed them. The buyers are out of capital and are now worried about a loss in their own positions. They are no longer buying and may begin to lighten up their positions, adding to the selling pressure. This imbalance in the demand-supply seesaw drives prices lower, triggering entry into your own short position.

Once the trade triggers by the price breaking below the consolidation low, enter the trade by using a sell stop–limit order. We usually set the stop $0.10 to $0.25 below the consolidation low and the limit $0.10 to $0.20 below the stop.

Bear Rally

The bear rally is a continuation pattern like the bull pullback, and like the bull pullback, it represents orderly profit taking in an established trend. Bear rallies present safe entry points for short positions in a strongly downtrending stock.

These mini rallies are often driven by hedge funds and other short-term traders who have previously taken a short position in a stock and find the current prices attractive for booking some profits. Short-term countertrend traders (those who are addicted to Maalox) will also take the opportunity to enter a long position in a downtrending stock that has become overextended to the downside.

At Maverick, we're not on the side of the trade that causes the bear rally, we're on the side that benefits from its creation, using the rally as an entry point into a short position.

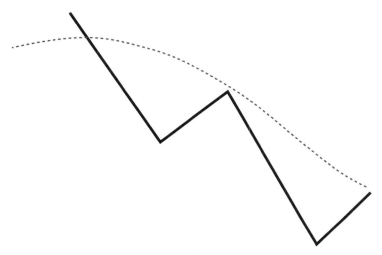

Figure 3-32   Bear Rally

The chart of a bear rally is shown in Figure 3-32.

Use the Top-Down Approach and screening criteria to find a downtrending stock in one of the two weakest-performing sectors. Again, there should be no earnings announcements scheduled in the next 10 trading days and no pending news.

Trade Setup The stock has established a downtrend and has recently made a new swing low. You should see a uniform rally of at least two to three days (possibly more). This rally should produce both higher daily highs and higher daily lows. You're looking for orderly and uniform buying as short sellers cover their positions and countertrend traders establish their long positions.

You want to see equal or lower volume on the rally as compared to the volume on the last down leg of the trend. The rally should bring the stock back to one of the following resistance levels:

1. The upper trendline of the trend channel
2. The 20-day SMA (short-term resistance)
3. The 50-day SMA (medium-term resistance)
4. Any reasonable retail price point

As with a bull pullback, don't try to be a hero when entering a short position. As much as it will often pain you to do so, wait until price confirms that the bear rally has finished and the downtrend has resumed. The trade trigger is when the stock breaks below the previous day's lows. It is also helpful, but not necessary, to see a reversal candle pattern at the area of resistance, either a doji or a shooting star. This is a clear indication that supply has equaled demand or that supply has overcome demand at the area of resistance. When price action breaks the previous day's low, that is the signal that short-term buying is over and the stock has resumed its downtrend.

We use a sell stop–limit order for a controlled entry into the position. The sell stop is placed directly below the previous day's low, usually $0.05 below. The limit is $0.10 to $0.20 below the stop, creating our window of entry.

The sell order is almost always a day order, canceled if it is not triggered the day it was entered. Unlike with the low base and the descending triangle, where we were waiting for a clear move below support and used a GTC order, with a bear rally, we look at the price action every day to see where the area of resistance actually occurs. The stock could rally through its 20-day SMA and find resistance at the 50-day SMA. We always wait for the price action to tell us when buying has ceased and sellers have resumed liquidating the stock.

The important concept is not to even attempt to call the short-term top. Concentrate on being profitable and entering the position when the trend has been reconfirmed rather than calling the top exactly.

Symmetrical Triangle Breakdown

Like the symmetrical triangle break*out*, the symmetrical triangle break*down* is a more complex chart pattern. The symmetrical triangle breakdown differs from the symmetrical triangle breakout only by where the stock has been and where it is likely to go in the future.

Symmetrical triangle breakdown setups should be used only by more experienced traders because they involve the same considerations as a symmetrical triangle breakout pattern. They are difficult to identify early in formation, they can break either way with little warning, they are more prone to failure than other bearish chart patterns, and they can stagnate or continue erratic performance.

Again, we recommend not searching for symmetrical triangles but viewing them as targets of opportunity when they do present themselves.

Trade Setup A bearish symmetrical triangle is formed when a stock has recently made a new swing low and then trades generally sideways from the swing low. During the consolidation period, the stock displays descending highs and ascending lows, so that the price action is being squeezed from both the top and the bottom. Trendlines drawn along both the highs and the lows should clearly define a triangle pattern, and the slope should be roughly the same at the top and the bottom. Any skew in the trendline slopes gives a good indication as to the next likely direction of the move.

Consolidation and formation of the triangle should last for a minimum of 5 days, and it could even take between 10 and 15 trading days to form. During consolidation, volume will often taper along with the triangle; wider price moves at the left side of the triangle will have more volume than the minor price moves at the right side of the triangle, often with minuscule price movement and volume immediately prior to the breakdown.

Symmetrical triangle breakdown patterns are found using the Top-Down Approach. Because of the volatility associated with symmetrical triangles, to maximize the chances of success, we recommend that all three escalators—market, sector, and stock—be in downtrends. You will probably already have the stock on your watch list as a candidate for a short position, possibly as a bear rally position.

Like the bullish symmetrical triangle, the bearish symmetrical triangle chart setup takes longer to develop than other chart patterns because some event caused price action to move significantly away from the mean it was following. Consequently, it takes the mean more time to catch up to the price of the stock.

Again, there are two equally motivated camps at work in a bearish symmetrical triangle. After the stock has made its new swing low, buyers come into the market because they feel that the price has become unsustainably extended from its mean of resistance. Once buyers have moved the price up partway, sellers come back into the market, halting the buying pressure and moving the price back down, but now the sellers don't have the strength or the conviction to completely overcome the buyers. The buyers come back in, in smaller numbers, halting the decline and driving the price back up, but not in sufficient strength to raise the price above the mini-swing high. The earthquake pattern develops, oscillating across a midpoint. The chart pattern is shown in Figure 3-33.

Figure 3-33   Symmetrical Triangle Breakdown

Be sure to use proper screening criteria for volume (more than 500,000 shares average daily volume), and check to make sure that there are no earnings announcements scheduled in the next 10 trading days and no significant pending news.

Immediately prior to the breakdown, volume and price movement should both be in very discrete ranges. Both buyers and sellers have committed all the capital that they are willing to commit to their positions. The time it took to form the triangle should bring the price back to one of the following resistance levels:

1. The upper trendline if the stock has been trading in a downward-sloping trend channel
2. The 20-day SMA (short-term resistance)
3. The 50-day SMA (medium-term resistance)
4. Any reasonable retail price point

A symmetrical triangle breakdown offers two trade triggers. For the more conservative trader, the trade trigger will be when the stock price breaks the last mini-swing low, signaling a breakdown in force as other institutions that sat on the sidelines during consolidation have determined that the downward trend is intact, the price is at a resistance level, and they had better get out while there is still time.

The more aggressive trader will enter the trade when the stock price breaks the lower trendline formed by the triangle. In either case, we recommend a sell stop–limit order for a controlled entry, with the limit $0.10 to $0.20 below the stop.

For traders using the more aggressive entry point of the lower trendline formed by the triangle, remember that depending on how you draw the trendline, the price may briefly fall below the trigger, filling your order, and then revert to the midpoint of the triangle or below. This may tie up your capital for an extended period of time before the price makes a genuine move, either confirming the trend or stopping you out.

The four basic bearish chart patterns that we've covered—low base, descending triangle, bear rally, and symmetrical triangle breakdown—will cover 80 percent of the bearish setups you will encounter as a trader. Using the Top-Down Approach and selecting the correct chart patterns, you will enter bearish positions in a safer manner rather than madly clicking the SELL button on something that just "looks" overextended or ready to move downward.

As with the bullish setups, identifying bearish chart patterns takes practice. Use the Top-Down Approach to identify weakness and then search for the chart patterns we've covered in the very weakest sectors. You may miss out on some gains in a downtrending stock that trades erratically, but you will have less stress and be more consistent and more profitable. As always, the goal is to be profitable, not right.

SIDEWAYS AND STAGNATION PATTERNS

There is an industry term for stocks that make no significant moves, up or down, for an extended period of time. They're called dead money. You can't make money on the long side, and you can't make money on the short side.

If you're trading only stocks, you want to stay away from these issues. All they do is tie up capital that can be put to better use in trending positions. But, as we'll see in the next chapter, if you're trading options, you can make money on stocks that are moving sideways and stagnating. That said, it's a good idea to recognize the chart patterns associated with these setups.

You will find stagnating stocks in all types of sectors: outperforming, market-performing, and underperforming. They will usually be the large-cap, behemoth names, but you will occasionally find some mid-cap stocks that make good stagnation plays. You want to know what the overall market and the stock's sector are doing so that you can give yourself a potential bias in whatever stagnation strategy you decide to execute.

When you see a stock that looks like it is stagnating, the first thing you want to do is identify the range that it's trading in. Looking at the chart pattern, you should see the stock meander up to the top of the range, slowly roll over, and then meander back down to the bottom of the range. You're looking for a trading range of 10 percent of the stock's price or less. If it's much more than that, the trading range will start to attract traders who will ride the stock up to the top of the range and then short it down to the bottom. If these traders begin to come in force and start to add significant volume, institutions will take notice and will either add to their positions or begin liquidating, knocking the stock out of its range and into a trend. Volume should be nearly uniform throughout the stagnation period.

The next items to look for are the 20-day and 50-day SMAs. The SMAs should be fairly flat, indicating no recent trend up or down. In the ideal situation, you will see the stock sitting above the 20-day SMA, which is stacked on top of the 50-day SMA. The difference between the 20-day SMA and the 50-day SMA should be minimal, with no large gaps between the averages.

The alternative setup is to see the stock price, still trading in a narrow range, dip up and down through the 20- and 50-day SMAs. In this pattern, the SMAs will show some oscillation, and sometimes the 20-day SMA will briefly cross through the 50-day SMA and then rise back above it.

In addition to individual stocks, sector ETFs exhibit stagnation patterns more often and are often a higher-probability trade than the underlying stocks. ETFs mute the movement of the individual stocks, and a stagnation period can reflect an institutional appetite for certain names within a sector, but apathy for the sector as a whole.

We'll cover the techniques for profiting from these chart patterns in the next chapter, but the rule of thumb is to attempt to enter the position when the stock is in the middle of the channel.

The nine chart patterns covered in this chapter (four bullish, four bearish, and stagnation) form the basis for entering positions using Maverick's systems. There are many more chart patterns available, but we have found these nine to be the most consistent and profitable.

As you extend your professional knowledge beyond what we've included in this book, you will be tempted to trade other, more complicated chart patterns. By all means, go ahead; just be sure that you understand the psychological underpinnings behind the charts: what are the institutional decision makers and traders thinking on a broad basis?

4

OPTIONS AND TRADING TECHNIQUES: THE SECRET SAUCE

Used correctly, options are an excellent tool that you can use to leverage your capital so that you achieve truly outstanding gains, hedge your portfolio during times of market uncertainty, and generate income during periods of market stagnation. Used incorrectly, options are an excellent tool for completely imploding your portfolio.

In the typical evolution of a retail investor, after he has learned how to short the market, the investor starts to see pop-up ads on his favorite financial sites touting the glorious benefits of options. The next step is usually to research options briefly, then download an options trading application from his broker.

After answering a few questions, the trader will be cleared to either sell covered calls or enter long positions in both calls and puts. To us, these are the most dangerous ways to use options. New traders are blinded by wildly unrealistic potential gains, so that they often enter positions that are too large or too expensive, and are counting on a wholly improbable move in a stock just to break even. Time is working against them, and they have no understanding of hedging, implied volatility, and time decay, and because of the restrictions on what their broker has allowed them to do, they have no ability to hedge their positions to reduce the effect of time decay.

When options are used properly, a trader can define down to the penny the exact amount of risk in each position as well as the exact amount of potential reward, and in some cases can leave room for performance that exceeds expectations. Additionally, the trader has to commit only a small portion of the capital required to establish an equivalent position in straight stock or in what can be called a synthetic long or short position. More than 90 percent of our trades involve the use of options, often to the exclusion of stock. This is a form of risk control and reward maximization that we have come to know and love, and profit from greatly.

Options are to be respected, but not feared. Brokers would have you think that options are dangerous, but it is a lack of education and tools that is dangerous. It is the same thing when you ask whether a gun is dangerous. A gun by itself is not dangerous at all. However, a gun in the wrong hands can lead to bad results. Options in the hands of an untrained user typically lead to disastrous results. A gun in the hand of a trained user who is implementing all possible safety measures can be quite safe overall.

WHAT ARE OPTIONS, AND HOW ARE THEY USED?

Plenty of books have already been written that describe what options are in eye-bleeding detail. We've read most of them. While some are good, in many cases we ended up wanting to jam pencils in our ears just to give us an excuse to stop reading. We'll tell you what we think you *need* to know about options. There's no reason to complicate an issue unnecessarily. If you want to learn about the more exotic (and less important) aspects of options, by all means do a Web search for options: you'll have reading material for the next month.

Buying an option gives you a right, but not an obligation, to buy or sell a stock at a given price within a set period of time. The price of an option is called the *premium*, the level that the option is good for is called the *strike price*, and the last date on which the option is good is called the *expiration date*. So how does this all work?

You actually see options in real estate quite a bit, especially in periods of uncertainty. This is the example that we use to orient new traders entering Maverick's training program.

Let's say you find a house that you like, and that house is listed at $100,000 (just play along; we know it's difficult to find a good house for $100,000). You may not be sure that you want to buy that particular house, but you don't want anyone else to buy it while you're out looking around.

You go to the owners and let them know that you like the house and you like the price, but you want some more time to think about it. You ask the owners for the option, the possibility, that you could buy their house in three months at their asking price of $100,000. For this right to buy the house in 90 days, you tell them that you are willing to pay them $1,000. If you don't buy the house after 90 days, they get to keep the $1,000. You've got all three aspects of an option right there: premium ($1,000), strike price of the house ($100,000), and expiration date (90 days).

So what happens now?

Scenario 1: The value of the house rises. Gold is discovered on the land the house is sitting on, and the current owners have mineral rights. Suddenly, the house is now valued at $150,000. You have the right to buy the house at $100,000. You are not obligated to buy the house, but since the owners sold you the option, they are obligated to sell it to you at the agreed-upon price of $100,000. The logical thing to do would be to exercise the option, buying the house for $100,000 and getting $50,000 in instant equity.

Scenario 2: The value of the house falls. A freak tornado lands on the house and rips off the roof (no homeowners were harmed during this scenario). Repairs are going to cost $20,000, so the house is now worth $80,000. It would make no sense to pay $100,000 to buy an $80,000 house, so you let the option to buy the house expire. The owners get to keep the $1,000 premium that you paid them for the right to buy the house at $100,000.

Scenario 3: The value of the house stays right around $100,000. Nothing happens to the real estate market or the house during the 90 days your option to buy was good for. You can make the decision to buy the house for $100,000, in which case your cost basis would be $101,000 (the cost of the house plus the cost of the option), or you can decide not to buy the house and let the option expire. You would then be out $1,000, the premium you paid for the option to buy the house.

In financial markets, options work the same way, both in rising markets and in falling markets. The buyer is buying the right to buy or sell something at a given price within a set time frame and is paying a premium for that right. The seller is selling the obligation to buy or sell something at a given price within a set time frame and is collecting a premium for the risk of doing so.

BREAD AND BUTTER: CALLS AND PUTS

Calls and puts are the DNA of trading with options; they are the building blocks from which we can build some very beautiful and profitable structures. Despite the length of "Characteristics and Risks of Standardized Options Contracts," which your broker will send you multiple times throughout your career, options are comparatively easy to understand.

To start off, all options are linked to an underlying instrument, which is why they are referred to as *derivatives*. They derive their value from the underlying instrument. In our case, the underlying instrument is a particular stock that we are contemplating taking a position in. Almost all sector and broad-market ETFs have options as well. This lets us take positions in a market, a sector, or an individual stock, which is very handy.

Here's some industry jargon for you to throw around at cocktail parties: the term *underlying instrument* is almost always shortened to "the underlying," with the instrument portion of the phrase left off for the sake of coolness. Example: "Yeah, I've got a bull put spread in [insert name of stock here], but I'm short the underlying to take advantage of theta decay." Your conversation partner will get a glassy look in his eyes and then say, "Well, yeah, of course. I'd do the same thing. So what do you think of the Redskins' chances this year?" Bam! Instant street cred, and your friends will stop giving you stock tips on the latest microcap dog they were spammed about.

The next characteristic is that each options contract represents 100 shares of the underlying. Prices are quoted on a per share basis. So if an options contract is quoted as having a $2 price at the ask, that particular contract will cost $200 to buy. Likewise, if you buy one contract, your effective position is 100 shares; if you buy 10 contracts, your effective position is 1,000 shares; and if you buy 500 contracts (the typical position limit for retail brokers), your effective position is 50,000 shares.

Each contract has an expiration date. ETFs generally have options expiring every month. Stocks will have expiration dates of the near month, called the *front month*, the following month, and then quarterly thereafter. Let's say that it's January 2 of any given year, and you pull up a list of options expiration dates for a stock you're interested in. You'll always see January's and February's contracts, but you will see March, April, or May expiration contracts (one of the three, not all three) as well. The methodology behind this occurrence isn't important. All that's important is that you realize that the situation exists.

The third Friday of every month is known as Expiration Friday. All the stock options contracts for that month expire on that day. Actually, they expire on the Saturday after Expiration Friday, but you can't trade on Saturday, so we're concerned only with the closing price on that Friday. Hey, we don't make the rules; we just make money off of them.

A consequence of Expiration Friday is that both the Thursday before and the Friday itself can be volatile as traders and options market makers roll their positions. You'll often see more volatile action on these days, so be prepared for it.

An emerging trend is to have weekly expirations for widely held stocks and ETFs. These expire every Friday. Quotes for the next week appear at market open on Friday, so these are really just eight-day options. Be aware that these options exist, because they can be very profitable in capitalizing on short-term moves.

Some contracts, like those on the S&P 500 Volatility Index (the VIX) are European-style options. Bless the Europeans, but they do do things differently. European-style contracts expire after the market close on Tuesdays. Usually the Tuesday of expiration is in the same week as Expiration Friday, but not always. Be sure to check the expiration date of the contract. If the Europeans have confused you again, just add it to the list of puzzling things about them, like berets, saying the word *Louvre*, and their love for soccer.

Each option also has a price above or below which it is effective. This is known as the strike price. We'll see how this works shortly.

As we mentioned at the start of the section, options come in two flavors, calls and puts.

If you buy a call contract (a long position), you are buying the right, but not the obligation, to buy the underlying stock at a set price on or before a set date. You are calling the stock to you ("Here, boy; come here"). If you sell a call contract (a short position), you are incurring the obligation to sell the underlying stock at a set price on a certain date.

If you are long (remember, being long means that you have purchased something) a put contract, you are buying the right to sell the underlying stock at a set price on or before a set date. You are putting the stock to someone else ("Please take this dog off my hands"). If you short (remember, being short means that you have sold something first) a put contract, you are incurring the obligation to buy the underlying stock at a set price on a certain date.

Here's where strike prices come in. Let's say you bought (went long) one call contract of XYZ stock at the $40 strike price. Between the time you bought the contract and the expiration date, XYZ went on a tear. It's now trading at $45. Your contract is said to be in-the-money (ITM).

Because you own the options contract, you have the right to buy 100 shares of XYZ at $40. You've paid the premium for this right, and the market maker took the premium to assume the risk. Since the stock is now trading at $45, the value of your contract is about $500 {100 shares × [(current price ($45) – strike price ($40)]}. Near the end of the trading day, the quote for this particular options contract will probably be about $4.90 bid and $5.10 ask.

Now, you can liquidate the position before the market closes and get $490 for the contract, or you can let the contract be exercised. When a contract is exercised, what the contract says, happens. So if your contract was to buy 100 shares of XYZ at $40, you will end up buying 100 shares of XYZ at $40. Most retail brokers will automatically exercise an ITM option if it's at least $0.25 ITM. At Maverick, we very rarely allow ourselves to get exercised. The amount of capital tied up is greatly increased, and we have to determine what to do with the shares after being exercised. That 40 strike XYZ contract that we may have bought for $2 and committed $200 in capital to is now 100 shares of stock at $40, which is $4,000 in capital tied up in the position.

But most important of all is that the risk parameter of our trade changes over the weekend, as we technically own the stock.

At this point, we have what is called "event risk," and anything bad (or good) that happens over the weekend will have risk profiles that are different from the risk profiles of the original position that you planned. We are anal-retentive about risk, and we make sure that our risk profile is always in line with our trading methodology.

What happens if the price of the stock falls below the strike price? Let's say that between the time you bought the option and its expiration, the price of XYZ fell to $39. The option is now out-of-the-money (OTM). The option expires worthless. A rational person wouldn't pay $40 for a stock that can be bought on the open market for $39.

When a stock is trading at the strike price, $40 in our scenario, the option is said to be at-the-money (ATM). Options pricing for ATM options is more volatile than that for ITM and OTM options.

Put options work the same way as call options, but on the sell side of the equation. The best way to understand a put option is that it gives you the option to short a stock at a set price on or before a set date. Let's look at the $40 XYZ puts. If you buy a put at the $40 strike and the price of XYZ goes down to $35, your $40 put is now ITM. If the price of XYZ rises to $41, your put is out-of-the-money. You wouldn't sell (short) something for $40 if you could get someone else to pay $41.

SPECULATION AND HEDGING

The options market serves two purposes: speculation and hedging. Of the two purposes, institutions primarily use options as a hedging tool. Remember that institutional positions take time to build and time to liquidate; institutions can't move into and out of the market as quickly as we can. Often, if a potentially detrimental event can be seen on the horizon, like a pending court case or even just a scheduled earnings announcement or conference call, institutions will go to the options market and buy protection in the form of puts. If they own 100,000 shares of a stock, they might buy 1,000 put contracts to provide downside protection for an event. They will pay a premium for the protection, but if the stock drops precipitously because of bad news, the downside will be covered.

When they are used to hedge a position, options actually work a lot like insurance contracts. An insurance contract you buy on your home will be very similar to a hedged put option. The premium on your insurance contract will be determined by the insurance company's analysis of three things: the amount of coverage, the period of coverage, and the perceived or implied risk. Obviously an insurance contract for a $1 million house right in hurricane alley in Florida will have a different insurance premium from a contract for a log cabin in North Dakota (no offense to North Dakota, of course). Option premiums in the market are determined by the strike price (insured amount), the expiration date (length of contract), and the perceived risk of the underlying option (implied volatility).

After the anticipated event, if the stock moves down, the institution can decide whether to keep the position as part of a longer-term strategy or liquidate it at leisure. If the stock moves up after the event, the institution is out the premium that it paid for the puts, but it probably didn't lose much sleep in the days leading up to the event. Some people would be upset if they lost money in this situation, but this would be the same thing as being upset that your house didn't burn to the ground, so you didn't get to use your insurance policy. We won't even mention the people who get upset on a monthly basis when they don't get to use their life insurance.

Likewise, large hedge funds that have a significant short position in a stock can use calls to hedge the risk that a stock will vault to the upside immediately after a news event. If the stock continues its downward move, the hedge fund sells back the calls.

If the stock does move to the upside, owning the calls will offset the losses in the fund's short position.

The second use of options, speculation, is the primary use of options in Maverick's system. Options allow a trader to control a significant block of stock with a relatively small outlay of capital.

Let's say that XYZ just broke to the upside in a high base. The trade trigger was $40. We could buy 100 shares of stock for $4,000, or we could buy one $40 call contract that expires in a month for about $200, one-twentieth of the capital required for the stock itself. If the stock goes up to $44, a 10 percent move, the straight stock is worth $4,400 (also a 10 percent gain). However, our single call contract is worth $400, a 100 percent gain.

If the stock drops to $38, both traders have a $200 loss, but the options trader hasn't tied up nearly as much capital. If the stock drops below $38, the trader with the stock continues to lose money, but the options trader is already at her maximum loss. If you look back to our ideals for risk control, we define what we're willing to risk prior to placing the trade.

By using options, we can focus our attention on the movement of a stock within a discrete range. In our XYZ case, we're interested in the stock only on any movement above $40. If there's any movement below $40, the stock doesn't interest us. We don't want to commit the capital and participate in potential losses below $40. We could take the same $4,000 that 100 shares of XYZ would cost us and get 10 or more different positions (remember trading as a basket). We're not pinning our hopes on one stock to make a 10 percent move. We're profiting on the probabilities that several of our positions will be successful and will make up for the losing positions.

HOW NOT TO LOSE YOUR SHIRT: COMMON PITFALLS WITH OPTIONS

Many retail traders, when first exposed to options, come to realize the power that they have at their fingertips. Visions of becoming a millionaire in a month dance in front of their eyes. They begin to pick out what yacht they want and consider whether to spend the Christmas holidays in Basel or Rio. Greed overpowers common sense. Consequently, they can do some very stupid things. We've seen some truly impressive blunders over the years. These pitfalls generally fall into three categories, or combinations thereof.

The first pitfall is buying options that are far out-of-the-money. New traders, and some experienced ones, buy these options because they are cheap. A stock could be trading at $40 and the $40 strikes could be trading at $2, but the $60 strikes could be trading at $0.20. We'll discuss options pricing shortly, but if you pull up an options chain, you'll see that the further OTM an option is, the cheaper it is as well.

Ebenezer Scrooge begins to emerge in the trader, and he starts conversations with himself along the lines of: "This stock could go to $65. Those $60 strikes will be worth $5, and the option costs only $0.25. I'll make 20 times my money! *Woooo ah ah ah ah*! I'll be *rich! Rich, I tell you!*"

Let's take a look at this. A $25 move in a $40 stock to $65 is a 62.5 percent move. Just to get the $60 strike to the ATM point is a 50 percent move, and the trader is probably looking at the front-month (closest month) contracts. So for these options to have any value in the next month, the stock needs to make at least a 50 percent move. How likely is that? It's likely to happen between two and three times out of a hundred. In general, if you do this, you'll be right once in every 30 to 50 attempts.

We see banner ads on websites touting such "investment systems" all the time. They usually have an attractive banner saying something like, "26-Year-Old Genius Becomes Gazillionaire with Never-Fail Options Strategy." On a personal level, each of us would happily stake these touts to a nest of red ants and pour honey over them. It is impossible to count the number of portfolios that have been damaged or destroyed outright by systems like this that rely on wildly improbable events.

What makes it maddeningly hard for Maverick's coaches in dealing with the people that come to trade with us who have been exposed to systems relying on buying OTM options is that very occasionally, these systems work. The profits on those 2 or 3 trades out of 100 are spectacular. The losses on the other 97 trades are forgotten, and these traders begin to have faith that they can reproduce these results consistently.

Looking at it strictly from a percentages point of view, when you're losing 97 times out of 100 and making 25 times returns the other three times, you're still behind 97 to 75, which is a bad score in any ball game.

Robb: Being cheap was a huge problem of mine when I began as a trader. I grew up in a family where Mom diluted the ketchup, mustard, and A1 sauce until they were 95 percent water and Dad somehow psychically knew when someone dared to put the thermostat in the house over 70 degrees. He could be at work, but he would call home and somehow know that we had had the audacity to move the heat up to 71. I grew up in an environment where every penny counted and you always looked for the cheapest way to do things. That has been a great lesson in life, but it has been a terrible strategy in the market and investing. I have learned very expensive lessons in my life that you get what you pay for, especially in the market.

In the first years of my career, I was always looking for a cheap stock that hadn't made a run yet. I would ignore all the other stocks that were running and focus on the ones that were "cheap," since they used to be $40 and were now trading at $15. This is called the value trap, and it should be left to long-term investors who understand how to read a company balance sheet and truly find value—not just a low stock price.

I had to learn the fundamental law as a trader. For a trader, *the only thing that matters is supply and demand.* I would ignore the stocks that were experiencing strong buying pressure and buy only the stocks that were experiencing strong selling pressure. Or I would short only the strongest, highest stocks, since they had gone up so much that they had to come down. This outlook caused me to take my biggest loss in a stock called Phone.com (this is a four-letter word in my house) in late 1999. Phone.com came public at $20 a share during the Internet boom and quickly ran to just under $100 per share in just a few weeks. The massive run attracted me to the stock, as I knew that anything that went up 400 percent in a few weeks was likely to have a pullback. Then I made the mistake of researching the company. Not only had Phone.com never reported a single dollar of profits, but it had not reported even a single dollar of revenue. That's right. It had never sold anything. It actually didn't even have a product to sell yet. It was in the process of developing a product that was going to work on either a phone or a computer, or maybe even both!

At this point, I became convinced that the stock was "expensive" because of the recent run it had had and the company's nonexistent earnings. So, I took a 1,200-share short position at 98^{1}/_{2}$ (we were still trading in fractions back then) and placed a stop at 99$^{7}/_{8}$ to lock in a loss around $1,500. Regardless of my personal opinion about the stock, there continued to be more buyers than sellers, and the stock went higher toward $100. I knew I was right on the trade and I didn't want to lose $1,500, so I canceled my stop order.

At around $120 a share, the position started to become real uncomfortable, and I decided to lighten up by buying back a couple of hundred shares. However, I didn't want to take the full loss, since the stock was now even more "expensive" and the fundamentals of the company were terrible. At $168 I took some more off the position, but not the entire amount, since I just *knew I was right*. At exactly 216$^{5}/_{8}$ I liquidated the rest of my position and wiped out most of my earnings for the year—with just one trade. I fell into every trap the novice trader can fall into, and it cost me about seven months' worth of work. The ironic thing was that

I was right! Phone.com did eventually go bust like many of the dot-coms . . . but it went to $320 first.

This trade and others by traders in the firm have given us the motto, "We would rather be profitable than right." So, when you trade the market, get rid of ideas like "cheap" or "expensive." Your concepts of "cheap" and "expensive" are just opinions and should never be part of your trading strategy. This was a very difficult mentality for me to break, since I had lived most of my young life with coupons, watered-down ketchup, and two-ply toilet paper being separated for more use (I am really not joking about that one). When it comes to investing and trading, you want to buy the "right" one and avoid the cheap ones (I hope you figured out that penny stocks are the cheapest and therefore most likely the worst).

The second common pitfall in using options is not allowing enough time for a move in the stock to occur. We'll see how time affects pricing in the next section, but pull up an options chain and you'll see that options with more time left until expiration cost more than the front-month options.

Even after a breakout or a breakdown, stocks take some time to make their moves. Sometimes after a breakout or breakdown, the stock will retrace to old support or resistance levels and hang out for a little bit before starting the move in earnest.

Traders often get in a rut and buy only the front-month options because they are cheaper than the longer-term options.

In the end, you could be right on direction but wrong on timing and end up with a losing trade. We would always prefer to be profitable than right. In later sections, we will explore how to reduce the effects of time decay and make it more profitable to give your trades a longer time period to work.

We often do use front-month options, especially when our experience tells us that the expected move will be short-term in nature, but we have techniques that allow us to experience less time decay.

A corollary to this pitfall is to ride a losing position to expiration in the hope that the option will magically come into the money before expiration. While we have techniques that allow us to weather some volatility, if we haven't hedged our time decay or if the chart pattern breaks down, we exit the position while there is still some value left in the option. A $1 loss is better than a $2 loss.

The third pitfall is position sizing. Traders often take on positions that are too large for their portfolio. The psychology behind this is understandable: if I'm going to be right on one contract, wouldn't it be better to be right on 100 contracts?

No. These traders have gotten hung up on being right rather than being profitable. This relates directly to the first chapter of this book, on risk management. Your position size should be directly related to your portfolio size and your risk tolerance.

On positions where we haven't hedged time decay, positions that are simply long calls and long puts, we have a 30 percent stop loss on our positions, which is tied to the Average True Range of the underlying stock. If we entered a position for a dollar, if the value of the option drops to 70 cents, we exit the position. Either the chart pattern failed or it is taking too much time to make its move. While we use trade triggers to minimize either of these events, they still happen.

At Maverick, we have strict position limits related to portfolio size. When you are trading on your own, you need to determine what the appropriate position size is for each position in your portfolio.

As an example, we'll use the same $10,000 portfolio we did in Chapter 1 and the same medium risk tolerance of 2.0 percent of the portfolio per position. In this case, that would be $200. Thus, $200 is the maximum loss that we are willing to take on any position.

It looks like our good friend XYZ Corporation has just broken out of a high base pattern and is trading at $40. Calls for the $40 strike are trading at $2. Our stop loss is 30 percent of the options premium, or $0.60. If the $40 strike calls trade at or below $1.40, we are going to automatically exit the position. With this stop loss, we are risking $60 per contract; $200 divided by $60 per contract gives us three contracts with a remainder. Throw the remainder away. Don't stretch it into a fourth contract.

If the option we were looking at was trading for $1 and we used a 30 percent stop loss, risking $30 per contract, we could get six contracts ($200 divided by $30). Seven contracts would put us over our risk limits. If the options were trading at $3, our stop loss would be $90 per contract, which means we could buy two contracts and stay within our risk limits.

These three pitfalls often combine, so that a trader's entire portfolio consists of cheap out-of-the-money options of short-term duration with position sizes that are too large for the portfolio. The trader has taken on too much risk in low-probability trades, and the result is an imploded portfolio and a fear of options.

Now that you know what the pitfalls in options trading are, you can avoid them easily. Just don't be guilty of falling into the traps. It's not like they've been camouflaged. They are out there for everyone to see.

OPTIONS PRICING: BLACK-SCHOLES AND WHAT YOU REALLY NEED TO KNOW

How are options priced? What determines how an option is valued? Why is one option more expensive than another? For the answers to these and other questions, we have three gentlemen to thank: Fischer Black, Myron Scholes, and Robert Merton. Their work in 1973 led to a reliable pricing formula for standardized options contracts and a Nobel Prize in economics in 1997. Here is a rare example of people with 40-lb brains bringing some order to chaos. Prior to their work, options pricing was very

Theoretical option price $= pN(d_1) - se^{-rt}N(d_2)$

where $d_1 = \dfrac{\ln(p/s) + (r + 1/2v^2)t}{v\sqrt{t}}$

and $d_2 = d_1 - v\sqrt{t}$

Variables:

p = stock price s = strike price t = time until expiration
r = current risk-free interest rate   (% of a year)
v = volatility (annual standard deviation) $\ln$ = natural logarithm
$N(x)$ = cumulative normal density function

Figure 4-1   Black-Scholes Options Pricing Model

much a from-the-hip affair. Finally, contracts became standard-ized and the computers to run the equation were able to keep up with the market, giving us the liquid options market we have today.

The Black-Scholes options pricing model is shown in Figure 4-1.

OK? Got it? Good. There will be a test on Friday.

Don't worry. We promised at the beginning of the book that you could be a successful and profitable trader with a grounding in fifth-grade math, and we intend to keep that promise. So what do you actually need to know about how options are priced? Just a few key concepts.

Intrinsic and Extrinsic Value

These are fancy terms for describing what portion of an option's value comes from how far in-the-money the option is and what portion is related to how much time is left on the contract and what the volatility of the stock is. Usually, we just lump time and volatility together and refer to the extrinsic value as *time value*.

To understand intrinsic and extrinsic value, we'll pull up an options chain for United Technologies (symbol: UTX). An options chain shows multiple strike prices grouped together by expiration date. The options chain in Figure 4-2 shows the March 2011 and April 2011 contracts that were trading when we pulled up the chain.

The last trade for UTX was at $82.89. For call options, every call $80 and below is ITM. For put options, every put above $85 is ITM. We'll look at the March 80 calls.

March 80 calls are currently trading at $3.27. The intrinsic value of the call is the current price of the stock minus the strike price of the call. For these options, the intrinsic value is $2.89 ($82.89 price of the stock – $80.00 strike price). The extrinsic value is the price of the call minus the intrinsic value, in this case $0.38 ($3.27 price of the call option – $2.89 of intrinsic value).

Let's take a look at the same strike, but with an additional month until expiration, the April 80 calls. April 80 calls are trading at $4.20. The intrinsic value is still $2.89, as the stock is still trading at $82.89 and the strike price is still $80. However, the extrinsic value of the April 80 call is $1.31 ($4.20 price of the call option – $2.89 of intrinsic value).

Symbol	Last	Time		Change	Bid	Ask	Open	High	Low	Close	Volume
UTX	82.89	2011-03-09 16:10:26		-0.37	82.57	83.07	83.13	83.2	82.03	83.26	3794251

Calls							Mar 2011	Puts						
Ticker	Last	EV	Delta	Gamma	Theta	I-Vol	Strike	Ticker	Last	EV	Delta	Gamma	Theta	I-Vol
UTX110319C00065000	18.50		0.16	0.97	0.007	-0.040	83.33%	65.0	UTX110319P00065000	0.02	0.04	-0.01	0.003	-0.013	66.87%
UTX110319C00070000	14.90		0.41	0.92	0.014	-0.077	76.56%	70.0	UTX110319P00070000	0.08	0.09	-0.03	0.009	-0.024	55.48%
UTX110319C00072500	10.80		0.46	0.90	0.019	-0.080	66.35%	72.5	UTX110319P00072500	0.11	0.10	-0.04	0.013	-0.025	46.61%
UTX110319C00075000	7.40		0.26	0.91	0.025	-0.049	45.68%	75.0	UTX110319P00075000	0.15	0.14	-0.06	0.022	-0.031	39.44%
UTX110319C00080000	3.27		0.46	0.79	0.077	-0.055	27.42%	80.0	UTX110319P00080000	0.41	0.36	-0.19	0.079	-0.046	24.86%
UTX110319C00085000	0.43		0.42	0.25	0.107	-0.047	21.44%	85.0	UTX110319P00085000	2.41	0.44	-0.75	0.106	-0.048	21.95%
UTX110319C00090000	0.02	200001.00	0.00	0.000	0.000	0.00%	90.0	UTX110319P00090000	7.50	0.09	-0.95	0.026	-0.021	30.36%
UTX110319C00095000	0.02		0.08	0.03	0.012	-0.022	44.31%	95.0	UTX110319P00095000	0.00	1.04	-0.82	0.023	-0.149	83.38%

Calls							Apr 2011	Puts						
Ticker	Last	EV	Delta	Gamma	Theta	I-Vol	Strike	Ticker	Last	EV	Delta	Gamma	Theta	I-Vol
UTX110416C00075000	8.05		0.56	0.87	0.028	-0.022	29.28%	75.0	UTX110416P00075000	0.44	0.45	-0.12	0.027	-0.019	27.44%
UTX110416C00080000	4.20		1.31	0.69	0.055	-0.030	23.73%	80.0	UTX110416P00080000	1.18	1.23	-0.30	0.057	-0.028	22.96%
UTX110416C00085000	1.31		1.30	0.36	0.069	-0.027	20.30%	85.0	UTX110416P00085000	3.80	1.34	-0.63	0.068	-0.028	20.78%
UTX110416C00090000	0.20		0.23	0.10	0.034	-0.012	19.20%	90.0	UTX110416P00090000	0.00	1.09	-0.77	0.035	-0.034	32.25%
UTX110416C00095000	0.03	200001.00	0.00	0.000	0.000	0.00%	95.0	UTX110416P00095000	0.00	0.94	-0.83	0.023	-0.037	41.41%

Figure 4-2 United Technologies Options Chain

An option that is out-of-the-money has no intrinsic value. The entire value of the option is extrinsic value. An OTM option has value because of the possibility that something could happen to make the option become ITM. This leads us directly to time decay.

Beating the Clock: Theta Decay

Imagine a teenager in high school who is given a project that is due at the end of the semester. This project accounts for a significant portion of the teenager's grade. What happens? For the first three months of the semester, the student sporadically does some work on the project. With six weeks left, at dinner one night, you ask him how his major project is coming along? After a briefly glazed look, he says, "Oh, yeah . . . the project. Fine . . . I guess. I think I might do some work on it this weekend. Could I have some more potatoes?" A great orator, our young scholar.

At four weeks out, our young student's heart starts to beat more quickly when he thinks about his project. The scope of the project, which could have been spread over the entire semester, now must be done in a few short weeks. At two weeks out, incipient panic sets in. He spends late nights at the computer trying to make online references actually sound like scholarly texts. One week out, he's bouncing off the walls of his room, trying to type out his project. Two days before the deadline, our teenager is staying up all night frantically trying to put everything into a coherent document. On the due date, after pulling an all-nighter, the teenager staggers into class, drops his completed project on his teacher's desk, and collapses into his seat.

The increasing panic that our student experienced could be graphed and would match the time decay of an option. When he had plenty of time, the panic factor was low (time decayed more slowly). As it got closer to the due date, the panic factor increased dramatically.

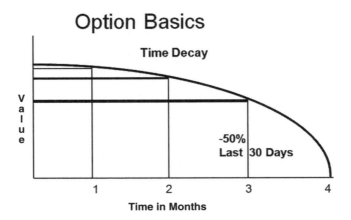

Figure 4-3   Time Decay

We refer to this time decay as *theta decay*. If you want to write it shorthand in Greek, the symbol is θ. Just remember that theta stands for T and T stands for time. This is one of the options Greeks that we pay attention to.

With options, you pay more for an option with a lot of time remaining than you do for an option with the same strike price that is closer to expiration. The final 50 percent of an option's time value is lost in the final 30 days before expiration. Figure 4-3 graphically shows the effect of time decay on an options contract. You'll notice that decay starts out slowly; the line is fairly flat. As the contract gets closer to expiration, the last bit of time value drops off quickly.

In an options chain, theta decay is expressed as a negative number, usually in dollars. On a proportional basis, ITM options will lose value less quickly than OTM options. Let's take another look at the options chain for UTX and our March 80 calls. For the March 80 calls, theta is listed as -0.055 (see Figure 4-4). That means that everything else remaining equal, the value of the March 80 calls will be $5^{1}/_{2}$ cents less the next day as a result of theta decay.

Symbol	Last	Time			Change	Bid	Ask	Open	High	Low	Close	Volume
UTX	82.89	2011-03-09 16:10:26			-0.37	82.57	83.07	83.13	83.2	82.03	83.26	3794251

Calls							Mar 2011	Puts						
Ticker	Last	EV	Delta	Gamma	Theta	I-Vol	Strike	Ticker	Last	EV	Delta	Gamma	Theta	I-Vol
UTX110319C00065000	18.50		0.16	0.97	0.007	-0.040	83.33%	65.0	UTX110319P00065000	0.02	0.04	-0.01	0.003	-0.013 66.87%
UTX110319C00070000	14.90		0.41	0.92	0.014	-0.077	76.56%	70.0	UTX110319P00070000	0.08	0.09	-0.03	0.009	-0.024 55.48%
UTX110319C00072500	10.80		0.46	0.90	0.019	-0.080	66.35%	72.5	UTX110319P00072500	0.11	0.10	-0.04	0.013	-0.025 46.61%
UTX110319C00075000	7.40		0.26	0.91	0.025	-0.049	45.68%	75.0	UTX110319P00075000	0.15	0.14	-0.06	0.022	-0.031 39.44%
UTX110319C00080000	3.27		0.46	0.79	0.077	-0.055	27.42%	80.0	UTX110319P00080000	0.41	0.36	-0.19	0.079	-0.046 24.86%
UTX110319C00085000	0.43		0.42	0.25	0.107	-0.047	21.44%	85.0	UTX110319P00085000	2.41	0.44	-0.75	0.106	-0.048 21.95%
UTX110319C00090000	0.02	20000	1.00	0.00	0.000	0.000	0.00%	90.0	UTX110319P00090000	7.50	0.09	-0.95	0.026	-0.021 30.36%
UTX110319C00095000	0.02		0.08	0.03	0.012	-0.022	44.31%	95.0	UTX110319P00095000	0.00	1.04	-0.82	0.023	-0.149 83.38%

Calls							Apr 2011	Puts						
Ticker	Last	EV	Delta	Gamma	Theta	I-Vol	Strike	Ticker	Last	EV	Delta	Gamma	Theta	I-Vol
UTX110416C00075000	8.05		0.56	0.87	0.028	-0.022	29.28%	75.0	UTX110416P00075000	0.44	0.45	-0.12	0.027	-0.019 27.44%
UTX110416C00080000	4.20		1.31	0.69	0.055	-0.030	23.73%	80.0	UTX110416P00080000	1.18	1.23	-0.30	0.057	-0.028 22.96%
UTX110416C00085000	1.31		1.30	0.36	0.069	-0.027	20.30%	85.0	UTX110416P00085000	3.80	1.34	-0.63	0.068	-0.028 20.78%
UTX110416C00090000	0.20		0.23	0.10	0.034	-0.012	19.20%	90.0	UTX110416P00090000	0.00	1.09	-0.77	0.035	-0.034 32.25%
UTX110416C00095000	0.03	20000	1.00	0.00	0.000	0.000	0.00%	95.0	UTX110416P00095000	0.00	0.94	-0.83	0.023	-0.037 41.41%

Figure 4-4   United Technologies Options Chain

In Maverick's training program for new traders, we explain theta decay using two ice cubes. The larger ice cube is the time value of the longer-dated option, and the smaller ice cube is the time value of the shorter-dated option. When you place those two ice cubes side by side, the smaller ice cube will melt faster as a percentage of the whole than the larger ice cube (see Figure 4-5).

This is why short-term OTM options are such a consistently money-losing strategy. Buying them is like pouring yourself a drink, throwing in a tiny ice cube, and watching it melt before you can take a drink (collect your profits).

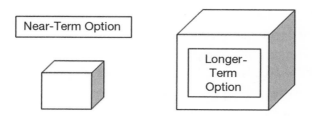

Near-Term Option

Longer-Term Option

Figure 4-5   Ice Cubes

Speed and Acceleration: Delta and Gamma

The second and third options Greeks that we're concerned with are delta and gamma. Delta is an option's "speed," or how much it gains or loses value compared to a move in the underlying. For those of you who are learning Greek, the shorthand symbol is Δ. This symbol is used because it is the customary symbol in mathematics and physics for difference (D, difference, delta) or change. Gamma is delta's "acceleration," or how much delta increases or decreases compared to a move in the underlying. We generally don't write this in shorthand Greek because the capital version, Γ, looks like you've forgotten what letter you were writing halfway through, and the lowercase version, γ, looks like a weird letter Y. We recommend writing it shorthand as "G."

Looking at our options chain for UTX and our March 80 call, we see that the delta is 0.79. The stock itself was trading at $82.89, and the March 80 call last traded at $3.27. So if UTX traded up $1.00 to $83.89, the March 80 call would trade up $0.79 to $4.06.

Right about now, we'll bet you're asking why the value of the March 80 call didn't go up by $1.00 as well. The simple answer is that some of the EV (extrinsic value) converted itself to IV (intrinsic value). If UTX stock rose to $83.89 from $82.89, the new IV of the March 80 calls would be $3.89 ($83.89 stock price − $80.00 strike price), and the EV would drop from $0.38 to $0.17 ($4.06 for the new value of the March 80 calls − $3.89 in IV).

Stock always has a delta of 1.00.

Another key trait in delta is that it represents the probability of that particular option expiring ITM at that particular point in time. At the time we pulled the option chain on UTX, the March 80 calls with a delta of 0.79 had a 79 percent chance of expiring at-the-money (ATM, or $80.00) or ITM (above $80.00).

This is another reason why buying OTM options is a low-probability play. Those deep OTM options that were trading for

$0.10 might look good from a cost perspective, but they also may have a delta of only 0.03, meaning that they have only a 3 percent chance of expiring ATM or ITM.

The deltas of a call and a put with the same expiration and the same strike price will theoretically add up to 1.00. In practice, they come pretty close. Since our March 80 call has a delta of 0.79, theoretically, the March 80 put will have a delta of 0.21. Looking at the options chain, the March 80 put actually has a delta of 0.19.

The deeper ITM an option gets, the greater the chance that it will expire ITM. This is where gamma comes into play. Gamma is the change in delta for a $1.00 move in the underlying. Gamma is always highest with ATM options.

If you keep in mind that delta is the speed of an option and gamma is its acceleration, then gamma is like third gear in a car, and the car is the option. The car is in a quarter-mile drag race with an ITM speed of 50 mph and starts off at a standstill (zero speed, delta of 0.00). The light turns green and the car takes off and slowly gains speed. The car shifts into second gear at about 20 mph and gains speed at a faster rate. At 35 mph, the car shifts into third gear and really hits its stride, rapidly accelerating through 40 mph, hitting 50 mph, and going on to 60 mph. At 60 mph, the car shifts into fourth gear. The car is still gaining speed, but it is doing so more slowly than when it was in third gear. With the engine screaming, the car shifts into fifth gear at 80 mph and claws its way to 100 mph before the end of the track (options expiration), finishing the race ITM (delta 1.00).

Looking at a graph of gamma for a single strike price, you can see that as the price moves closer to the strike price of the option, gamma rises, peaks at the strike price, and then declines. This is commonly called a *gamma spike*. Figure 4-6 shows a gamma graph of a SPY 130 call with about five weeks to expiration.

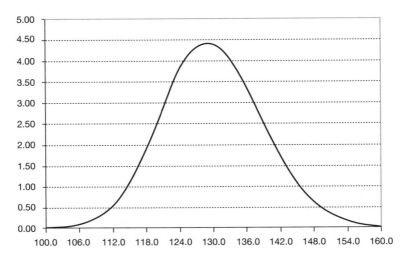

Figure 4-6   Gamma Spike

For this ETF, gamma peaks right at the strike price of 130, causing a change in delta of just under 4.5. To go back to the car analogy, $130 is the point where the acceleration/deceleration will be the greatest during the race down the track.

Gamma also changes with time. The closer the option is to expiration, the more pronounced the gamma spike will be, which makes sense if we think of theta decay as a panic factor. When there are five weeks left, we've got quite a bit of time to see what happens. When there is just a day left until expiration, any price change will dramatically affect whether an ATM option closes ITM, therefore having value, or OTM, and thus worthless.

Figure 4-7 shows a gamma graph of the same SPY 130 call, with each week until expiration shown by a different line.

With five weeks until expiration and SPY trading near the strike price of $130, gamma is pronounced, but sedate, causing a change in delta of 0.045 with a $1.00 move in SPY. Just prior to expiration, with SPY trading near the $130 strike, that same $1.00 move in SPY changes the delta of the option by 0.26.

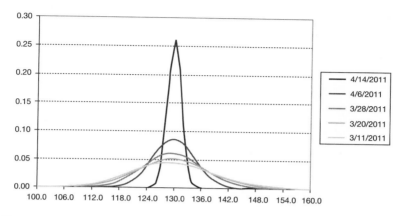

Figure 4-7   Gamma Graph with Different Times to Expiration

The relation between delta, gamma, and the value of the option is important to us because we want to focus on trading options that take advantage of the gamma spike, adding more delta to the option in a short period of time, and price movement, making the value of the option greater.

Figure 4-8 is a graph of the same SPY 130 call showing the delta curve. At opposite ends of the graph, you can see that delta is nearly zero at $110 and nearly 1.00 at $150. The curve slowly slopes up and begins to gain momentum at $124. Delta increases at a nice rate between $128 and $136 and then rapidly begins tapering off.

When deciding which strategies and strike prices to use for our trades, we want to position ourselves so that we can enjoy the steepest slope of the delta curve. This point varies depending on the particular strategy we are using, but the more time we can spend in net delta between 0.25 and 0.80, the faster we will make money on our trades. After a net delta of 0.80 is reached, we often have to make a decision as to whether the amount of time that our capital will be tied up is worth the wait to see delta approach 1.00.

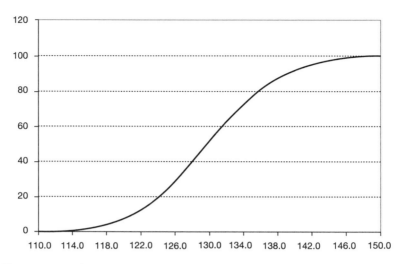

Figure 4-8   Delta Curve

Pricing Neurosis: Historical and Implied Volatility

The last factor we pay attention to in options pricing is volatility. There are two types of volatility. Historic volatility is a statistical measure of the craziness of a stock. A stock that makes sedate, consistent price moves, either up or down, has low historic volatility. A stock that has wild price swings and erratic behavior has high historic volatility.

Stocks with low historic volatility have options that are less expensive than stocks with high historic volatility. The reason is risk. The options market makers have to balance their risk and still turn a profit on the premiums they get for facilitating the options trades.

Options market makers are pretty smart people. They don't last long in the business unless they hedge their risk. There are basically two ways for them to hedge their risk: they can be either contract-neutral or delta-neutral. The safest position to be in is to be contract-neutral, meaning that they've bought as many of the same options as they've written (sold). At that point, their profit is the cumulative differences between the bid-ask spread of the option times the number of contracts they've written and bought. This may be ideal, but it rarely happens. The market will almost always have a bias to one side or the other.

The more common method of hedging for an options market maker is to be delta-neutral. For example, you buy a call option in the market that has a delta of 0.60. You are now long 60 points of delta, and for every dollar that the underlying stock rises, the value of your option will rise 60 cents.

The market maker is short 60 points of delta because he wrote (sold) you the option. The market maker probably isn't just going to write the option and wait to see what happens at expiration. If the stock has moved up appreciably, he's going to have to buy that stock on the open market to give to you if you exercise your option. To hedge his position, as soon as he writes you the option and is short 60 points of delta, he will buy 60 shares of the stock, which has a delta of 1.00. He is now delta-neutral because being long 60 shares of stock with a delta of 1.00 offsets the short 60 points of delta that he incurred when he wrote the call option. If the stock keeps rising, the market maker will continue to add to his long stock position to keep his delta balance as close to zero as possible. If the stock falls in price, he will sell portions of his long position to keep his delta balance in line.

On a stock with low historic volatility, the market maker will be able to hedge his risk without much trouble. On a stock with high historic volatility, however, hedging his risk becomes more problematic. If the stock gaps up or down, he could be caught being hedged too much or not being hedged enough. To compensate for this additional risk, options on highly volatile stocks are more expensive.

The other aspect of volatility is implied volatility. Implied volatility is best described as the demand-supply seesaw for the options themselves. When the demand for options is greater than the supply, the price of the options rises. When the supply is greater than the demand, the price of the options falls.

Let's say that there is some anticipated event coming up in the near future. Earnings announcements are always good to use. A couple of weeks before the scheduled earnings announcement, both institutional and retail traders get interested in the options of a company. Some people want to hedge their positions in case earnings fall short of expectations and the price of the stock falls, and some people want to speculate that the price of the stock will rise because the earnings will be better than expected. Regardless, the demand for options has increased.

Immediately after the earnings announcement, the demand for options falls off dramatically. Fewer people are interested in hedging their stock position, and fewer people are seeking to speculate on a dramatic news-induced move. Because supply now weighs more than demand, the relative price of the options decreases.

Sports betting is a perfect example of how implied volatility works. When you go to Vegas to place a bet on an NFL game, the bookie doesn't simply let you bet on who will win the game. Let's say the mighty New England Patriots are set to play the lowly Buffalo Bills (for full disclosure, this is Robb's favorite NFL team. Nice pick!) next Sunday. The bookies know that the Patriots are most likely going to win the game, and if they let people just bet on who wins or loses, they will be out of business. So, they implement a spread, or an amount of points that they think the Patriots will win by, and have the line of Patriots +9. This means that if you bet on the Patriots, they will need to win by more than nine points. If you bet on the Bills (bad idea—ask Robb), if they can either win or lose by less than nine points, you win the bet. This is exactly how implied volatility works in the options market. The market makers know that some stocks are likely to move more than others and are likely to move around news and earnings reports. Just like a bookie, they price a "spread" into the options to account for this implied volatility.

Newer traders will often try to capitalize on news-driven events and take long positions in either puts or calls right before the event. They may end up being right in their analysis, and the stock may move the way they anticipated, but because of implied volatility, they probably paid too much for the option and got less of a profit than they anticipated. In cases where the stock made no significant move after the event, these traders probably lost money because the value of their options deflated as a result of the removal of implied volatility.

Knowing the factors that influence options pricing will help you determine which options strategy is best for a particular situation.

TRADING TECHNIQUES: *SETTING* UP THE TRADE

With every trade we do, we have a plan for its execution. This is what separates us from the amateurs, and it's what allows us to be consistently profitable on both sides of the market. If you're not trading with a plan, you're trading on emotion. Emotion will keep you in a bad trade too long, get you out of a winning trade too soon, and generally cause you to lose sleep and impair your performance.

Trading with a plan removes emotion from the decision-making process. With a plan, when A happens, you do B, automatically and without discussion. It doesn't matter what A is; whether a stock hits your target exit point or your stop loss, B is either exit and book your profits or exit and take a small loss. C is always move on to find the next trade.

At Maverick, the meat of every plan has three parts that are price points of the underlying stock we are trading. From bottom to top, they are the Stop, Entry, and Target. Our teaching acronym for this is SET.

We've already discussed entry points in the previous chapter. The entry point of a trade is the trade trigger for that chart setup or the actual price at which the stock was trading when you pulled the trigger on the trade.

In our first chapter, on risk management, we introduced the concept of having a loss limit, a maximum amount that you were willing to risk on the trade. Accepting the concept of having a predetermined price at which you will exit the trade with a small loss is the key to a career in trading. The problem is that if you use an arbitrary number for your stop loss (for example, $2) for every stock, you will be stopped out of what are actually good trades and stay in trades that have clearly gone against you. The amount of the stop loss is dependent on the trading range of each stock and where the support and resistance are for each stock.

Equally important is establishing target prices at which you will exit the trade and book profits. Again, using an arbitrary number (for example, a $6 move in a stock) will have you leaving reasonable profits on the table and will also result in wholly unrealistic profit targets. To be effective, targets must be directly related to the stock you are trading, or to the underlying if you are trading derivatives like options. Far too often, we have seen traders, even those who purport to be professionals, have a trade reach their target price, and then those traders get greedy and watch all their profits evaporate. The "just one more day" syndrome can affect trades that work for you as well.

An absolute must is to have all three pieces of the plan ready to execute, whether or not you are watching the market. We accomplish this through contingent orders. The order to execute the trade is contingent on the trade's triggering through price action in the stock. The order to exit the trade with a small loss is triggered when the price action of the stock breaks your stop price. Finally, the order to exit the trade and take profits is contingent on the stock's reaching your target price.

The first 20 times you make a trade, take a sheet of notebook paper and write out your trade contingencies in a flowchart. Your flowchart should look something like this:

IF [insert the ticker symbol of the stock you are interested
in] trades [above or below] this price [trade trigger]

THEN enter the trade [long, short, specific options
strategy]

IF the trade is triggered

THEN

STOP OUT the trade if the stock trades [below if long,
above if short] this price [enter stop price]

OR

STOP OUT the trade if the price of the options strategy
trades below [enter stop price on options premium]

EXIT the trade if the stock trades [above if long, below if
short] this price [enter target price]

OR

EXIT the trade at market price at 15:59:00 EST on
[enter expiration date]

With this flowchart, you aren't entering the trade until it
triggers based on the chart pattern that the stock is forming. You
are protecting yourself if the chart pattern fails or the trade takes
too long to develop after triggering (keeping theta decay in mind).
You are also taking profits at a predetermined price or exiting the
trade right before the market closes on expiration day to keep
from being exercised.

We will discuss trading platforms in a later chapter, but at
this point, suffice it to say that if your broker doesn't support contingent orders, then you need to find a new broker. Once your
flowchart is in place (call it an algorithm if you are technically
inclined), you leave it and resume looking for new trades.

Protecting the Portfolio: Setting Protective Stops

Your first protective stop loss is your most important because your
risk is highest immediately after the trade triggers. This is the
point where your potential loss is greatest. But where do you put

the stop? You don't want it too close to your entry price because if it is, you will probably be stopped out quickly, and you don't want it too far away from your entry price, because if it is, you could needlessly risk capital. What's the best fit?

We've found that the best tool for setting stops related to price action in a stock is the Average True Range (ATR). The ATR takes the trading ranges for each of the past 14 days (you can usually set the period, but 14 days is standard) and then averages them. If the stock has been making large moves, the ATR will be proportionally larger than that for a stock making smaller moves.

Figures 4-9 and 4-10 show two charts, one of General Electric (symbol: GE) and one of Google (symbol: GOOG). GE was trading around $19, and GOOG was trading around $550. The ATR is the lowest line on the chart and is set for a 14-day period.

The ATR for GE is $0.61. Over the past 14 trading days, GE has averaged a trading range between the daily high and the daily low of $0.61, or about 3 percent on a daily basis.

The ATR for GOOG is $11.21, or about 2 percent of the stock price between the daily high and the daily low.

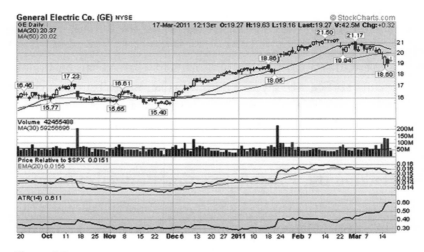

Figure 4-9

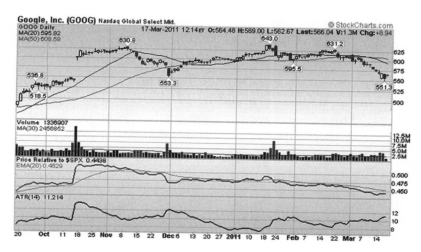

Figure 4-10

Based on this comparison, GE has actually been the more volatile stock in the past three trading weeks on a percentage basis (which is what we *always* use for analysis).

Now, we wouldn't make a trade in either of these stocks at the time we pulled these charts; neither has established a tradable pattern. But if we were to make a trade, we would want to give the trade some room. For the sake of argument, let's say that we thought that GE had bottomed and that GOOG still had room to move to the downside, and we wanted to take a long position in GE and a short position in GOOG.

For our long position in GE, we entered the trade at 19.27, and we want to give GE a chance to move 1 ATR below our entry point; $19.27 minus 1 ATR of $0.61 gives us a sell stop of $18.66. If GE trades below $18.66, we will exit the trade and take the loss. But how large a position do we take?

Going back to our example $10,000 portfolio and a medium risk tolerance of 2.0 percent of the portfolio per position ($200), we divide our maximum risk by the ATR. Thus, $200 divided by $0.61 gives us a maximum position of 327 shares (this would take $6,300 in capital, so you can see why we like options).

The entry price for our short position in GOOG is $566.04. For a short position, we add the ATR to our entry price ($566.04 + $11.21 = $577.25 stop loss). If GOOG trades above $577.25, we will automatically exit the trade. If our maximum risk is again $200, our position size would be 17 shares ($200 divided by $11.21). This position would take more than $9,600 in capital.

You'll have noticed in Chapter 3 that most of our chart setups relied on prices meeting and touching their moving averages, usually either the 20-day or the 50-day SMA. If you are entering a long position, you can set your stop loss 1 ATR below the support provided by the SMA that the stock bounced off of. If you are short, you can set your stop loss 1 ATR above the SMA that provided resistance.

We've found that using support and resistance levels formed by SMAs is a good practice. We've also found that when price breaks through the SMA by more than 1 ATR, it usually signals a failure of that SMA as support or resistance, often resulting in a technical breakdown. When a technical breakdown occurs in a chart setup that's triggered a trade, get out. Stops are there for a reason; use them.

The rule for stops is that they can always be moved tighter, but they can never be loosened. Once you've entered a trade and you have 1 ATR of profit in the trade, there is nothing wrong with moving your stop to your breakeven point. This ensures that if the trade goes against you, you'll get out without taking a loss. Breaking even on a trade that goes against you is infinitely better than taking a loss on a trade.

Target Acquired: Booking Profits

The last price point of the trading plan is establishing a target where you will take profits and exit the trade. There are two methods for accomplishing this: a working crystal ball and prior performance. Since there is a shortage of working crystal balls, we rely on analysis of prior performance.

Remember that market performance is based on the collective actions of the institutions and their traders. In the same way that patterns emerge to create tradable chart formations, recent prior moves give an indication of performance in the near future.

In plain language, if an uptrending stock is making a series of bull pullbacks in its uptrend, and if the difference between the last low of the last bull pullback and the swing high of the new pullback is $10, it's a decent deduction that the difference between the next low of the current bull pullback and the next swing high will be around $10.

Institutions and their traders are creatures of habit. If something works once, chances are that it will work a second time. Their thinking is that if they were able to trade a stock for a $10 move last time, they will be able to trade the same stock for another $10 move this time.

You see the same moves in any trending stock time and again. The chart makes a series of identifiable moves with roughly the same interval between the swing highs and the swing lows.

A second technique that works well in trending stocks is to actually print out the chart, draw in the support and resistance lines of the trend channel, and extend them off the chart. Once the trend channels have been drawn, use the slope of the last move to draw a new slope from the recent swing point in the chart. Where the drawn line intersects the drawn trend channel is a reasonable target price.

What happens when your trade reaches its target? We'll see shortly that you can have two types of trades with respect to the potential profit: limited reward and unlimited reward. In a limited-reward trade, your profits are capped; movement past that price point won't bring you any more gain. When you're in a limited-reward trade and your stock hits its target price, you've gotten as much as you have any right to expect from the trade. Exit, book your profits, and move on to the next trade.

In a trade with potentially unlimited reward, if the stock reaches your target faster than you anticipated, there may be some more unanticipated gains out there. There are several techniques to capitalize on this. Why leave money on the table, especially if you can protect your gains?

The first technique is to move your stop up to your target price. If the stock falls below your target price, you've still maximized your gains in accordance with your plan, which is a good day's work in anyone's book.

If the stock rockets past your target and shows no sign of slowing down, you can use a trailing stop. Trailing stops can be used on both stocks and options. Like the name implies, a trailing stop trails behind your position like a guard dog, protecting your profits. A trailing stop will always move in the direction of a profit but will never move in the direction of a loss. It works similar to a ratchet.

Let's say you took a position in our friend XYZ. It broke through resistance at $30, and you had a target of $35 for the trade. After the bell on the day you made the trade, XYZ made a surprise announcement that it had just completed a major deal for exclusive widget manufacturing rights in some distant locale. The next day, the stock gaps up to $35 and continues to trade higher throughout the day on massive volume. Now, you've hit your price target and your trade is profitable. There is nothing wrong with exiting your position and walking away with a profit. But XYZ looks as if it could go even higher. Why leave money on the table?

As the stock trades up through $36, you decide to put on a $1 trailing stop. That means that if the stock trades down to $35 from $36, the stop will execute and liquidate your position. If the stock moves up to $37, the trailing stop moves up to $36, and so on. Eventually, XYZ will run out of energy and fall back down to the trailing stop. But on the way up, the stop automatically moved up with the stock.

Trailing stops work the same way with options. Let's say that instead of going long stock, you bought a $27.50 call option for $3.50. The day the stock gapped up to $35, that $27.50 call option is worth around $8.50. A $1 trailing stop on the option would mean that if the option traded down below $7.50, the stop would liquidate your trade, preserving your gains. If the value of the option rose to $10, the stop would automatically raise itself to $9.

Preserving your profits is second only to limiting your losses. Profitable trades will run their own courses, and it is important to harvest those profits while they are still ripe. Too many traders let greed get in the way of objectivity and allow a profitable trade to fall back to breakeven, or, worse yet, turn into a loss, because they didn't take the profit when it was available to them.

CHAPTER

5

WHAT ARE THESE THINGS IN MY TOOLBOX?

TECHNIQUES AND RISK GRAPHS

In your career as a trader, you will come across many scenarios. Some will be bullish setups, some will be bearish, and others will be plays to make money on volatility and stagnation. Choosing the right technique can be just as important as identifying the right setup. Is your plan short-term, medium-term, or long-term? Is this trade something that you want to tie up significant capital to execute? Do you want to capture a discrete move in the underlying stock, or do you want to give yourself more upside potential?

Each technique has its place, and in many cases more than one technique would be equally justifiable. That doesn't mean that you can choose a technique at random and hope it works. To be successful, you need to use the Top-Down Approach and, once you identify a potential trade, build a trading plan using SET (Stop, Entry, and Target).

With each technique in this chapter, we've provided a risk graph for that technique. Risk graphs show profit, loss, and breakeven points along a price continuum. For the most part, we will be showing risk graphs as they would appear at expiration.

At Maverick, our traders use specialized software that allows us to produce risk graphs for all our positions and compare the different strategies over time. We are also able to see what the probabilities of the trade's being profitable are, based on historic volatility. Tools like these should be part of your toolbox before you make any trades. You need to know where you will be profitable and which strategy best suits your risk appetite and time frame before you make a trade.

BULLISH TECHNIQUES

Long Stock

Although we use this technique very rarely, it is one to keep around in your toolbox. It is the technique that everyone starts out with: buying a stock itself. It is technically a limited-risk, unlimited-reward trade, in that your risk is limited to the amount you paid for the stock, and the stock could theoretically keep rising in price forever. The risk graph (Figure 5-1) is a straight line sloping up and to the right. An increase in price raises the value of your position, and a decrease in price lowers the value of your position.

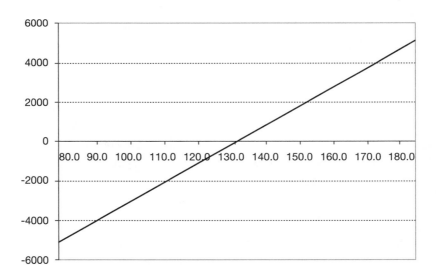

Figure 5-1   Long Stock

The chart setup for a long stock position is a bull pullback, a high base, an ascending triangle, or a symmetrical triangle breakout.

Long stock is a strategy that we will use when something catches our eye that looks as if it would be worth a long-term trade. At major market bottoms, when the recovery is just beginning, options are sometimes too expensive to be worth the risk because of the overall level of volatility in the market.

In other situations, we may end up with long stock if we've decided to let options from another strategy be exercised. A tertiary use of long stock is to hedge ourselves if we are in a bearish options strategy and we foresee the potential for the strategy to incur some volatility.

Finally, in an uptrending broad market, we may park the trading capital that we aren't currently using for specific positions in a broad-market ETF like SPY or QQQQ.

Long Call

The first true options strategy that most people use is the long call. The majority of investors and traders have a bullish bias, and the long call is an extension of that bias using options. Long calls are a limited-risk, unlimited-reward strategy: your risk is limited to the premium you paid for the option, and the reward is theoretically unlimited.

The chart setups for long calls are a bull pullback, a high base, and an ascending triangle. We don't enter a position with long calls on a symmetrical triangle breakout because of the higher failure rate of that pattern and often higher implied volatility, as traders on both sides have driven up the price of the options to the point where the reward-risk ratio doesn't work out.

After you've completed the Top-Down Approach and determined that the current chart pattern is bullish, you need to choose which option to buy.

With long calls, there are two primary rules: (1) no front-month options, and (2) a delta of 0.65 or greater. The reason for these two rules is time decay. Unlike other strategies that we will look at shortly, long calls are completely unhedged when it comes to theta decay. Entering a position with an option with two to three months until expiration keeps the daily theta decay fairly flat compared to theta decay in an option with less than 30 days until expiration. Additionally, a call option with a delta of at least 0.65 has a lower proportion of extrinsic value (EV) in the premium than an option with a lower delta.

The breakeven price in a long call strategy is the strike price of the option plus the premium paid for the option. Our standard risk on a long call position is 30 percent of the premium paid for the option. We use this benchmark because we are buying fairly deep in-the-money (ITM) options when we look for deltas above 0.65. The 30 percent benchmark on the option premium is highly correlated with a move of 1 average true range (ATR) of the underlying stock. This way, we will exit our option position when the stock has a greater than 1 ATR move against us. The 30 percent risk parameter can be made wider as long as you adjust your position size for a larger percentage of risk.

Figure 5-2 is a risk graph for the SPY ETF, which tracks the S&P 500. At the time of this example, SPY was trading at $126.18. The 123 call options two months from expiration had a delta of 0.65 and were trading at $6.93. Our maximum risk is $2.08, so if the price of the call option trades below $4.85, we will exit the trade. Our breakeven point for this trade (at expiration) is $129.93 ($123 strike price of the option plus $6.93 option premium). For us to be profitable on the trade at expiration, SPY must rise at least 3.0 percent in the next two months. Anything above that is profit.

However, remember all the Greeks that we have working for us and against us during the trade before expiration. For the first

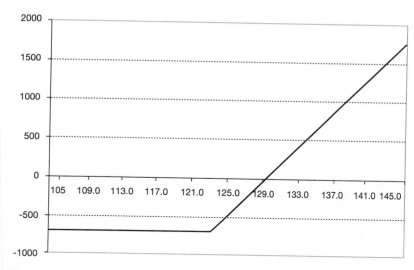

Figure 5-2   Long Call

$1 the SPY moves for us, we will experience a $0.65 gain in our long calls. If the SPY moves another dollar, we now get the benefit of an addition of gamma to the delta. If gamma was at 0.04, the next $1 move in the SPY would be worth around $0.69. Don't forget about theta, though, as a long call is a negative-theta position. If theta is 0.04, you could expect to lose $0.04 each day you hold the option position.

The minimum reward-risk ratio that you are looking for in a long call position is 2:1.

To calculate your potential reward, take your target price and subtract the price of the stock at the time you enter the position, then multiply the result by the delta of the call. In this example, we calculated a probable price target for SPY of $135.

Risk = 30% of premium = $6.93 × 0.3 = $2.08
Reward = (target − price of stock at entry) × option delta
        = ($135.00 − $126.18) × 0.65 = $5.73
Reward-risk ratio = $5.73 reward/$2.08 risk = 2.76

Trade management for this position:

- **Stop losses.** If the option trades below $4.85 or if the stock trades 1 ATR below our entry point.
- **Exit stops.** When the option trades above $5.73 or when the stock trades at or above $135.

Bull Call Spread

Bull call spreads are limited-risk, limited-reward strategies. These strategies are useful in capturing short-term moves in a stock. They are also a form of vertical spread because you are dealing with one strike above another in the same month of expiration. Bull call spreads are also debit spreads because when you enter the position, your account will incur a debit.

For a bull call spread, the stock must be in an uptrending chart pattern. You will buy a short-term (three to eight weeks until expiration) at-the-money (ATM) call. At the same time, you will sell an out-of-the-money (OTM) call with a higher strike price, but with the same expiration date. The premium you bring in from selling the OTM call works to reduce the cost of the ATM call that you bought. Vertical spreads have the added benefit of reducing theta decay. While the ATM call that you bought is losing money daily because of theta decay, you are gaining money from the theta decay of the OTM call that you sold. You will never completely eliminate your theta decay, but you can reduce it to a point where you can give the trade time to work.

When choosing which options to enter in a bull call spread, you need to calculate your Stop, Entry, and Target first. The entry point will determine which option you buy (the closest to ATM or the first ITM call). The target price will determine which option you sell to offset the cost of the position. If your calculated target is $5 away from your entry price, you usually don't want to sell an option that's $2.50 away because you're potentially leaving $2.50 on the table, nor do you want to sell an option that's $7.50 away from the entry price because you're also leaving money on the table in the form of the premium that you could have brought in to offset the cost of the ATM option.

In a bull call spread, the ATM call that you buy costs more than the OTM call that you sell, so your account will initially incur a debit (this is why it's called a debit spread). The maximum amount of your debit should be less than 45 percent of the amount of the spread, so if you were looking at establishing a 125/135 bull call spread in SPY (a $10 spread), you shouldn't pay more than $4.50 for the spread. Anything more than 45 percent of the spread and the reward-risk ratio doesn't work out.

We think ATM vertical spreads give a trader the best opportunity of profiting from vertical spreads. Traders can use any combination of strike prices to put together their vertical spreads, from having both of them out-of-the-money to having both of them in-the-money. Out-of-the-money spreads will be very cheap, since you are dealing with cheap options; they have a great reward if the stock moves far enough, but they also have a very low statistical probability of profit. An ITM spread will have a low profit potential compared to the risk, but will have a very high statistical probability of profit. We find that the best results come from having one strike in-the-money and one strike out-of-the-money. This is for two reasons: spreads and commissions. Stock and option spreads (the difference between the bid and the ask) are determined by volume. The more volume the stock or option has, the tighter the spread will be. When there is less volume, the market makers widen the spreads to make up for the lack of volume. ATM options almost always have the highest volume and open interests, which lead to the smallest spreads on a percentage basis. The other reason is commissions. If you are using OTM vertical spreads, you will need to place much bigger orders to get the same reward-risk profile as that of an ATM vertical spread. With options, you typically pay per contract, which leads to more commissions.

Table 5-1   Bull Call Spread

Option	Price	Delta	Theta
Long 40 call	$1.53	0.53	−0.02
Short 45 call	−$0.14	−0.09	+0.01
Total	$1.38	0.44	−0.01

In a bull call spread, your net delta should be at least 0.25. We say net delta because the ATM call that you bought gives you a positive delta, but the OTM call that you sold gives you a negative delta, which is subtracted from the delta of the call that you own.

Let's take a look at a bull call spread with Hewlett-Packard (symbol HPQ). Let's say our analysis shows that HPQ has just triggered a trade to the upside. HPQ is trading at $40.14. The nearest ATM option is a 40 strike price. We feel that HPQ could move to $45 in the next month, so we would look at selling a 45 strike call to bring in some premium and offset our theta decay (see Table 5-1).

To enter this position would cost us $1.38, which is 27.6 percent of the spread ($1.38 cost/$5.00 spread amount). This is also our maximum risk. Our maximum reward is $3.62.

Our breakeven point for the trade is the lower strike price plus the net cost of the spread, in this case $41.38.

Our risk graph looks like Figure 5-3.

For position sizing, divide your established loss limit by the net debit of the trade. With our example $10,000 portfolio and a $200 loss limit, we can safely enter into a one-contract position because the total cost of the position is $138 (per share price of the contract × 100).

Note: we typically do not use stops on vertical spreads, since we are using spreads to give us the opportunity to sit through volatility in the markets. Remember, with a spread, you are long and short an option on the same stock, and the

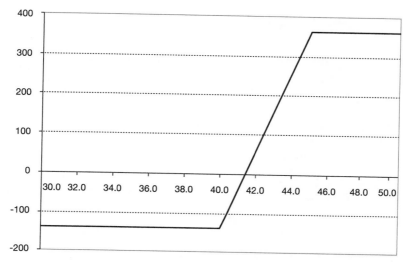

Figure 5-3 Bull Call Spread

movement in your position value will be muted, since one option will be working for you while the other is working against you. We love vertical spreads, since you can sit through a lot of volatility in the markets and let your trades move to fruition without getting knocked out early on a one- or two-day move. The most aggravating trade is not a trade where you lost money. The most aggravating trade is one that would have been profitable, but you lost money because you got knocked out as a result of temporary volatility. Only when the trade has clearly violated the chart pattern will we exit a vertical spread.

Diagonal Call Calendar Spread

Diagonal call spreads are excellent trades to use either in a sideways to uptrending market with a sideways trend or in an uptrending market with an uptrending stock that you feel could have a multi-leg run. The beauty of the diagonal spread is that as the trade develops, you have multiple opportunities to sell front-month premiums, and you could end up with what is essentially a free position.

To enter a diagonal call spread, buy an ITM call with an expiration that is at least four months out. Check to make sure that there is no pending news or earnings announcement in the next six weeks. At the same time, short an OTM call that expires no more than six weeks out. The reason these trades are so great is that the long call you bought doesn't expire for at least four months, so its time value will deteriorate at a much slower rate than the time value of the short-term option you sold, giving you a positive theta. This means that the trade will make you money each day because of time decay even if the stock consolidates and moves nowhere. These are good trades to do on or immediately after an Expiration Friday so that you can take advantage of selling the most of a rapidly depreciating premium in the OTM call. The short-term OTM call premium needs to be a minimum of 25 percent of the longer-term call premium.

For our example, we'll look at Joy Global (symbol: JOYG). At the time we created this scenario, JOYG was trading at $91.20. Looking at options with four months until expiration, the first ITM call is the 90 strike, trading at $9.20. Since our theoretical outlook for JOYG is sideways to slightly positive, the first front-month call that is OTM is the 95 strike, trading at $2.49 (see Table 5-2).

Time works for us on a diagonal spread. If the price of JOYG goes sideways for the next month, our long 90 call will lose only $0.04 per day, while the 95 call that we sold will be losing $0.07 per day. This will only accelerate as we get closer to expiration of the front-month 95 call.

Table 5-2   Diagonal Call Spread

Option	Months to Expiration	Price	Delta	Theta
Long 90 call	4	$9.20	0.57	−0.04
Short 95 call	1	−$2.49	−0.38	0.07
Total		$6.72	0.19	0.03

With regard to stop losses, on a diagonal call spread, we're primarily concerned with the lower breakeven point because it is the closest and the most likely to affect us in the near term. The software that we use for options analysis tells us that our lower breakeven is $88.78. Our upper breakeven is $110.43. Our maximum gain at expiration is at the strike price of the option we sold, in this case $95. Any price between $88.78 and $110.43 and we make a profit.

The risk graph looks like Figure 5-4.

Position sizing requires a little math (we're sorry), and you need to use some judgment based on your risk tolerance. If the stock is in a sideways pattern, we recommend that you place your stop 1 ATR below the consolidation low. You'll need to calculate that price, look on your risk graph to see what the loss would be at that price, and then make your calculations accordingly. For example, if a protective stop 1 ATR below the consolidation low turned out to be at $87, then you would lose about $100 per contract. Using our example $10,000 portfolio and 2.0 percent risk limit, we could buy two contracts.

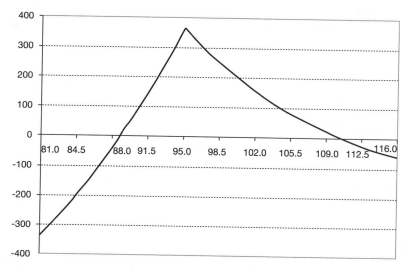

Figure 5-4   Diagonal Call Calendar Spread

If you're entering the position from a consolidation or continuation pattern, place your stop 1 ATR below support, calculate your loss at that point, and size your position accordingly.

What happens when the trade goes your way and you make a profit? If you've calculated the target correctly and the stock closes close to your target price at expiration, you have two choices: exit the entire position or roll the position to the next front-month option. If your analysis indicates that the stock has some more room to move sideways or slightly up, you can sell another front-month option at a new target price and further reduce the cost of the longer-term call option that you originally bought.

Let's say that we entered the JOYG trade just described, and at expiration, JOYG is trading right around $94.50 and is consolidating. We are still long our 90 call, and the 95 call we sold will expire worthless. As the 95 call expires worthless, we could sell the 100 call for around $2.50. The next month at expiration, JOYG closes at around $99.50. As the 100 call expires, we could sell the 105 call for the next-month expiration and bring in around another $2.50. The final month would turn into a vertical spread because the original call we bought is expiring that month along with any call we wanted to sell against it. Let's say that JOYG is trading around $104.50, and we can get a final $2.50 for the 110 call. In this magical example, we'll say that JOYG closes at $109.99 on expiration of the 90 call that we bought four months previously.

We paid $9.20 for the call, and we brought in about $10 in premiums, so the call was essentially free. To top it off, the 90 call we bought is now worth $19.99 at expiration. We made nearly $2,000 per contract with no capital of our own.

Darren: Immediately prior to our going to print, both our attorney and our editor read this example and suffered cardiac events within hours of each other. They are both expected to recover fully, and we wish them a speedy recovery. In accordance with both of their wishes and best advice, we feel obligated to say that if a scenario like the one just described were to happen to you in trading, you must have been continuously sitting on a horseshoe for several months and now have four-leaf clovers growing out of your ears. Please buy a lottery ticket right away. This scenario was illustrative in nature and was meant to show how a series of diagonal spreads can greatly reduce the cost basis of the long call portion of the position. You get the picture.

As we discuss more advanced option strategies, like rolling a position, you need to look carefully at your trading platform and your broker to make sure that they support rolling a position. In more advanced platforms, it is usually a simple order form to roll a position. When you roll a position, you buy back the short option that is about ready to expire and simultaneously short another option of your choice. If the option you shorted the month prior is ITM, the broker should automatically debit the difference from the premium you collect from shorting the new option.

Naked Put

A naked put is shorting a put on a stock that you haven't shorted. It is a great cash-generation tool to use at market bottoms, before volatility drains away, as it does in an uptrending market. The naked put can be used in a bullish retracement, a high base, or an ascending triangle.

You have to be selective in your trade setup when you are using naked puts. There is significant downside risk in using naked puts; you could end up being exercised and having to buy the stock above the market price. The margin requirements for naked puts are also much greater than the margin requirements for the other strategies that we use. Depending on the broker, your margin requirement may be from 30 percent of the strike price of the put up to 100 percent of the strike price for a cash-secured position.

The safest trade setup in which to use a naked put is a bullish market, a bullish sector, and a bullish chart setup. The ideal trade setup is a market bottom, a bullish sector, and a bullish chart setup. At the very least, you should have a bullish sector and a bullish stock. Volatility is high across the board at market bottoms as the last investors capitulate and seek downside protection. As the market rises, investors remove their hedges and volatility decreases, making the price of the put that you shorted decline even faster.

The underlying stock itself needs to be trading above $5 and be one that you want to own, and possibly own through some volatility; you may end up with it. The closer to a strike price the underlying stock is, the better. The gamma spike will work to your advantage. Again, especially with this technique, there must be no earnings announcement or news expected prior to expiration of the option. The biggest risk you have on selling a put is that you can and sometimes will get the stock put to you, which means that you have to buy it. If you sell a $50 put and the stock goes down to $1, guess what? You get to buy it at $50. Congratulations.

To enter a naked put, you will sell a short-term (six weeks or less until expiration) ATM put. The premium return needs to be between 5 and 10 percent of the price of the underlying.

Your breakeven point is the strike of the option you sold minus the premium that you collected.

Trade management is easy: buy to close the position at your breakeven point. No ifs, no buts; close it out.

If the underlying is trading below the strike price of the put you sold but above your breakeven point, you need to decide if you want to allow yourself to be exercised and buy the stock at the strike you sold, then either keep the stock or hold it over the weekend and sell it at the market on Monday. When we do use naked puts and the underlying is trading below the strike but above our breakeven point, we nearly always close out the position in the last minutes before the market closes on Expiration Friday because we don't feel that being long the stock is an efficient use of our capital.

For our example, we're going to use Whole Foods (symbol: WFMI). Our analysis of WFMI indicates that the stock is in a bullish pattern, has shown strength in the market for the past six months, and has no earnings announcements in between the time we put on the position and expiration of the option.

WFMI is trading at $60.44, making the 60 puts the closest to ATM. With about six weeks to expiration, we can sell the 60 puts for $3.77. Our return is 6.2 percent ($3.77 divided by $60.44), so we're good there. Our breakeven point is $56.23 ($60.00 strike – $3.77 premium). Happily, our breakeven point also coincides with an area of support, so we're protected there.

Figure 5-5 shows the risk graph for a naked put on WFMI.

If the stock holds above our breakeven point during the time between the trade and expiration, we will make a profit. If WFMI is trading anywhere above $60 per share at expiration, the option

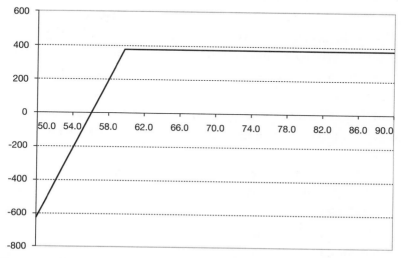

Figure 5-5   Naked Put

buyer will not exercise the right to sell it to us at $60 (since she can sell it for more in the open market) and will let the option expire. You keep the premium of $3.77 for not doing a whole heck of a lot. If WFMI looks as if it will close below our strike of $60 but above our breakeven, we can simply close the position by buying back the put option for a lower price. Let's say the stock looks as if it will close at $59 per share. You will be able to buy back the option close to expiration for around $1.05, since there is little or no time value left, only intrinsic value (IV). If you do nothing, remember that your broker will exercise all options that are $0.25 ITM or greater, and you will effectively buy the stock over the weekend at $60. You are now sitting on a $1 loss on the stock, but you have the $3.77 option premium to offset any loss.

Covered Call

A covered call is a sideways to bullish strategy with limited reward. Covered calls are a good way to generate cash in a stagnant to mildly bullish market. Most novice traders don't understand the covered call, and selling a put gives you the exact same risk graph and is essentially the same trade. The biggest difference will be the margin requirement your broker applies to you holding the position. Everything we talked about wanting in the naked put strategy will apply to covered calls as well. The best stocks to use for covered calls are those that are priced between $5 and $30. The reason is that options for lower-priced stocks are proportionally more expensive than options for higher-priced stocks. Since you're selling options, you want to get the most premium possible.

Covered calls are especially useful if a stock has just completed an extended runup and is beginning to consolidate. A good rule of thumb is that consolidation after a long move will take just about as long as the move itself. So if a stock was in an uptrend for one month and begins consolidating in a high base, it's entirely reasonable to expect that the high base will last about a month.

Covered calls are so named because if the option you sold gets exercised, you already have the stock in your account to sell at the strike price. You are covered if your options are exercised. If you were selling calls without having the stock, you would be uncovered or naked, and you would have to buy the stock at the market price to sell to the options holder.

The trade setup for a covered call position is a stock in a sideways or mildly bullish pattern. Some platforms have a covered call trading option. If your trading platform doesn't, the procedure is to buy the stock itself in lots of 100 because if the options you sell are exercised, you will have to deliver the stock in lots of 100.

The next step is to choose which option you want to sell against your long stock. Your decision should depend on your outlook for the underlying stock. If your analysis tells you that the stock will consolidate sideways for quite a while, you can maximize the premium you generate by selling an ATM call. If the stock unexpectedly moves down, the greater premium generated by the ATM call will lower your breakeven point.

If your analysis indicates that the stock will make a base for a while but then possibly move up gradually, you can sell an OTM call. The premium that you generate will be less than that for the ATM call, but you won't necessarily have the stock called away. However, if the stock moves down, your breakeven point will be higher than if you had sold an ATM call.

Trick of the Trade. Options market makers are pretty smart cookies. They have to be. They're juggling not only their inventory of stock but their contract ratios and their net deltas. When a stock is trading close to a strike price, say just a few cents ITM, take a look at the price of both the ATM call and the ATM put of the front-month contracts. Add the price of the call to the ATM strike and subtract the price of the put from the ATM strike. This will give you the expected trading range from the current time until expiration, all things remaining equal.

For example, Yahoo! (symbol: YHOO) is currently trading at $16.03, and YHOO options trade in $1 strikes. With one month to expiration, YHOO $16 calls are trading at $0.67, and YHOO $16 puts are trading at $0.63. Based on historic and implied volatility at this point in time, the options market makers expect YHOO to trade between $15.40 and $16.70 ($16.03 – $0.63 for the put premium and $16.03 + $0.67 for the call premium).

Using this technique, you have the choice of selling the $16 calls for $0.67, with the result that your return would be 4.2 percent for the next month, but you would have a pretty good chance of having the stock called away, or you could sell the $17 calls for $0.33 and get a 2.1 percent return, but have a better chance of keeping the stock.

You don't have to view having the option you sold get exercised as a bad thing, especially if you sold an OTM option. Using YHOO as an example, if you bought 100 shares of YHOO at $16.03 and sold a $16 call with one month to expiration, your return would be 4.2 percent for one month's work if the stock were called away at expiration. That annualizes to a 50.4 percent return.

If you bought 100 shares of YHOO for $16.03 and sold the $17 call with one month to expiration, and the call was exercised, your gain would be $1.30 ($17.00 strike of the call – $16.03 cost of the stock + $0.33 premium for selling the $17 call). That comes out to an 8.1 percent return for the same month. That annualizes to a 97.2 percent return.

There are several annoying aspects of a covered call. It takes a significant amount of capital to establish a position because you have to buy your stock in 100-share lots. You have to hold on to your stock as long as you are short the call. To liquidate the position, you have to buy back the call and then sell the stock. This doesn't present so much of a problem close to expiration because most of the time value has already accrued to you, but if the stock falls immediately after you sell the call, the decrease in the price of the short call will not be as great as the decrease in the price of the stock. The third annoying aspect of a covered call is that when the price of the stock rises above the strike price of the option you sold and then an additional amount exceeding the premium you received for selling the option, you've essentially left money on the table, and there is nothing you can do about it. The analytical part of you tells you that you should be happy with a profit. The greedy part of you tells you that you were less than intelligent for giving up some gains.

Figure 5-6 shows the risk graph for our YHOO covered call, selling the 17 call with one month to expiration. You'll notice that the covered call has the same shape risk graph as the short put. Our maximum gain is $1.30, and our breakeven is $15.70 ($16.03 price of the stock – $0.33 premium from selling the $17 call).

At Maverick Trading, we use covered calls and naked put selling as building blocks to train our traders to use much better strategies. While covered calls and naked put selling can seem like

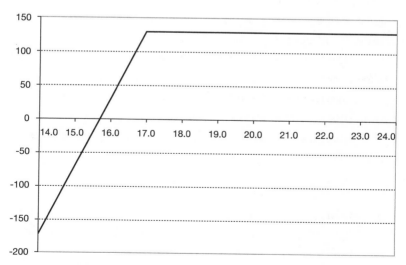

Figure 5-6   Covered Call

a winning strategy on paper, in real life they rarely generate long-term profitable results. The crux of the problem is the uneven reward-risk distribution for the trade. With both the covered call and the naked put, you have a small amount of gain with a large amount of downside risk. The typical result when a novice to intermediate trader uses these strategies is to be consistently profitable in her trades for four or five months in a row, profiting 3 to 7 percent per month. On a $10,000 account, this could be a move up to between $11,500 and $12,000 in a couple of months. Then, she will inevitably pick a losing stock that drops 30 percent during her trade (statistical probability states that this will happen several times per year), which moves the account from $12,000 down to $8,400 for an overall loss. Here was a trader who was correct 83 percent of the time and produced a −16 percent return over six months—a lot of time and work to lose 16 percent. When using a covered call or selling a put, you are selling away your upside potential in the stock, and if the stock jumps 30 percent, you will profit by only a small amount. Yet, if the stock drops 30 percent, you will take the full loss. That's not the kind of long-term reward-risk profile we are looking for in positions. However, these strategies are the building blocks of better option selling strategies, and everyone must have a complete understanding of how call and put selling works if he is to comprehend the advanced strategies. In the advanced strategies, we will be looking for ways to lower the overall risk of the trade on the downside and give us more ways to profit from upside movement. We do this by replacing the underlying stock with synthetic option positions.

Call LEAP Write

Some very liquid stocks have extremely long-term options called LEAPS. LEAPS stands for Long-term Equity AnticiPation Securities. LEAPS expire on Expiration Friday of every January and usually go out two years.

Brokers don't allow you to buy options on margin. They want cash on the barrelhead. However, the Chicago Board Options Exchange (CBOE) and brokers view LEAPS with more leniency. For options with more than nine months to expiration, some brokers will allow you to post only 75 percent of the cash value of the option.

For the trade setup, the stock should be in a bullish retracement, a high base, or an ascending triangle. Just because you're buying an option with a long time to expiration doesn't mean that you can ignore the fundamentals. It is helpful if the market and the sector are bullish as well. Your analysis of the stock should indicate bullishness for the long term.

The next step is to make sure that the stock has LEAPS available. Not all stocks do.

For a LEAP write, the long leg of your position should be a LEAP call with a delta of at least 0.80. This will be deep ITM, and the extrinsic value of the option will be a minor percentage of the option premium. At the same time, you will short an ATM or slightly OTM call against the long LEAP call. The time to expiration should be six weeks or less. To determine which call to short, use the same criteria you would for deciding which option to sell in a covered call strategy.

For our example, we're going to enter a LEAP write on the S&P 500 ETF, SPY. At the time of this example, SPY was trading at $127.76. For our long LEAP leg, we are going out 21 months until expiration. The first LEAP option for that expiration with a delta above 0.80 is the 100 call, trading at $32.19 with a delta of 0.84.

We want to keep this position for a while, so we're going to sell a slightly OTM call for the short leg of our LEAP write. Looking a month out, market makers are expecting a high for the trading range of SPY to be between $130.50 and $130.85, so we're going to sell the 131 call. The 131 call is trading at $1.31 and has a delta of 0.32 (see Table 5-3).

Table 5-3   Call LEAP Write

Option	Months to Expiration	Price	Delta	Theta
Long 100 call	21	$32.19	0.84	−0.01
Short 131 call	1	−$1.31	−0.32	0.04
Total		$30.88	0.52	0.03

Now, this isn't a cheap position to enter. One LEAP write will cost us $3,088 to enter. So why do we even like LEAP writes? For one thing, since LEAPS are 25 percent marginable, the day after we enter the trade, we have to maintain a margin requirement of only $2,316 instead of the full $3,088 ($3,088 × 0.75 = $2,316). That's going to free up some cash for other trades right away.

Second, the 100 call option with 21 months to expiration has an IV of $27.76. The EV of the option is only $4.43. The 131 call we sold has no IV, so the entire $1.31 premium that we got for selling the option is EV. By selling that option, we effectively reduced the EV in our long LEAP by nearly 30 percent, and after expiration we'll have another 20 months' worth of options that we'll be able to sell against our long LEAP.

But wait ... there's more. Some options have weekly expirations. SPY has weekly expirations. The weekly expirations get posted each Friday and expire the next Friday.

The weekly options are indicating a likely high trading range of just over $129 for SPY. We know that we're going to roll our position, so we're going to look at selling the 129 call with one week remaining. The 129 call is trading at $0.94, and the theta decay is $0.12 per day and will only increase (see Table 5-4).

Table 5-4   Call LEAP Write with Weekly Options

Option	Months to Expiration	Price	Delta	Theta
Long 100 call	21	$32.19	0.84	−0.01
Short 129 call	0.25	−$0.94	−0.37	0.12
Total		$31.25	0.47	0.11

Even just selling the OTM option with only a week remaining, we've still eliminated 21 percent of the EV of our long LEAP. Instead of making $0.03 per day in theta decay, we're now making $0.11 per day.

To top it all off, we have about 90 weeks until our long LEAP expires, and we can collect premiums during each of those weeks while we hold the LEAP. After the unfortunate incident with the diagonal call spread, our new attorney and our new editor have asked that we let you do the math and refrain from any theoretical calculations.

The LEAP write allows you to sit through sideways movement and get paid to do so.

Because the LEAP write is a premium generation machine, depending on your risk tolerance, you can afford to sit through minor pullbacks in an overall bullish market. For a protective stop, we recommend exiting the entire position when the stock breaks down through a major trend channel, as the market did in late July and early August 2011.

Figure 5-7 shows the risk graph for the SPY LEAP write with writing weekly options. As with the diagonal call calendar spread, our maximum profit (each week) is at the strike price of the option we sold. Our weekly breakeven on the low end is $126.90, and the upper breakeven is at $144.76. That is a range of 13.8 percent movement of the SPY in a week's worth of time. Sure, there have been one or two weeks in the last 50 years in which the SPY has moved more than this, but you can see that the profit window is huge. Since we have so much time on our LEAPS, we can adjust our strikes on our short calls every week, selling the option that brings in the most premium.

We can't stress enough that this is a long-term play in either a stock or, as in our example, an ETF. There is a tendency, even among traders, to become married to a LEAP write position, because they are such long-term positions and premium generation machines. But they are still long positions, and were entered

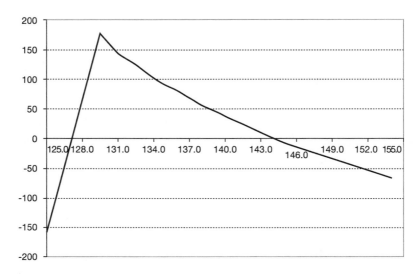

Figure 5-7   Call LEAP Write

on the thesis that the long-term outlook was bullish. When that situation changes and the stock, ETF, or broad market breaks through a major trend channel or major support like the 200-day SMA, it is best to exit the entire position.

The reason is that the market can go down more quickly than you can generate premium by selling calls against the LEAP. When things turn bearish, especially when they turn violently bearish, it is simply not safe to buck the trend and be in a long-term bullish position like the LEAP write.

BEARISH TECHNIQUES

As we've said before, we trade both sides of the market. We are what we call Market Agnostic: we don't care whether the market is rising or falling; we intend to make money either way. In order for us to accomplish this, we have to trade a bearish market.

By and large, the public has a psychological bias toward the long side of the market. It's natural because we want things that we own to be worth more than what we paid for them. Institutions have this same bias to the long side. Most professionally managed funds, including mutual funds, are long only in their investment theses. Even large university endowments with more than $1 billion in assets and investments across a variety of asset classes, including stocks, bonds, venture capital, private equity, real estate, and commodities, allocate only about 21 to 25 percent of their portfolios to alternative assets like hedge funds that can benefit in all market environments. The interesting fact, however, is that the larger and more successful the university endowment, the greater its exposure to hedge funds.

Because of the public's bias toward the long side of the market, people have a tendency to view those who make money on the short side of the market as being just a little bit evil, or if not evil, then unsavory company at the least.

To top it off, short sellers don't do themselves any favors, either. Go to a cocktail party during a market correction or a genuine bear market, and while 90 percent of the people at the party have just seen their retirement funds take a substantial hit, there's always that one guy who can't help crowing about how he's making a killing on the short side. You usually don't see him at the next cocktail party.

There is nothing wrong with just participating in bull runs and then sitting on the sidelines in cash during corrections and bear markets. If your risk tolerance doesn't support making money on the short side of the market, don't force the issue; you'll just cause yourself stress and end up losing money.

If your risk tolerance does support making money on the short side of the market, it's best to keep quiet about it and just take the money as it comes. For those who can grasp and embrace the idea of making money on the short side, there is something viscerally satisfying about making money while other people are losing money. Frankly, there's probably an element of schadenfreude involved as well.

As professional traders, we're interested in riding the fastest bus, whether it's headed uptown or downtown. We're not going to stand in front of the bus, no matter who thinks we should, or even if the whole crowd is standing in front of the bus because of what their investment advisors told them or because they somehow feel that it's a show of solidarity with the rest of the crowd to do so. Either get out of the way of the bus and sit on the sidelines or hop on the bus and make some money.

To be successful and not get run over, you have to trade the market in front of you, not the market you would like to see.

Short Stock

That being said, the first bearish technique that traders are introduced to is short stock. At Maverick, we tend to short stock more often than we go long stock, but we do so for similar reasons.

We will sometimes end up in a short stock position if we allow a bearish strategy that we were in to be exercised. This happens rarely, and only if we feel that there is further downside for the stock, rolling to a new bearish strategy is too expensive, and we don't have any better trade setups where we can put our capital to use.

We will also sometimes short stock against a bullish position when our short-term analysis tells us that the original bullish thesis is still valid, but there may be some near-term volatility in price. This is using short stock to hedge a bullish position.

The risk graph for short stock is exactly the opposite of that for long stock. It is technically a limited-reward, unlimited-risk trade because the price of the stock can only fall to zero and the price could theoretically rise forever.

The trade setups for short stock are a bear rally, a low base, a descending triangle, and a symmetrical triangle breakdown.

Figure 5-8 shows the risk graph for short stock.

Shorting stock is a very difficult concept for some people to grasp. When we tell people that they can sell a stock first and buy it second, they usually look at us with that glazed, far-off look that they get when someone is telling them about her alien abduction

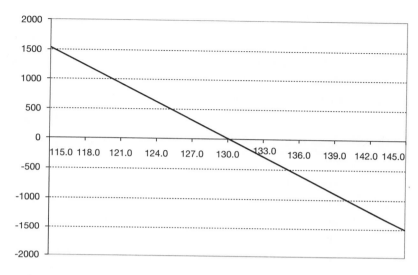

Figure 5-8   Short Stock

experience. Shorting happens all the time in our economy in things we deal with every day.

The best analogy to shorting stock is to take a look at how a bank works. A bank is simply a company that a large number of people have chosen to hold their money for them. When you walk into your bank with a $1,000 deposit and walk up to the teller, does someone take the money back to the vault, find your little shoebox, and put the money in there? Then, when you come back in for your money, does someone have to tell you to wait while he goes back to the vault, reaches into your shoebox, and brings your money back? No. The money goes into the pot of money that the bank has, and you will withdraw a completely different $1,000 from what you deposited in the first place. You don't care as long as it is $1,000. In return, the bank will provide services and may even pay a small amount of interest, even though this seems to be becoming as rare as the once-popular mullet haircut.

This is exactly what your brokerage (Schwab, E*TRADE, Morgan Stanley, and so on) is doing for your investment accounts.

Brokers hold stock, bonds, mutual funds, and other securities for their clients. What you need to understand is that if you own 200 shares of Microsoft, there is no shoebox at Charles Schwab with your specific 200 shares tucked away sweetly to bed. The broker throws everything together into the pot, just like a bank. So, when you sell your 200 shares of Microsoft, you will not be selling the exact shares you bought years ago. Everything is together in the pot.

The primary way a bank makes money is by loaning out the money that people brought into it at higher interest rates. I could walk into your bank and get a loan from the bank for $1,000. I will be required to put up collateral, but that $1,000 is the exact $1,000 you brought in and deposited earlier in the day. When you try to get your money out of your bank account, the bank isn't going to tell you, "Sorry, but we lent your money out to some guy, and as soon as he brings it back, we will let you know." It will give you $1,000 out of the pot.

When you short stock, your broker (Schwab, E*TRADE, Morgan Stanley, and so on) has millions of shares of stock sitting in the pot. As long as you have a margin account, you have the ability to borrow and sell any of the stocks it has available in its pot. Whenever you borrow something from your friend, you need to give it back sometime in the future. When you borrow stock from the broker, you need to give the broker back the same number of shares you borrowed.

Let's say you borrowed 200 shares of Microsoft (ticker: MSFT) from your broker and sold it short at $25 per share. At this point, since you have sold short, you must eventually return 200 shares of Microsoft to your broker. There is no time limit on how long you can stay short stock—except for your death. (Side note: brokers are required to cover all shorts in your account upon your death. But don't worry . . . it won't be your problem anymore.) To complete the trade, you will need to buy

200 shares of Microsoft on the open market to return to the broker. If you can buy Microsoft shares for less than $25 (where you sold them short), you will have a profit. If you purchase them for more than $25, you will have a loss. It's exactly the same as buying a stock, except in reverse.

Shorting has been around for as long as the markets. The first documented short in history was in 1609 by Dutch merchant Isaac Le Maire. He had invested 85,000 gilders in the Vereenigde Oostindische Compagnie (Dutch East India Company), and when the company stopped paying dividends and its ships were under constant attack by the British, he sold his entire stake and more. This was considered "an outrageous act," and the practice of short selling got its first but not last attempted ban.

We don't typically short stocks, since there are much better ways to play stocks moving down—a multitude of synthetic bearish option positions that give a trader better reward-risk profiles and the ability to tie up less capital.

Long Put

Long puts are the first bearish option strategy that people use. The risk graph of long puts is the mirror image of that for long calls. Your risk is limited to the premium paid for the option, and your reward is limited because the stock can only go to zero.

The setup for long puts is a bear pullback, a low base, or a descending triangle. The ideal setup for long puts is a bearish market, the weakest sector in the market, and a bearish chart formation. You can still enter a long put position in a bullish market, but the sector and the stock have to be weak and bearish.

Once the stock has triggered your entry point, the option you should choose should have a delta of at least 0.65. (Technically, the delta is -0.65, but for the sake of clarity, we're going to use absolute numbers.) The next rule with a long put position is no front-month options. Even after a breakdown, stocks can linger near resistance before beginning their next move downward in earnest. You need to give the trade time to work, and the theta decay in front-month options is horrendous. Finally, you want to see a reward-risk ratio of at least 2:1.

Using your SET procedures, you should already have calculated your anticipated target price. To calculate your anticipated reward, take the difference between your target price and your entry price and multiply by the delta of the put. As with long calls, your stop loss is 30 percent of the premium of the option.

For our example, we're going to use SPY again. We'll say that SPY showed that it was in a downtrend and just bounced off resistance in a bear rally. SPY is trading at $127.75, and our SET analysis said that a likely target would be $121. The option with two months to expiration (no front-month options on long puts) and at least a 0.65 delta is the 132 put, trading at $6.30 with a delta of 0.66.

Our stop loss is 30 percent of the premium, or $1.89. If the value of the put falls below $4.41, we'll be stopped out of our position. Our expected reward is the difference between our entry price and our target price ($127.75 entry price − $121.00 target price = $6.75) multiplied by the delta of the option (0.66), giving us a reward of $4.46 ($6.75 × 0.66). Our reward-risk ratio is 2.36 ($4.46 reward divided by $1.89 in risk).

This is true for any trade, but it's especially true for long call and long put positions: if the reward-risk ratio does not pan out, don't adjust your target price to make the ratio work; find another trade.

Position sizing for long puts is the same as for long calls. With our example portfolio ($10,000) and medium risk tolerance (2 percent of the portfolio = $200) and a maximum risk for the position of $189, we can safely enter a one-contract position with an initial outlay of $630.

The risk graph for a long put is shown in Figure 5-9.

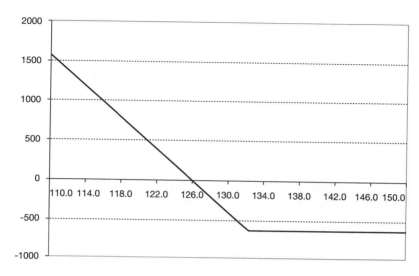

Figure 5-9   Long Put

Bear Put Spread

The bear put spread is a directional, limited-risk, limited-reward trade. Like the bull call spread, the bear put spread is a vertical spread and a debit spread. Delta is muted, but theta decay is hedged. The bear put spread is used to capture discrete short-term moves to the downside once a stock breaks through support or confirms a continuation pattern.

The ideal trade setup for a bear put spread is a downtrending broad market, a stock in a weak sector, and the stock itself making a bear rally, a descending triangle, or a low base pattern.

To enter a bear put spread, as the trade triggers, buy the short-term (three to eight weeks until expiration) ATM or the first ITM put. Using the target price generated from your SET procedures, short an OTM put with the same expiration as close to your target price as possible. As with the bull call spread, the metrics for the bear put spread are net debit no more than 45 percent of the spread amount and a net delta of at least 0.25 (the more the better).

Table 5-5   Bear Put Spread

Option	Months to Expiration	Price	Delta	Theta
Long 41 put	1	$3.01	0.51	−0.04
Short 36 put	1	$1.13	−0.24	0.03
Total		$1.88	0.27	−0.01

Your maximum risk is the debit to enter the spread. Your maximum gain is the amount of the spread less the debit to enter the spread. The breakeven price in this trade is the higher strike of the long put less the debit.

Our example position is Apollo Group (symbol: APOL). At the time of this example, APOL was trading at $40.32 and had just broken through support. Our SET analysis indicated the likelihood of a $5 move to the downside.

We're looking one month out, and the first ITM put is the 41 put (APOL options trade in $1 strikes), trading at $3.01 with a delta of 0.51. Since we're expecting a $5 move to the downside in APOL, we're going to short the 36 put with the same expiration. The 36 put is trading at $1.13 with a delta of 0.24 (see Table 5-5).

We have a $5.00 spread with a maximum risk of $1.88 (debit to enter the position) and a maximum reward of $3.12. Our debit-to-spread ratio is 38 percent, and our net delta is 0.27. This trade meets our criteria. Our breakeven price for the trade is $39.12. Any close at expiration below $39.12 is profit.

The risk graph for our APOL bear put spread is shown in Figure 5-10.

Position sizing for the bear put spread is the same as that for the bull call spread: divide your per trade risk tolerance by the per contract debit of the spread. Remember, we don't like to have stops on vertical spreads, as these trades allow us to sit through a lot of volatility because we are both long and short the same stock

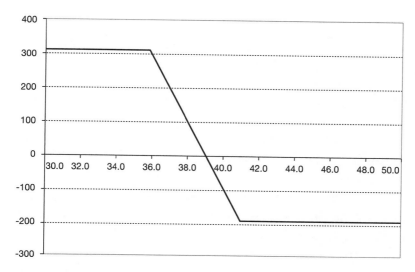

Figure 5-10   Bear Put Spread

through different options. So, make sure to calculate your position size for the maximum loss just in case.

Diagonal Put Calendar Spread

Diagonal put spreads are excellent trades in sideways to downtrending markets. The stock you choose should be moving sideways and/or your Top-Down Approach should indicate that the stock could experience a multileg run to the downside. Like the diagonal call spread, the diagonal put spread gives you multiple opportunities to sell front-month premiums, drastically reducing the cost of the trade as it progresses.

To enter a diagonal put spread, buy an ITM put with an expiration that is at least four months out. Again, check to make sure that there is no pending news or earnings announcements in the next six weeks. At the same time, short an OTM put with an expiration no more than six weeks out. The short-term OTM put premium needs to be a minimum of 25 percent of the longer-term put premium. If you are entering a diagonal put spread in a stock or ETF with weekly options, depending on your risk tolerance, you could reduce your criteria for selling the OTM put to 15 percent of the premium of the long put. This will adversely affect your breakeven point, but will allow you to roll your position more easily without the risk of owing cash in the case of a sudden down move.

We're going to use the same stock that we did for the bear put spread. Our top-down analysis indicated that APOL was probably just beginning a multileg downtrend, and we want to stay in the trade for as long as possible to catch the majority of the move, and also to generate premium as the stock consolidates on its way down.

As in our bear put spread scenario, APOL was trading at $40.32. We are going out five months until expiration, and we see that the first ITM put is the 41 put, trading at $4.45 with a delta of 0.48. Now we need to find an OTM front-month contract that is trading for at least 25 percent of the premium of the 41 put, or at least $1.11. Looking out one month, we see that the 38 put is trading at $1.24 (see Table 5-6).

As with the diagonal call spread, time works for us in the diagonal put spread. We're losing $0.01 per day in theta on our long 41 put, but we're gaining $0.04 per day on our short 38 put. This gain will accelerate as the front-month 38 put approaches expiration.

With regard to our breakeven points and stop losses, on our diagonal put spread, we're concerned with the upper breakeven point. It's the closest, and it could also tell us if our

Table 5-6   Diagonal Put Calendar Spread

Option	Months to Expiration	Price	Delta	Theta
Long 41 put	5	$4.45	0.48	−0.01
Short 38 put	1	$1.24	−0.31	0.04
Total		$3.21	0.17	0.03

analysis was incorrect. Our upper breakeven point for this trade is $42.28, and our lower breakeven point is $28.88. Our maximum gain at expiration is at the strike price of the option we sold, $38. At any price between $28.88 and $42.28, we make a profit.

The risk graph for our position is shown in Figure 5-11.

As with a diagonal call spread, position sizing is based on your judgment and risk tolerance. If the stock is in a sideways pattern, we recommend placing your stop 1 ATR above the consolidation high. In this example, the consolidation high was at $41.27 and the ATR for APOL was $1.11. Using these criteria, that would put our stop at $42.38, just $0.10 above our breakeven point of $42.28.

Here's where judgment comes into play. If you put the stop at $42.38 and incurred a $10 loss per contract, simply using the risk parameters in our example portfolio, you could theoretically take a position of 20 contracts. You can get into each contract for

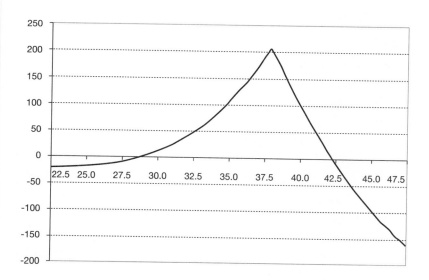

Figure 5-11   Diagonal Put Calendar Spread

$321. If you made your position 20 contracts, your debit would be $6,420.

Please don't do this. No one should have 64 percent of his portfolio in a single trade, even if the stop loss makes it look appetizing. It's a poor use of capital, and you'll find yourself thinking about the position constantly. This will impair your judgment and cause stress. As a rule of thumb, don't put more than 10 percent of your capital into any single position. Using that criterion, with a $10,000 portfolio, we'd recommend establishing a three-contract position.

As we mentioned earlier, diagonal spreads can turn into multimonth positions, continually selling options against the long leg of the position and receiving premium. If the first month of the trade has been profitable and your Top-Down Approach indicates that there is still room either in a sideways movement or in a continued downtrend, you can consider rolling your position to the next month.

Short Call

One of our bullish strategies was short puts. Then it stands to reason that in a bearish stock, you should be able to short calls, right? Ummm, no.

Naked shorting of calls is the epitome of a limited-reward, unlimited-risk play.

In most of our bullish techniques, we've shorted calls, but we've always had something beneath them, either stock or another long call at a lower strike price, to cover us if the price of the underlying moves above the strike of the call we shorted. We've always been covered.

If you want to be in a situation where a gap up could decimate your portfolio, then by all means, find a broker who will let you short calls and have at it.

The more advanced brokers will actually let you write naked calls. You just have to have about $500,000 in liquid cash at all times, and the margin requirements are usually an additional 30 percent of the strike of the call you are shorting.

For mere mortals, the rule is, "Be smart; don't start."

STAGNATION AND VOLATILITY TECHNIQUES

Sometimes the markets just don't go anywhere for an extended period of time. For those traders who are shackled to stocks, those times are frustrating because the traders aren't making any money. They're dead in the water and going nowhere fast. It's usually at those points that desperation for any movement sets in and stock-only traders start doing really stupid things in an effort to make money.

Most novice to intermediate traders are directional traders only, with a strong bias toward the bullish side of the market. A directional trader plays only bullish or bearish trades and needs the stock and the markets to move in order to make profits. This means that most traders will think they are great traders when they are trading in a bull market, and they will slap high fives and tell you about their successes. However, whenever the inevitable bear market or stagnant market comes, they get wiped out, ending the high fives and the overconfidence. We notice a big difference in prospective traders who are looking to join Maverick Trading during different market conditions. In bull markets, every applicant likes to tell us how great she is and how she knows it all, but in bear markets, the applicants have been humbled and are looking for more help and structure that they thought they didn't need before.

If you truly want trading to be your long-term profession, you need to be able to trade in all three market environments. During our 14 years in business, we have seen two periods of bubbles followed by two of the worst crashes in history. But in our opinion, the most difficult year in which to make money as a trader was 2003, between the crash and the next bull market. That year the S&P traded in a 14 percent range from high to low, causing volatility to drop to 40-year lows. If you wish to make it as a long-term trader, you need to know how to make money in bull, bear, and especially sideways markets.

Horizontal Calendar Spread

Since we have options in our toolbox, we can use periods of stagnation to generate cash through the selling of options. One of the best techniques to use in a stagnant market is a horizontal calendar spread.

In a calendar spread, you can either use calls or puts. When your Top-Down Approach indicates that the trend in a stock is sideways to slightly positive, use calls. When the Top-Down Approach indicates that the trend in the stock is sideways to slightly down, use puts.

To enter a calendar spread, buy a slightly ITM option (call or put, depending on your outlook) that expires a minimum of four months out. At the same time, sell a short-term option (less than six weeks to expiration) with the same strike. The premium of the short-term option should be at least 40 percent of the longer-term premium. Conduct your research to ensure that there is no pending news or earnings announcements between the time you enter the position and the expiration of the option you sold.

We're going to provide two examples of a calendar spread on the same stock, one using calls and the other using puts. The stock we're going to use is Steel Dynamics (symbol: STLD). At the time of the example, STLD was trading at $18.10. It had established support at $17.40 and met resistance at $19.20.

Our first example will use a call calendar spread on STLD. STLD options trade in $1 strikes. The 18 calls with five months to expiration were trading at $1.70, and the front-month 18 calls were trading at $0.78. Our return was 45.9 percent ($0.78 premium of the calls we sold divided by $1.70

Table 5-7   Call Calendar Spread

Option	Months to Expiration	Price	Delta	Theta
Long 18 call	5	$1.70	0.56	−0.006
Short 18 call	1	$0.78	−0.54	0.014
Total		$0.92	0.02	0.08

premium of the calls we bought). Our maximum gain occurs when STLD closes at $17.99 on the day the front-month option expires. Our gain would then be $57 per position. Our breakeven points are at $16.81 on the low side and $19.48 on the high side. For position management, we'll set our stops for a break above or below the resistance and support levels we identified during our SET procedures, $17.40 and $19.10 (see Table 5-7).

You'll need to wait at least a week before you see any appreciable profit or loss in the position, and during the first few days of holding the position, any up or down movement in the stock price, even over a normal range, will have the position showing a small loss. Time decay has yet to begin working to your advantage.

Position sizing is a function of trade management. If the position begins to move against you and breaks through either support or resistance, you have the choice of either liquidating the entire position or turning the calendar spread into a diagonal spread.

If you are using calls for your calendar spread and the position breaks to the downside, the best thing to do is liquidate the position and take a small loss. If it breaks to the upside, you can buy back the short calls for a small loss and resell calls with a higher strike, turning the position into a diagonal call spread.

Likewise, if you are using puts and the position breaks to the upside, liquidate the position. If the position breaks to the downside, buy back the short puts and resell puts with a lower strike, turning the position into a diagonal put spread.

If you intend to liquidate the entire position if it moves against you, you could safely allocate up to 5 percent of your portfolio to a single position. In this case, with our example portfolio, you could have a five-contract position because your net debit to enter the position is $92. If you think there's the possibility of a break to the upside or downside and you intend to turn the calendar spread into a diagonal spread, calculate your position size for a diagonal spread and use that position size for your calendar spread.

Alternatively, you could go with a larger position size for the calendar spread, and if the underlying breaks in the direction needed for a conversion to a diagonal spread, convert the appropriate number of calendar spreads into diagonal spreads and liquidate the excess calendar spreads.

The risk graph for the STLD call calendar spread is shown in Figure 5-12.

For comparison, we'll set up a put calendar spread for STLD as well. The 18 puts with five months to expiration were

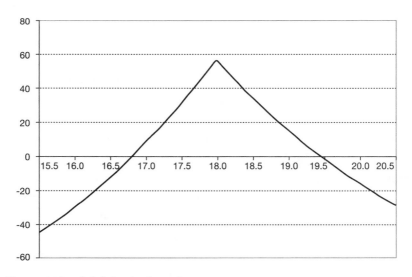

Figure 5-12   Call Calendar Spread

trading at $1.88, and the 18 puts with one month to expiration were trading at $0.83. Our return was 44.1 percent ($0.83 divided by $1.88). Our maximum gain at expiration of the front-month puts was $82 per position, and our breakeven points were identified as $16.25 on the low side and $20.30 on the high side (see Table 5-8).

The risk graph for the STLD put calendar spread is shown in Figure 5-13.

Table 5-8   Put Calendar Spread

Option	Months to Expiration	Price	Delta	Theta
Long 18 put	5	$1.88	0.44	−0.01
Short 18 put	1	$0.83	−0.46	0.02
Total		$1.05	−0.02	0.01

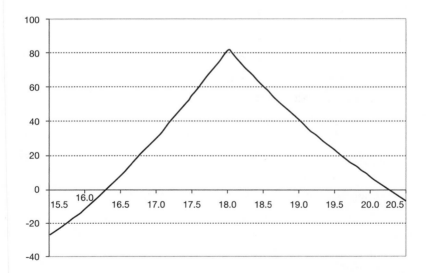

Figure 5-13   Put Calendar Spread

Table 5-9   Comparison of the STLD Call Calendar Spread and Put Calendar Spread

	Debit	Maximum Gain	Low Breakeven	High Breakeven
Call calendar spread	$0.92	$0.57	$16.81	$19.48
Put calendar spread	$1.05	$0.82	$16.25	$20.30

In situations where support and resistance are clearly established and you have two choices for how to enter a position, a comparison of the two positions is helpful to determine which one gives the greater reward-risk ratio. Table 5-9 gives a comparison of the STLD call calendar spread and put calendar spread.

All things being equal, placing a calendar spread on STLD using puts would be the better decision. Our gain-to-debit ratio using calls is 0.62, while our gain-to-debit ratio using puts is 0.78. Additionally, the profit range using calls is $2.67, centered on $18, and the profit range using puts is $4.05, nearly 52 percent greater.

Condors and Butterflies

Our next stagnation techniques are condors and butterflies. The difference between a condor and a butterfly is that a condor sells options at two different strikes and a butterfly sells options at a single strike. Condors and butterflies can be established with all calls or all puts. Using both calls and puts turns the strategy into an iron condor or an iron butterfly. The basic formula for any condor or butterfly is to "buy one, sell two, buy one" as you work your way up the strikes.

The ideal setup for a condor or a butterfly is a broad market displaying sideways action, a stock sector displaying sideways action, and a stock in a sideways pattern. There should be no scheduled earnings announcements or other catalysts during the period of the trade.

After you've identified a candidate for a condor or a butterfly, you need to identify the upper and lower ranges of the consolidation pattern. If the stock is trading at or very near a strike price, usually the best strategy is to use a butterfly. If the stock is trading in between two strikes, the best strategy is usually a condor. A butterfly has greater profit potential, but a smaller profitable range. Condors have a lower profit potential, but a greater range of profitability.

Table 5-10 shows the different legs of condors and butterflies.

Butterflies and condors are strategies that we want to work as quickly as possible to take advantage of theta decay. Because of this, we almost never establish a condor or butterfly more than five weeks out. We're comfortable projecting sideways movement for up to a month, but beyond that time frame, we've found that you're holding on to the firecracker just a little too long before throwing it.

When you pencil out the trade, your maximum gain should be greater than or equal to 50 percent of the spread amount. With a time decay strategy, we'll risk a dollar to make a dollar, but we're not going to risk two dollars to make one dollar.

For our example, we're going to take a look at a butterfly with all calls on JPMorgan (symbol: JPM), then a condor with all puts, and finally an iron condor. At the time of the example, JPM was trading at $45.63 in a consolidation pattern with support at $44 and resistance at $48. JPM's front-month options have about four weeks to expiration.

Since JPM options trade in $1 strikes, we're going to establish a 44/46/48 call butterfly; $44 and $48 are where support and resistance are, and $46 is the closest strike to where JPM is trading. In condors and butterflies, the distance between the midpoint of the spread and the outlying strikes needs to be equal. If they aren't, you're weighting your trade in one direction and will incur unnecessary risk in the position.

Table 5-10   Condors and Butterflies

	First Strike	Second Strike	Third Strike	Fourth Strike
Call butterfly	Long ITM call	Short 2ATM calls, same strike		Long OTM call
Put butterfly	Long OTM put	Short 2ATM puts, same strike		Long ITM put
Call condor	Long ITM call	Short call at low range of consolidation	Short call at upper range of consolidation	Long OTM call
Put condor	Long OTM put	Short put at low range of consolidation	Short put at upper range of consolidation	Long ITM put
Iron butterfly	Long OTM put	Short ATM put and ATM call (same strike)		Long OTM call
Iron condor	Long OTM put	Short put at low range of consolidation	Short call at upper range of consolidation	Long OTM call

Since our formula for a call butterfly is to be long one call at the lower end of the spread (support), short two calls at the strike nearest to where the underlying is trading, and long one call at the upper end of the spread (resistance), we will buy one 44 call, short two 46 calls, and buy one 48 call.

The 44 call is trading at $2.28, the 46 calls are trading at $1.07, and the 48 call is trading at $0.38.

The two long calls are debits totaling $2.66. The two short calls are credits totaling $2.14. We'll be entering this position with a $0.52 debit.

At expiration, our maximum gain will be $149 and will come if JPM closes at $45.99, right below the two 46 calls we sold. The 44 call that we own still has $2 in value, and the 46 call we were also long has expired worthless. Our breakeven points are at $44.51 and $47.49.

Figure 5-14 gives the risk graph for the JPM call butterfly.

How do things look for the put condor? We're going to examine a 44/45/47/48 put condor. We will buy a 44 put, trading

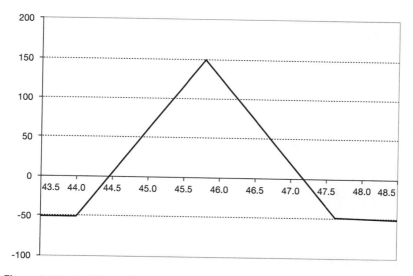

Figure 5-14   Call Butterfly

at $0.81; short a 45 put, trading at $1.17; short a 47 put, trading at $2.25; and buy a 48 put, trading at $2.97. We shelled out $3.78 for the two long puts and took in $3.42 in premium from the two short puts.

In this position, our maximum risk is $36, which occurs at a close on expiration either below $44 or above $48. Our maximum gain in this trade is $64, lower than that for the butterfly, but we receive the maximum gain on any close at expiration between $45 and $47. Our breakeven points are $44.36 on the low side and $47.64 on the upper end.

The risk graph for the put condor is shown in Figure 5-15.

To enter the iron condor in this example, we're going to buy the 44 put, trading at $0.81; short the 45 put, trading at $1.17; short the 47 call, trading at $0.66; and buy the 48 call, trading at $0.38. In this case, our long call and long put will cost us $1.19, but the short call and short put will bring in $1.83, meaning that we'll start off the trade with a credit of $0.64. This is our maximum gain on the trade. Our maximum risk is still $36. Our

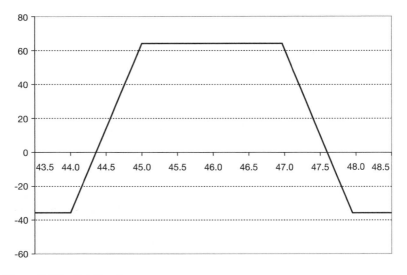

Figure 5-15   Put Condor

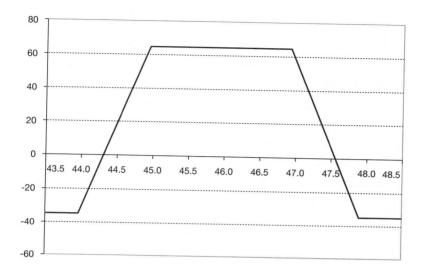

Figure 5-16   Iron Condor

breakeven points for the trade are $44.36 and $47.64. If you've been following the box score at home, the maximum reward, maximum risk, and breakeven points are the same for a butterfly and an iron butterfly and the same for a condor and an iron condor. The difference is that with a straight call or put butterfly or condor, you start off the trade with a debit that is your maximum risk and work your way to profitability as time decays. With an iron butterfly or iron condor, you start off with a credit that is your maximum reward and decrease your credit as the position moves within (or outside of) your profit range.

To prove it, Figure 5-16 shows the risk graph for the JPM iron condor.

It's exactly the same as that for the put condor.

Straddles and Strangles

Straddles and strangles are useful when it looks as if the underlying stock could break either way, usually because of an upcoming catalyst, like earnings or a court decision. If you are entering a straddle or a strangle in anticipation of an earnings announcement, make sure that the stock has not seen large moves immediately after the last two earnings reports.

You want to enter these positions only on stocks that experience swings in price greater than those of the overall market. These are called high-beta stocks, and you want a stock with a beta of over 2.0. What this translates to is that if the market goes up 10 percent, that stock is likely to rise close to 20 percent.

There are two market conditions that will help these trades be profitable: either the broad market is in an extreme consolidation, making the options for the stock less expensive, or the broad market is wildly volatile (that is, volatility over 40 on the S&P Volatility Index, symbol: VIX). In a wildly volatile market, the options will be more expensive, but the stock is likely to make a move that will put you in an area of profitability.

You need to use your SET procedures to calculate realistic price targets for your stock. In choosing which options to buy, you need to look at the medium-term options with expirations two to five months out. Your expected catalyst should also be scheduled for between three and five weeks away. If the catalyst is any closer, institutions that want to either speculate on a position or hedge against their existing positions will have begun to drive up the implied volatility, making the options so expensive that it will be difficult to actually profit from a move in the stock. If the catalyst is any further away, you're going to be losing too much time value waiting for the catalyst to occur.

Remember when we discussed implied volatility and compared it to the spread in sports betting? The same thing happens in the options market when there is an earnings or major news announcement upcoming for the stock. The market makers know that there is going to be a move, and they begin to price the options accordingly. In sports betting, one day you will see the bet on the Patriots favored by 9 points, and the next day the spread might be down to Patriots by 7. This comes from bettors placing more bets on the Bills winning, so the house adjusts the spread to reflect supply and demand. The highest point of implied volatility is immediately before the announcement, making options most expensive at that time. After the announcement, there is typically a tremendous crumbling of implied volatility, since the traders now know exactly what the news or earnings are. This is known as the volatility crush.

To enter a straddle or a strangle, you are going to buy both a call and a put. For a straddle, you will buy the call and the put at the same strike price, whatever the ATM strike is. For a strangle, you will buy your put and call at different strikes, both OTM. A straddle is more expensive to enter but will achieve profitability with a smaller move in the stock. A strangle is less expensive, but the maximum risk portion of the risk graph is larger, and you need a larger move to achieve profitability. The key consideration in whether to choose a straddle or a strangle is how close to a strike price the underlying is trading. If it is close to a strike, enter a straddle; if it is between two strikes, choose a strangle.

For our example, we'll take a look at a straddle and a strangle on InterMune Pharmaceuticals (symbol: ITMN). At the time of this example, ITMN was trading at $44.30, and its options trade in $1 strikes. During our SET analysis of ITMN, we saw that it bases for a very long time and then is capable of making wild moves. Our analysis indicates that a $15 move up or down is not out of the question for this stock. The expiration period we are looking at is four months out.

We're going to look at a straddle at the 44 strike and a strangle between the 42 and 46 strikes (see Table 5-11).

Table 5-11   Straddle and Strangle

	Call Strike	Call Premium	Put Strike	Put Premium	Total
ITMN straddle	44	$4.60	44	$4.23	$8.83
ITMN strangle	46	$3.90	42	$3.45	$7.35

To calculate your breakeven points for either a straddle or a strangle, add the debit to the strike price (upper strike for a strangle) and subtract the debit from the strike price (lower strike for the strangle). The lower breakeven for the straddle is $35.17, and the upper breakeven is $52.83. For the strangle, the lower breakeven is $34.65, and the upper breakeven is $53.35.

Figure 5-17 shows the risk graph for the straddle, and Figure 5-18 shows the risk graph for the strangle.

Ideally, both breakeven points should be closer to the strike prices than the targets. This increases your probability of success because the underlying doesn't have to move as far in order to turn a profit.

Position sizing and trade management for the straddle and the strangle are straightforward. Done correctly, these are expensive positions to enter, so a lower position size is warranted. Too many times we've seen traders enter straddles and strangles with less than a month until expiration and then watch their positions go nowhere and time decay and the volatility crush set in rapidly.

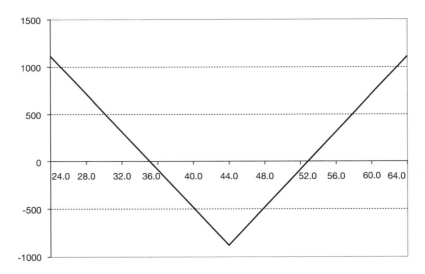

Figure 5-17   Straddle

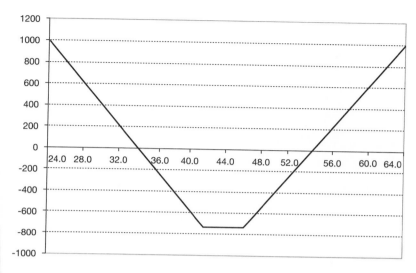

Figure 5-18   Strangle

As the catalyst event approaches, implied volatility will rise, temporarily reducing the effects of theta decay on your position. Once the catalyst occurs, implied volatility will fall off a cliff. This will cause the value of your straddle or strangle to lose money the day after the catalyst event.

Since these positions are used to capitalize on expected movement after a catalytic event, once the event has occurred, it's usually best to exit the position at the market open the day after the event, unless the stock gaps up or down and continues to move in that direction for the entire trading day on which the event occurs. If the stock makes no appreciable move or a lackluster move the day after the event, exit the position and recover as much time value as possible from the options. Don't hold on to the position in the hope that the move will occur later. It won't.

GETTING INTO THE GAME: TECHNOLOGY AND BROKER SELECTION

If you listen to any financial-centric cable channel for more than half an hour, you'll be bombarded by commercials for retail brokers clamoring for your business. You'll see the whole gamut, from private wealth management firms catering to accredited investors and institutions, to full-service brokers who are there to assist you with every investment decision you want to make, and on to discount brokers who provide access but no advice.

Choosing the right broker will help you to generate a profit as long as you know what you are doing. If you just aren't a good trader and you don't understand proper position sizing and risk management, it doesn't matter who you choose. Remember, the broker has no vested interest in your account growing, since it will be making money from commissions or yearly management fees. The broker will sit on the sidelines and let traders run their accounts down to zero without even a phone call, hiding behind the firm's risk disclosures and stating that the trader was doing this at his own risk. However, choosing a broker that is unsuited to your trading style and trading system will hamper your efforts and eat into your profits.

The analytical tools that you use prior to making a trade are in some ways more important than your selection of a broker. You can make money on a good trade setup with a bad broker, but a good broker can't help you make money on a poorly designed and executed trade setup.

At Maverick, we use several separate programs in addition to the software provided by our broker. We have a screening program, a charting program, an options analysis program, and our strategy and setup sheets. We use these programs outside of our broker interface for two reasons: (1) each of these programs performs its specialized task better than any other we've found, and (2) it helps to ensure that we fully understand the setup, entry, stops, targets, and profit areas of each trade before we enter the trade. When you try to do your entire setup within your broker interface, those BUY and SELL buttons are just too close for comfort. Anything you can do to remove the temptation to trade on emotion rather than analysis is a good thing.

Using the right tools from analysis to execution will make trading easier, and you will feel more confident about each trade that you make.

CHEAP IS COSTLY

As we continue with this chapter, we ask that you take one premise as given and run with it. That premise is that *cheap is costly*. We're not the military, and our weapons aren't made by the lowest bidder. Our tools provide the access, functionality, and capabilities that we need if we are to execute our business plans successfully.

We're not saying that you should flagrantly throw money at every new tool or system that comes down the pike. We're saying that you, as a professional trader, need to make a holistic cost-benefit analysis of every aspect of your business support tools and pick the ones that best fit your needs.

You can view your support tools in one of two ways: either as an expense or as an investment. If you view them as an expense, you will do everything you can to reduce their cost, even to the detriment of their capabilities. When you view your support tools as an investment, however, you evaluate the capabilities of a particular support tool with an eye toward what return those capabilities will generate for you. You should always expect a return on your investments.

We use terms like *professional trader, support tools, return on investment*, and *business* for a reason. Professional trading is a business, and you need to treat it like one if you are to be successful. Just beginning to classify your trading career as a business is a step in the right direction.

There are certain tools that you will need if you are to execute Maverick's trading system successfully. There are also other tools out there provided by brokers that are frankly unnecessary and really just serve to keep you logged in to your trading account and as close to the BUY and SELL buttons as possible.

Keep in mind that your broker and service providers get paid before you do and regardless of whether you make money on your trade. Your making money on a trade is a wholly secondary consideration for them. If you do make money, or at least have the impression that you are making money, you are more likely to remain a repeat customer.

Since you are running a business as a trader, your primary focus needs to be on turning a profit on as great a percentage of your trades as possible. Your focus shouldn't be on getting the latest gadget, service, or newsletter every time one pops up in front of you. That practice quickly turns a business into a hobby, and we've yet to find a hobby that is consistently profitable.

That said, what do you really need if you are to be successful?

STARTING THE BAND: NECESSARY INSTRUMENTS

The first question that you need to answer is where to put your trading account. You want a broker that will support your trading strategy and that provides the tools you need in order to execute those strategies. Using Maverick's system, you will need to be able to go long and short stock and to buy and sell options.

Each broker has its own levels of trading authority, but Table 6-1 is a good guide.

If you talk to most discount brokers and tell them that you want to trade options, they will give you Level 1 trading authorization (short stock; write covered calls) without much discussion. If you press the issue, you can usually get Level 2 trading authority (buy calls and puts; write cash-secured naked puts), but they will want you to tell them that you have at least $50,000 in investable assets, exclusive of your primary residence.

Huh?

It's true. Most discount brokers are stock- and mutual fund–centric. Many don't even offer options trading, or if they do, they don't give their customers more than Level 2 trading authority. They are just trying to protect themselves from their customers imploding their accounts. So many people have

Table 6-1   Levels of Trading Authority

Trading Authority Level	Capabilities
Level 0	Buy stocks, bonds, mutual funds
Level 1	Sell stock short; write covered calls
Level 2	Buy calls and puts; write cash-secured naked puts
Level 3	Enter debit spreads
Level 4	Enter credit spreads; write naked puts
Level 5	Write naked calls

destroyed their portfolios by falling into one, two, or all three of the common options trading pitfalls (OTM options, too little time to expiration, too large a position size) and then blamed their broker for letting them do it that many discount brokers just relieve themselves of the headache.

If you are currently at one of those brokers that don't offer professional-grade trading authority and you want to implement Maverick's trading system, you're probably going to have to move your account to a broker that either offers services for professional traders or is options-focused.

Options-focused brokers cater to a more educated type of retail trader. They take the position that if you request specific authorization, you presumably know what you are doing. These brokers have account minimums, so be sure to check with each broker. The upside is that if you go to an options-focused broker and request a certain level of trading authority, the broker will grant the authority with a minimum of fuss. If you aren't in a structured trading program, the broker may start you off at Level 2 trading authority and raise your authorization upon request after you survive the market for a certain period.

All the techniques covered in this book except for iron butterflies, iron condors, and naked put writing can be accomplished with Level 3 trading authority (debit spreads). In our trading at the firm, Maverick's traders use some more advanced techniques and as a matter of course have Level 4 trading authority (credit spreads; naked put writing).

We can't, in good conscience, recommend that anyone attempt to secure Level 5 trading authority. The only additional capability that Level 5 provides is the ability to write naked calls. You're not a market maker. There's no need for you to write naked calls. Even a delta-neutral strategy with a naked call can blow up in your face and decimate your portfolio. Added to that risk are the margin requirements for writing naked calls. This varies from broker to broker, but plan on having half a million dollars sitting in cash in your account and then having margin requirements equal to 30 percent of the strike price of the calls you write. We can think of better uses for our capital.

DATA FEEDS AND COMMISSIONS

We're going to let you in on a little secret. If you're with a discount broker that doesn't charge for data feeds from the markets, you're paying for the data feed in the commission. That "every trade for one low price" model amortizes the cost of your data feed over the range of all your trades in a month.

Here's a situation where cheap can get expensive. Let's say there are two brokers that you are deciding between. The first broker offers trades for $10 commissions but doesn't charge for data feeds. The second broker charges $100 per month for data feeds, but charges only $1 commissions.

With the first broker, your commission for the total trade, the round trip of entry and exit, is going to be $20, not $10. Unless you hold your strategy to expiration and allow yourself to be exercised, you've got to liquidate the position at some point.

At Maverick, over the course of a year, we will make between 150 and 200 trades. This averages out to between 12.5 and 16.67 trades per month. If you go with the broker that doesn't charge for data feeds, you will be paying at least $250 per month in commissions. With the broker that charges $100 per month in data feeds but has $1 commission, your total cost will be around $125 ($100 in data charges and 12.5 trades × $2 round trip).

A major tenet of a sound risk management policy is to trade as a basket. You need to decide how big that basket will be, calculate your expected monthly trading volume, and compare costs accordingly.

OPTIONS AND STOCK PRICING

The next question you have to ask is whether you are getting the best bid and the best ask in your broker's quotes and executions.

Right alongside that consideration is whether your broker offers penny pricing for options. Many options are now so liquid that they are quoted on the major exchanges in penny increments. If your broker doesn't pass this on and offers options pricing only in $0.05 increments, not only is your profit area smaller, but you're consistently leaving money on the table.

But the amounts are so small—do they really affect me? Yes, they do.

Let's say that for a fairly liquid stock, the difference between the best bid and the best ask at the major exchanges is $0.01. Let's also say that your discount broker adds a penny to the ask and subtracts a penny from the bid. The bid-ask spread is now $0.03. Carrying on our example, let's say that you make 150 trades per year, each of 100 shares of stock. Over the course of the year, you've paid an extra $150 for the stocks you bought and left an additional $150 on the table for the stocks you've sold, for a total of $300. Where did that $300 go? Your broker kept it.

For options, not only does best bid/best ask matter, but so does penny pricing. For the sake of argument, we'll say that the average difference between penny pricing for options and nickel pricing for options is $0.025 on both the bid and the ask. You make 150 trades per year and trade an average of five contracts per trade. The math looks like this:

> 150 trades × 5 contracts per trade @ 100-share contract size = 75,000 shares
> 75,000 shares × $0.025 difference on buy side = $1,875
> 75,000 shares × $0.025 difference on sell side = $1,875
> Total difference between penny pricing and nickel pricing = $3,750

Even scaling this down to one contract per trade, you still end up with $750 in lost profits.

We don't know your feelings on the subject, but we're not keen about giving someone we don't even know the cost of a fairly nice vacation. The market does what it can to throw you without adding insult to injury in the form of overpaying for trades.

MARKING THE CARDS: ANALYTICAL TOOLS THAT PUT THE ODDS IN YOUR FAVOR

As we mentioned earlier, we spend more time with our analytical tools than we do logged in to our broker's trading platform. We log in to our broker's platform to place trade triggers and set stops. For the most part, we stay logged off outside of those reasons. It's not that we don't like our broker's platform. It is a tool that serves our needs well when we want to place and execute our trades, but beyond that, we want to remove the temptation to trade by the seats of our pants.

Retail brokers have come a long way since the late 1990s, when retail trading first gained popularity. Today, retail brokers are bundling analytical tools with their trading platforms and making both the analytical tools and the execution tools easier to use. They are now marketing these platforms as one-stop integrated platforms, offering pattern-recognition modules, strategy back testing, volatility studies, paper trading, and what-if scenarios.

Let's talk about the elephant in the room. Although no broker's representative will publicly say so, the primary purpose of these modules, tools, and add-ons is to give you the opportunity to trade more. If they actually help you make more money, that is a secondary concern for the brokers. Let us back up just a little bit. Larger accounts will make more trades, so if you come to them with a smaller account, they will want you to be successful so that you will have a larger account and can make more trades.

In all honesty, they would prefer that you came to them with a larger account rather than build the account up. You'll be trading in higher volume from Day 1, making them more money, and they'll have a better return on investment from all the advertising they do.

Don't get us wrong. We want our brokers to generate revenues and turn a profit. They provide us with a method for accessing the market, and they deserve to be compensated for that service. But we're going to make a trade only when it benefits us, not when it benefits our broker. We're happy to let our broker make more money off people who are less disciplined about their trading. It doesn't affect us either way.

So, our advice is to stay off your broker's platform unless you are entering a trade setup or a stop (or unless you are liquidating positions on expiration day, but the more professional brokers will allow you to automate that as well).

THE TRADING CAVE: YOUR PERSONAL SPACE

Each of us has an office at home that we use for trading and other business. Robb and Jon are able to use Maverick's corporate offices for trading and teaching, but they also do some of their trading from their home offices. Whatever your personal situation, it is important that you carve out a space where you can comfortably concentrate on trading.

Maverick's trading system is not intellectually demanding, but there are procedures that need to be followed. Having distractions in the background leads to inattention, inattention leads to mistakes, and mistakes lead to losses.

As you read through this section, please keep in mind that we aren't interested in giving you another full-time job. We are interested in giving you a full-time life. When you trade with the system we've developed, more free time, excess capital, lower stress, and a greater sense of personal fulfillment are the by-products of successful trading. We instruct every new trader entering our firm that his primary focus should be on trading itself, not on the rewards. The rewards come with the trades.

Since most retail traders, and most of Maverick's affiliated traders, do their trading from home, it's important that you minimize distractions in the home when you are evaluating trade setups and placing execution orders and triggers. Most of us have some form of a "Red Rule" at our homes: if you're not bleeding or on fire, please don't bother me when I'm in the office.

When you first begin trading professionally, you will need to emphasize the professional nature of your activities to your family. When you're in the office, you are at work. You just work from home.

Unless your pets are firmly ground-based, keep them out of the office, especially if you are logged in to your trading platform. If Fluffy jumps up in your lap while you're placing an order, that conservative position of 100 shares or 10 contracts could accidentally turn into 10,000 shares or 1,000 contracts. Don't think it hasn't happened.

You'll need a desk or some other flat surface to accommodate your computer and monitor and to provide a place where you can pencil out trade setups and review charts and risk graphs. Keep within your means; it's just a flat surface. However, when it comes to a place to park yourself, while a chair from a card table set is functional, it's not something that we'd want to sit on for a couple of hours at a time. Find a chair that is nicely padded and has some back support. You can find functional and comfortable chairs on sale for less than $100.

For computer equipment, your needs are actually modest. While the gear geek in each of us would like to be able to tell you that you need an ultra-high-end custom-built computer with dual-core water-cooled processors and a six-monitor display, you really don't.

A PC-based system can be purchased for under $1,000, and often much less. A second monitor is handy, but not necessary. We will throw you a bone, though. If you've still got a CRT screen, join the twenty-first century and buy a flat-panel monitor. It will free up an impressive amount of desk space.

One place where we do advocate getting the best is Internet access. If you have the option of a cable modem, by all means take it. We've found that DSL just doesn't have the bandwidth to handle live data feeds. Dial-up access isn't even an option because it is even slower than DSL.

Throw in a printer to print out charts and such, and you're ready to go.

For ambiance, whatever makes you comfortable is the rule of the day. If you like sunlight, open the blinds. If you like working in a cave, keep them closed. If you work best in pin-drop quiet, close the door. Like working with music in the background? Turn on some music.

Out of habit, we will generally have a financial news channel playing in the background. We're not listening to it for trade ideas; we're listening to see if there are any news events affecting the market.

Whether you have a dedicated office line or your home phone pulls double duty, you need to decide if you are going to answer the phone when you are working. If you are not, turn off the ringer until you are done working (don't forget to turn it back on). If you are going to answer the phone while you work, make sure that the phone is within arm's reach, and buy a headset. This little investment will pay dividends because it keeps your hands free and doesn't put a kink in your neck from trying to pin the phone to your shoulder.

If you need a cup of coffee while you work, get it before you go into your trading cave. Your productivity will soar if you take care of your little needs before you start work rather than hopping up and down every five minutes to get something that will make you more comfortable.

Finally, take a break every couple of hours. Give your eyes a rest. Don't go blind trying to analyze 200 charts in one sitting. One of the worst thing a trader can do is be behind the market every second of the trading day. The days can get long, and traders will be tempted to trade out of boredom. We have all done it many times. In Chapter 9, we will talk about over-trading and the destruction it can cause in a trading account.

The markets will be open, and the lights on your monitor will be blinking. Your job is to trade the markets on *your* terms, not based on what is happening on your monitor at the moment. Take breaks during the day, and make sure you aren't there during the middle parts of the day, where the volume is typically low. Trading may be your profession, and you need to treat it like one, but that doesn't mean it has to be a penal sentence.

7

BATTING PRACTICE: PAPER TRADING

At our firm, before being permitted to trade with the firm's capital, all new traders are required to paper-trade for at least two months. It's part of our testing procedure, and it serves several purposes.

Primarily, it ties together all the lessons taught in our training program and establishes a track record of applying those lessons, including risk management, position sizing, trade setup evaluation, strategy selection, and trade execution. We're not going to turn new traders loose with live capital without seeing that they have the ability and discipline to apply Maverick's system without being supervised.

You should feel the same way when you are trading with your own capital. For all intents and purposes, this is a totally new system for you. We know it is because this book is the first time that we've let our trading system out from behind the wall of our firm and our member traders.

If there is a lesson that should be learned from the financial crisis of 2008 to 2009, it's that you should never outsource your due diligence. Probably the best example of this was pension funds investing money in mortgage-backed securities and collateralized debt obligations. Pension funds and other institutions essentially relied on ratings agencies to conduct due diligence on these products. On the ground, we could see that these products were of questionable value. When a "no doc" stated-income, stated-assets loan for a $500,000 house for people who have a questionable employment and credit history is approved, all you have to ask yourself is whether you would have loaned them the money for the house yourself.

You are the only person who truly has a vested interest in your financial well-being. Don't blindly adopt and follow a new system without testing it and exploring its strengths and weaknesses. You should understand when an investment system works best and in what market conditions it doesn't work well. For Maverick's system, because we analyze both broad markets and individual sectors before we take a position in a stock, at market tops and bottoms, our portfolios tend to end up delta-neutral until the market asserts its direction. This can and has led to short periods in which a good percentage of our positions weighted in one direction are stopped out for small losses before our positions weighted in the other direction can begin making gains in earnest. The important fact is that we recognize this and begin to get very cautious when a market going in either direction is starting to get long in the tooth.

Not only do you need to make a frank assessment of whether a system works, but you need to make an honest assessment of whether that system works for you in particular. Use the time you invest in paper trading to conduct that assessment. You may be able to see the benefits of a system and see that it works, but something in your mentality may not let you fully capitalize on it.

Whatever system you use to invest or trade needs to resonate with your natural tendencies. We're not talking about the bad habits that all traders pick up; we're talking about the natural psychological traits that each person develops over a lifetime. If you are naturally risk-averse and shy away from the prospect of any type of loss, perhaps equity trading is not for you. You may be better suited to investing in high-grade corporate paper or government notes and bonds. If you are an adrenalin junkie and eschew risk controls of any type, you may have trouble with a system that requires the use of risk controls.

Maverick's system pitches a pretty large tent with regard to the psychological makeup of people who would benefit from the system. The system is designed to accommodate both the risk-averse and the risk takers through position sizing.

If a system doesn't resonate with you on a visceral level, either you need to go back and try to understand the tenets of the system or the system is so at odds with your psychology that you should find another system. Don't try to force the issue because you'll end up trading against your natural inclinations, violate key rules of the strategy, cause yourself unnecessary stress, cloud your judgment, and end up losing money.

If a system does resonate with you, there will still be a learning curve, a period of time in which you learn to put all the steps together and execute trades. Paper trading allows you to experience this learning curve without the danger of losing money. You can make mistakes in paper trading and not suffer the consequences in the real world.

Experiencing this learning curve in safety helps to build confidence in a new system. Humans are naturally skeptical creatures. It's a survival instinct developed over millions of years. After all, there may be a large and angry saber-tooth tiger in the back of that nice-looking cave. Don't fight nature.

On the conscious surface of your mind, you may tell yourself that everything you are studying and reading makes sense and absolutely has to work. However, deeper down, you still have an element of skepticism in you that will fight with your conscious mind *until you've seen the effectiveness of the system for yourself.*

We take the existence of accurate maps for granted. GPS guidance systems for cars are options in the same way that air conditioning was an option 30 years ago. We would venture to say that 30 years (or even less) from now, GPS systems will be a standard feature in cars.

But 500 years ago, the existence of accurate maps and nautical charts was not taken for granted. On each oceangoing ship, the navigator, or pilot, kept his own charts and logs, called rutters, of how he got from port to port. No pilot truly trusted another pilot's rutter until he had traveled the course that it laid out, arrived at his location, and returned to his home port.

You're the pilot of your financial ship right now, and we've just given you a rutter. It may lay out a course that you've never taken before, and it may use vessels that you've never used. This rutter seems to be well made and answers many of your questions about how to get to your destination, but you won't truly trust it until you see it work repeatedly. Paper trading can help to give you that trust in your new rutter, so that when you actually leave port with your ship on the way to your destination, you will be able to get there more quickly and with fewer storms.

Even after seeing a system work and developing trust in that system, you may find the need to refine some of the particulars in order to make yourself more comfortable. Paper trading helps you to tune and refine your execution of a system, again without the risk of losing money.

In your paper trading, you may find that you are setting your trade triggers too close to the chart formation. You'll be able to see that you are getting triggered on trades whose chart formations subsequently fail and then stop you out of your position. You can refine your execution to give the stock more room to break out of its formation before triggering your trade.

You may find that you're setting your triggers too loosely and missing out on some profitability. Experiment with setting your triggers closer to the chart formation until you find a balance between being triggered too early and being triggered too late.

You may find that you're getting stopped out of quite a few trades that subsequently rebound and perform exactly the way your analysis indicated they would. Take a closer look at where you are setting your stops, and consider reducing your position size and giving your trades more room to run. The reduction in position size will offset the greater size of the stop loss, so that your total risk exposure remains the same.

In the course of paper trading, you may see that your trades consistently reach the targets you've designated, but then continue on. Review your practices in establishing targets and determine whether you are being too conservative. Conduct a couple of trades where you increase your targets from your initial estimate and see what the results are.

While it is not a substitute for live trading, paper trading will allow you to begin to determine your natural risk tolerance. You won't suddenly begin to think of the notional capital in your paper-trading account as real money, but you can examine how both the wins and the losses affect you. If a paper-trading loss of 2.0 percent of your notional portfolio bothers you, you can probably deduce that a 2.0 percent risk tolerance is too large for your natural inclinations. Likewise, if a 2.0 percent loss in your paper-trading account doesn't bother you and you find yourself wishing for a larger position size on your winners, you can probably safely increase your risk tolerance in 0.5 percent increments until a notional loss causes psychological pain. At that point, ratchet down the per trade risk until you are satisfied with your gains, and your losses don't cause undue stress.

After you have been paper trading for a couple of months, or, better yet, until you feel comfortable with the analysis, research, trade setups, execution, and exit in each of your trades, you will find that when you do make the transition to live trading, you will be more confident, less hesitant, and more successful in your live trading.

However, in order for paper trading to be effective, you have to keep track of your results. If you don't keep track of the results of each setup, execution, profit or loss, and after-action critique, you may develop confidence, but it will be confidence based on emotion rather than fact.

At Maverick, during the paper-trading period of training, we provide each trader with an automated spreadsheet to track her paper-trading progress. Again, we deliberately keep this record separate from whatever platform the trader is using to paper-trade. We want to reinforce the idea that a trading platform is for execution only and that the less time the trader spends logged in, the fewer emotional trades she will make.

Our tracking spreadsheet records what the setup was, what the trigger was, the entry price of the position, where the stops were, where the targets were, where the trade was exited, the profit or loss, and, finally, a critique of the trade.

It is important that you fill out a trade tracking spreadsheet as soon as any event happens. You want to capture information while it is fresh in your mind. If you fill out a trade tracker weekly or inconsistently, you will forget some pertinent information and end up with cryptic notations that not even Nostradamus could decipher.

You want to capture the full spectrum of information. Enter each setup immediately after you've worked it out using the Top-Down Approach and your SET procedures. If the trade never triggers, include that in your critique. Did the chart pattern fail? Did it take too long to develop? Did the stock gap up past your entry window? List it all. If your trades consistently fail to trigger, you may benefit from reviewing how to conduct the Top-Down Approach and establish trade triggers. You may even learn how to better identify the beginning of a market top or market bottom.

On the trades that do trigger, what was the result? Were you stopped out? Did you forget to put your stop in after the trade triggered and end up with a larger than acceptable loss? Did the trade trigger and go nowhere?

Explore how close you are coming to your targets. Did the trade expire halfway in your profit area? Did the trade hit your target and begin to consolidate? Did the trade hit your target and then continue to move? Did the trade hit your target price and then move back down?

Take a close look at how you're harvesting your profits. Did you use a contingent order so that the trade liquidated when it hit your target price? Did the trade hit your target, and then you used a trailing stop? Did you get greedy and let the trade run, only to see it hit your target and then turn back down for a lower profit or even a loss?

The ultimate confirmation that your trading system works and that you are ready for real capital is that your numbers are consistently profitable. The key word in trading is *consistency*. The only way to develop a profitable trading system is to treat every trade exactly the same way as the last, with no deviation. Only by doing this can you get a logical idea of what kinds of returns you will be able to generate over long periods of time. You should have periods of bull markets, bear markets, and stagnant markets that show that you can be consistently profitable during any kind of market behavior.

Jon: During the course of a year, we give out a lot of trade recommendations. By no means do we want every trader to simply piggyback on these trades and follow us blindly. We offer our trade recommendations so that our traders can see what we are seeing and why we are making the choices we are, then follow our reasoning through our Top-Down Approach and SET procedures, including trade management and adjustments when necessary.

I think the best thing traders can do is place all of the trades we send out in a demo account and watch how they react to market conditions in real time.

When I'm coaching a trader, I have him put in multiple strategies on the same underlying trade so that he can see the differences side by side. For instance, if we have a bullish trade setup, the trader might have a hard time deciding between a bull call spread and a diagonal call calendar spread. With a demo account, he can put both strategies into the account and then determine later which one would have been the better choice. This reinforces recognitional decision making, so that the next time a similar situation occurs, the trader will have a higher probability of choosing the more profitable strategy to capitalize on the setup.

Additionally, a demo account provides a safe place to try out new strategies that a trader is just learning or is not entirely comfortable with. If a demo account is used properly, it's a phenomenal asset in the learning curve. Perfect practice makes perfect.

The two biggest numbers to a trader are her win-loss percentage and her reward-risk ratio. In common English, this means how many times out of 100 you made money when the trade was completely exited and how much you made in comparison to your losses. A good goal to shoot for is a win-loss percentage above 60 percent and a reward-risk ratio above 1.5, meaning that your average winner was $1.50 for each loser of $1.00. Market conditions will definitely affect these numbers; our reward-risk ratio jumped to 4.3 to 1 in 2008, since we had some monstrous winners on the short side during the market collapse, then moved back to more moderate levels in 2009.

These numbers mean something only if you are consistent in your management of all your trades and treat them all the same. If you sometimes sell early and sometimes use a stop, you will not be able to count on your numbers to stay consistent in the future. A trading system works only when you use it with complete and utter consistency.

Success is a consistently growing portfolio. This can be determined from a month-to-month glance at your account balance, but a fact-based analysis of your actions will help to develop you into a professional trader. It will give you insight into whether you are taking on unnecessary risk or unnecessarily leaving profits on the table.

Even after traders exit from Maverick's training program, we encourage them to continue with their trade tracking. If you track your trades in both paper-trading and live-trading situations, you will be able to consistently refine your approach, increase your win-loss ratio, and increase your reward-risk ratio.

8

THE BIG TIME: LIVE TRADING

When is the best time to begin trading live, with real capital, risking real money and taking real profits? The simple answer is, when you are comfortable that you will be able to make money and you have proof of this in your virtual trading journal. The irony about trading is that everyone who gives it a shot is pretty convinced that he was going to make a bunch of money or he never would have tried it in the first place. You can even tell people before they begin that more than 90 percent of people will fail at trading, and they will tell you how sorry they feel for the other 90 percent who won't make it. Confidence is a good thing, but false confidence is a nail in the coffin of an unproven trader.

The markets are a scary place, and they have eaten up people who are a lot smarter than you and we combined. This is why it is so important that you not only understand the market, but also understand yourself and how you will react in certain situations. We are convinced that the reason that most people who fail at trading do so is not from lack of knowledge but from lack of discipline and consistency. Do yourself a favor and spend the time necessary building these skills before you enter the market.

Jon: In my experience, nobody should ever begin trading live unless she is entirely confident of her abilities and she truly understands how to mitigate risk. Without these traits, there is absolutely no way that she will be able to generate consistency, which is the key to profitability. The reality is that trading isn't about knowledge. Learning how the bid-ask spread works and what calls and puts do isn't going to make anyone rich. The X factor is always the trader. Is she passionate about trading? Is she confident? Is she disciplined? Is she diligent and committed? Is she focused? Is she consistent?

The reason we make our traders jump through a few hoops before we let them loose on the market isn't for our benefit nearly as much as it is to make them recognize for themselves when they are ready to be professional traders.

By now, you should understand the forces that drive price movement in individual stocks, their sectors, and the broad markets as a whole. You should be able to conduct market analysis using the Top-Down Approach; identify high-probability trades through chart analysis; establish stops, entry points, and trade triggers; and estimate likely targets for a successful trade.

You have a grounding in what strategies work for particular setups and targets and the mechanics and risk graphs of those strategies. We've taken you through the step-by-step procedures for entering a trade, and you should have invested some time in paper trading to ensure that you understand and are confident about the basics of Maverick's system.

Now would be a good time to jump right in and use real capital, right?

Hold on for one second. We don't know when you'll be reading this book or what the market will be doing when you reach this point.

You need to make an assessment of what the market is doing right now. Is it trending bullish or bearish, is it moving sideways, or does it look like it's at a near-term top or bottom?

If the market is moving sideways or looks as if it's topping or bottoming, wait until the market asserts its direction. Cash is always a viable position—something that many people and many trading systems forget or ignore. In times of uncertainty, sometimes it's best to take a vacation and wait for the market to decide what it wants to do. Most traders don't consider cash a position. Cash is the best position if you are trying to find the least amount of risk for your money.

If the market is trending bullish or bearish, take a moment to be a little introspective. Is there any portion of the material we've covered so far that you'd like to reread and explore in more depth? Do you want to paper-trade for another few weeks or wait until the Monday after an expiration Friday to enter a position? That's fine.

Be sure you are comfortable trading, or as comfortable as you feel you can be, before you begin risking capital on trades.

CALM DOWN: THE DANGERS OF READY, FIRE, AIM

Unfortunately, paper trading can take you only so far in establishing comfort with and confidence in a system. Some doubt will remain. Your confidence and understanding will help alleviate that doubt, but only after you take that last step and begin trading live with real capital will you become fully confident of your abilities and the capabilities of the system you are using.

That said, people will often try to power through that last bit of doubt and hesitation. They will have to make a leap of faith at some point, so why not now?

The problems occur when people build up their courage too much. They may have had a really good run in their paper-trading account in the last month and begin to kick themselves for not having started to trade live earlier.

They start to see trade setups everywhere. Gradually, self-imposed pressure for performance builds, and they start to think of the money that they're not making by trading as money that they're losing. Finally, the pressure becomes too great. They're going to trade now, today, at market open, come hell or high water. Damn the torpedoes; full speed ahead!

They log in to their trading platform an hour before the market opens, reviewing trade setups, allocating capital, queuing up trades for execution, checking the clock every five minutes, listening to market commentary prior to the opening bell. They've got this market thing figured out. There's no way they can lose.

Ding, ding, ding. Opening bell. And they're off. Never mind contingent orders; they've got to get in the game. Click, click, click. BUY . . . BUY . . . SELL . . . BUY. "I'll be rich! *Rich*, I tell you! RICH!"

Ten minutes after the opening bell, 100 percent of their capital is allocated. They collapse back in their new office chairs in a fevered sweat, watching charts of their positions, tick by tick. Hey, this trading thing isn't hard at all. They should be able to retire to the Caribbean by the end of the year.

Oh . . . hello. What's that? The market just reversed direction? Earnings were announced this morning? Why is that chart pattern failing? Why didn't my stop trigger? Oh—I didn't put the stop in yet. "*Nooooo!* I'm ruined! *Ruined*, I say! I'll be stuck in my cubicle until they wheel my cold corpse out of the office and into a pauper's grave."

You can call situations like this by many names. The most common are "spray and pray" and "ready, fire, aim." No matter what you call it, the outcomes are rarely pretty.

All the time that you've invested in learning a new system step by step, all the time that you've invested in paper trading, and all the time that you've invested in picking high-probability trade setups has just given you a negative return because you got too excited.

When this happens, it's a confidence-shattering experience. Doubt reasserts itself in a much louder voice, and your judgment is impaired by emotion and stress—emotion because it looks as if everything you've worked for was for naught, and stress because now you have to decide whether to liquidate your positions and start over or let them run and risk greater losses.

Trade setups will come and go. If you miss one, or several, believe it or not, more will come along, and in short order.

When you take the step and begin trading live, there are several steps that you should take to avoid the dangers of the ready, fire, aim syndrome.

PENCIL IT OUT

Your procedures in live trading should be no different from your procedures in paper trading. The only difference is that you're logging in to the account that has the real money in it.

You will be excited. You will want to log in to your trading platform, enter the trade, and hit BUY. Put steps in place to slow yourself down and avoid this.

For your first few trades, print out a chart of the broad market, a chart of the stock sector, and a chart of the stock itself. Annotate each of them: what is the market doing, what is the sector doing, and what is the stock doing? On the chart of the stock, physically mark your entry price, your stop price, and your target price.

Once you've marked up the charts, choose your strategy. Better yet, choose two or more strategies and print out risk graphs for each of them. Mark up and evaluate each strategy and write down on the risk graph of the strategy you choose the reasoning behind your choice.

Placing these speed bumps between you and the trade slows you down and makes you think about why you're placing the trade. You may decide that the trade actually isn't as good as you thought it was. That's fine. Abandon the trade and start over on another trade.

Do this during market hours the first few times and you'll erode the emotional need to get in right at the market open. The only time you should be entering a trade at the market open is when you input the setup previously and it triggers at the market open. Doing so at any other time feeds a perceived emotional need; it doesn't follow a disciplined plan.

START SMALL

You may have graduated to trading 10-, 20-, 50-, or 100-contract positions in your paper-trading account. It doesn't matter. For your first 10 to 20 live trades, consider just trading single-contract positions. This is the last step in building confidence in your system and removing the last bit of doubt that is in your psyche. You don't need to confuse the situation with position sizes that are too large.

Paper trading will give you a good idea of what your actual risk tolerance is, but until you are actually trading with your own capital, you won't be able to truly know and understand your risk tolerance. You shouldn't feel stressed about the size of any particular trade. You can always increase your position sizes after you've built confidence in your system, your ability to execute, and your ability to manage risk and take profits, and removed that last bit of natural doubt.

Additionally, when you start live trading, don't expect to enter all your trades in a single day, or even a single week. At Maverick, a busy week is setting up ten trades and having four of them trigger. It may take you three to four weeks or more to build your basket of trades. During that time, some trades will be stopped out and some will be liquidated because they hit their targets. In a slow week or a period of uncertainty, we may not enter any trades during a given week.

Limiting your position size when you first start trading live also has another positive effect: you don't allocate all your capital all at one time. Some of our traders have only about 10 percent of their capital allocated at any single time. Very rarely will we have more than 50 percent of our capital allocated to active trades. You aren't a mutual fund whose charter says that you have to be fully invested at all times and carry no more than 5 percent cash.

Determining your risk tolerance involves determining not only how much capital you are willing to risk on each trade, but how much of your total portfolio you are comfortable having at risk at any point in time. You may find that you are comfortable at a point where 20 percent of your capital is at risk, but that when 30 percent of your capital is tied up in trades, you start to think about your trades and watch them more often, even when you have protective stops in place. If you are worried about a position or a portfolio, your position size is too large or you have too much of your portfolio working.

It is satisfying to increase your position sizes after a period of success. It is humbling to decrease your position sizes after a period of losses, especially when you are first starting out.

FOLLOW ORDER ENTRY PROCEDURES

If you have followed the steps just given and are still ready to enter the trade, enter it as a contingent order, even if the stock is trading at or above your trigger. If the stock is trading above your trigger, the order will execute immediately anyway. You want to build good habits, and one of those habits is trading with a plan and using contingent orders.

This may seem like an unnecessary step, and it is, but it keeps you from getting into the habit of clicking the BUY button and reinforces the habit of trading with a plan.

Another habit to develop is to trade with limit orders. If you've calculated your entry price for a single-leg strategy or a spread strategy, stick to that calculation. If your trade calculations had you entering the trade at $1.80, but the strategy is trading at $1.90 or more, put in a limit order for $1.80. Either you'll get filled or you won't. If you do get filled, you've traded to a plan on your terms. If you don't get filled, the trade wasn't in accordance with your plan, and you would have either been assuming more risk than you calculated or decreasing your expected reward had you executed the trade at market prices.

If you can see that a trade setup has triggered, but you haven't entered the order yet, enter it as a contingent order, but also split the difference between the bid and the ask. It may be a matter of only a few dollars on each trade, but those few dollars probably just paid your commission or a good part of your commission. Also, you've made the market come to you instead of you going to the market.

When you follow these steps when you are beginning to trade with live capital, you'll be able to make the transition from paper trading to live trading without succumbing to buck fever and incurring unnecessary risk as you start out. The transition will be less stressful, your confidence will continue to build, and the last of your natural doubt will finally be put to rest. In combination, this will reduce your stress and keep your mind clear, allowing you to make better decisions.

You Versus You

You can be given the best tools in the world on a silver platter to analyze the market, have the best data feed and charting software available, be running the best risk analysis tools in the industry, have the perfect chart setup sitting in front of you, and still lose money trading the market.

You may ultimately call the setup, the entry, the target, and the timing correctly and still lose money.

What do you mean? How can this happen? Is it possible to stop it? If this is true, what's the point of trading in the first place? Those are all excellent questions.

The simple answer to what causes people to lose money with a winning system is psychology. The trader is causing losses by taking actions outside a proven system.

How does this happen? When a trader is learning and applying a new system, he is actively concentrating on applying all the precepts and lessons that are inherent in that system. He's learning to do things the right way. He's a teenager with a learner's permit learning how to drive a car with Mom or Dad in the passenger's seat.

"Hands at 10 and 2. Slow down; don't speed. Here comes the curve . . . start turning now. Look out for the pedestrians. Don't hit the stop sign. *No, no, no. The brake! The brake! That's the gas!* Oh, hell. Pull over right here. Hello, officer. How are you today?

Yes, sir, new driver. Absolutely. We'll be more careful next time. Thank you, and have a nice day."

Compare that to how you drive after 5, 10, or 20 years' experience. Cruise control is a brick. You steer with one hand most of the time, and sometimes with just a knee. The vehicles in front of you are an impediment to your progress, and the drivers behind you are crazy maniacs who don't know how to drive.

You can see the difference. When you're learning something new, you're paying attention all the time and following all the rules. Once you've learned a new skill, even a complex one, experience teaches you what you need to pay attention to and what you can relax on. It's natural, and we all do it.

At this point, most trading and investment books would lay this next gem on you: "You just need to learn/exercise more discipline. Discipline is the key. Discipline, discipline, discipline."

We can't think of more useless advice.

Don't get us wrong. A baseline of discipline is necessary in any trading system. With Maverick, you need to use a Top-Down Approach, you need to pencil out your trades, and you need to use your SET procedures. This does take discipline, and it will become natural over time. It's after you've learned the basics that problems begin.

Once you've learned the basics and become comfortable with a trading system, you will revert to type. You will begin to cut corners. Your personality and tendencies will begin to reassert themselves and will show up in the way you trade.

The key to overcoming this is not to change your personality, which is what many investment systems would have you do. The key is to understand what your trading personality is and then put systems in place to ensure that any less than desirable traits are bypassed.

When you trade against your personality, it just confuses your brain. We believe the technical term is that it screws you up.

Take a minute to stretch and grab a piece of notebook paper. It's test time. You're going to take a five-minute test to gain some insight into your personality. Don't worry, there's no passing score. At the end, you will have a basic understanding of your probable strengths and weaknesses as a trader.

Ready? Here is a series of 20 statements. For each question, write down on your notepaper which statement (A or B) resonates with you the most. We'll categorize everything in a little bit. Please, be honest with yourself. Write down the answer that suits you best, not the answer that you think represents the ideal trader.

1. A. Expend energy; enjoy groups
   B. Conserve energy; enjoy one-on-one
2. A. Interpret matters literally; rely on common sense
   B. Look for meaning and possibilities; rely on foresight
3. A. Logical, thinking, questioning
   B. Empathetic, feeling, accommodating
4. A. Organized, orderly
   B. Flexible, adaptable
5. A. More outgoing; think out loud
   B. More reserved; think to yourself
6. A. Practical, realistic, experiential
   B. Imaginative, innovative, theoretical
7. A. Candid, straightforward, frank
   B. Tactful, kind, encouraging
8. A. Plan, schedule
   B. Unplanned, spontaneous
9. A. Seek many tasks, public activities, interaction with others
   B. Seek more private, solitary activities with quiet to concentrate

10. A. Standard, usual, conventional
    B. Different, novel, unique
11. A. Firm; tend to criticize; hold the line
    B. Gentle; tend to appreciate; conciliate
12. A. Regulated, structured
    B. Easygoing, "live and let live"
13. A. External, communicative, express yourself
    B. Internal, reticent, keep to yourself
14. A. Consider immediate issues; focus on the here and now
    B. Look to the future; global perspective; "big picture"
15. A. Tough-minded, just
    B. Tender-hearted, merciful
16. A. Preparation; plan ahead
    B. Go with the flow; adapt as you go
17. A. Active; initiate
    B. Reflective; deliberate
18. A. Facts, things, seeing "what is"
    B. Ideas, dreams, seeing "what could be," philosophical
19. A. Matter-of-fact, issue-oriented, principled
    B. Sensitive, people-oriented, compassionate
20. A. Control, govern
    B. Latitude, freedom

Great. Let's see what kind of personality you have. In Table 9-1, by each question number, mark whether answer A or answer B to that question resonated more with you. Don't worry if for each trait, you have some answers in column A and some answers in column B. You're trying to see how your personality is biased, not to definitively label yourself in a particular box.

After you have made your marks for each aspect of your personality, one column will have more marks than the other. Circle or make a mark next to the letter below the higher total. This will give you your personality bias for each aspect. We'll explain those in a little bit.

Table 9-1   Personality Profile Answer Sheet

Energy		
Question	A	B
1		
5		
9		
13		
17		
Total		
	E	I

Attention		
Question	A	B
3		
7		
11		
15		
19		
Total		
	T	F

Decisions		
Question	A	B
2		
6		
10		
14		
18		
Total		
	S	N

Lifestyle		
Question	A	B
4		
8		
12		
16		
20		
Total		
	J	P

Table 9-2   Personality Aspects Matrix

Energy	Decisions	Attention	Lifestyle
Introversion (I)	Intuition (N)	Thinking (T)	Judging (J)
Extroversion (E)	Sensation (S)	Feeling (F)	Perceiving (P)

By now, you should have four letters marked or circled, one for each personality aspect: Energy, Decisions, Attention, and Lifestyle. Now we're going to take a look at what all this means and how it influences you as a trader (see Table 9-2).

- **Energy.** Introverts find energy in the inner world of ideas, concepts, and abstractions. They want to understand the "whys" of the markets. They concentrate and tend to be reflective thinkers. Introverts want to develop systems that integrate or connect the information that they learn about the markets and use this information to make more informed decisions.

  Extroverts find energy in things and in people. They prefer interaction with others and tend to be action-oriented. They will learn about the markets best in groups or by talking with others. They also tend to think on their feet and talk more than they listen.

- **Decisions.** Intuitive traders seek out patterns and relationships among the facts that they have gathered. They trust hunches or "gut feelings" when they are researching the markets. Chances are, they like using charts as indicators, and therefore spend a majority of their research time looking at historical charts.

  Sensing traders choose to rely on their five senses. They are detail-oriented; they want facts, and they trust them. Sensing traders prefer organized, linear, and structured research.

- **Attention.** Thinkers decide things impersonally based on analysis, logic, and principle. They place great weight on objective criteria in making a financial decision. They naturally see flaws and tend to be critical of research. Thinking traders prefer clear goals and objectives.

  Feelers focus on human values and needs as they make decisions or arrive at judgments. They are more apt to make a trade based on their understanding of market psychology. Their objectivity is often clouded by emotions, however, and this can lead to poor trades. Feelers need to be mindful of their emotions.

- **Lifestyle.** Judging traders are decisive; they are self-starters and self-regimented, and they probably trade because they "want to." They also focus on completing the task and knowing the essentials, and they take action quickly. They plan their trades and trade their plan.

  Perceptive traders are curious, adaptable, and spontaneous. They start trading wanting to know everything about it, and they often find it difficult to trade successfully. Perceptive traders often postpone doing research until the last minute. They are not lazy; instead, they are merely seeking information up to the very last minute.

Now that you've completed the exercise to determine what your personality profile is, we need to provide a little caution. Don't think of this exercise as putting yourself in a series of boxes. Think of it as the start of understanding where you fall on a continuum for each personality trait. Think of the personality traits as sliding scales on a four-channel sound mixer.

Your position on each of the traits can and will shift from day to day—not by a lot, but it will shift. External factors in your life will move you along the continuum of each trait. Time, life experience, and trading experience will also have an effect on your position with regard to the personality traits. Periods of sustained success may have the effect of making a person more extroverted; judging people may become more perceptive as they relax with age; any number of things can happen over time. We'll give you 2:1 odds right now that some aspect of your personality will be different five years from now.

STRENGTHS AND WEAKNESSES OF EACH PERSONALITY TRAIT

Each personality trait has its own strengths and weaknesses. The trick is not to try to change your personality. We've seen people try that too many times, with disastrous results. Instead, you need to have a good grasp of what your strengths are and an even better understanding of what your potential weaknesses are. By understanding your potential weaknesses, you can build systems and put procedures in place to help keep you from succumbing to your weaknesses and making bad trades.

Energy: Extrovert versus Introvert

> **Extrovert strengths.** Extroverts are energetic. They trade well in a group setting. They are not afraid to act; once they develop a plan, they want to execute that plan. Extroverts often think on their feet and will adjust the plan as conditions dictate.
>
> **Extrovert weaknesses.** In addition to being energetic, extroverts can be excitable. If the market goes against their positions, they can resemble Chicken Little: "The sky is falling! The sky is falling!" They don't trade as well on their own as they do in a team or group; they can become distracted when there is no one to talk with about a trade setup. While they like to talk with

others about their trades and potential trades, they often take too much advice. These are the people who need to try every new tool or newsletter that worms its way into their junk-mail folder, or who take advice from people who don't really know what they're talking about (such as stock tips from the local vagrant).

One of their most dangerous weaknesses is the tendency to overtrade. These are the people who will fall victim to clicking the BUY button just because it is there.

Introvert strengths. Introverts are introspective; they will want to fully understand all aspects of a trade—entry, stop, target prices, and exits—before entering the trade. They make informed decisions and are less likely to take advice from someone who is touting a surefire pick. Introverts want to understand the reasoning or methodology behind a trade, and they are thorough in their research and analysis.

Introvert weaknesses. Introverts can fall victim to analysis paralysis and let good trades go by because they felt they didn't have a full understanding of the trade, when in retrospect, they had more than enough information to make the trade. At the same time, they are hesitant about making decisions. Introverts are less comfortable trading with a team or group, even when valuable ideas and critiques from the group would make them better traders.

Decision: Intuitive versus Sensing

Intuitive strengths. Intuitive decision makers are often the best chart readers in the business. They like charts and indicators. They look for relationships. These are the people who take the benefits of Maverick's Top-Down Approach to a new level.

Intuitive weaknesses. While these people can take the Top-Down Approach and make it purr like a race car, they often throw away the system and trade on hunches and gut feelings. They can overuse technical indicators; sometimes they have so many indicators on their charts that our coaches have a hard time finding the price/volume action of the stock itself. This can lead to "wag the dog" trading, where a complicated relationship among chart indicators will trigger a trade when the price/volume action of the stock has already reversed. Intuitive decision makers have a tendency to look for things that support their bias; they can't remain objective for long periods.

Sensing strengths. Sensing decision makers are detail-oriented and often pick out key points and indicators that other people miss. They enjoy structured research and procedures. They are linear in their approaches, rarely, if ever, deviating from their evaluation procedures in a trade; they won't be rushed into action. Finally, they are organized and can produce supporting material and analysis in an instant.

Sensing weaknesses. Sensing decision makers are prone to overanalyzing a trade and hesitate to make decisions. Once the decision has been made, they can be as stubborn as mules in exiting the trade. They spent so much time on analysis that they feel they can't possibly be wrong. This reluctance to admit to a mistake also leads to a reluctance to learn from their mistakes.

Attention: Thinkers versus Feelers

Thinker strengths. Thinkers have clear goals and objectives. You won't find a thinker making a trade "just to see what happens." They would make a Prussian general weep with admiration at their skill in using the limited-objective attack: "I am trading this stock from *here* to *there*, and then I am *exiting*." Thinkers conduct logical analysis and are objective when conditions change.

Thinker weaknesses. Thinkers are as flexible as an iron rod; they can get sideswiped by rapidly changing market conditions. Coupled with this, they are skeptical of changing market conditions, often thinking them only momentary noise and not recognizing them for what they are. Thinkers can also think too much in winning trades; they are more likely to fiddle with their position in a good trade, often to the detriment of the trade.

Feeler strengths. Feelers can channel market psychology in a way that can be truly scary to someone who hasn't seen it before. This trait can, at times, have a prophetic feeling. They are in tune with the markets, and they understand how the big picture influences the smaller picture, picking and panning trades with a high degree of accuracy. They understand the why behind a particular trade and the market above it.

Feeler weaknesses. Their biggest strength, their empathy for a setup, can become their biggest weakness, keeping them in losing trades because of an unforeseen reversal or kicking them out of winning trades for the same reason. They are prone to having their feelings enter their trades. They also have a tendency toward emotional trading. If a feeler wakes up on the wrong side of the bed, there is a good chance that she will short more than is warranted. Feelers rely so much on their strengths that they can fall into the trap of ignoring data and facts. Finally, they are the eternal optimists and can be seriously hurt in a bear market.

Lifestyle: Judging versus Perceptive

Judging strengths. Judging traders are decisive. They are self-starters, and they don't have to be coerced into trading a particular market. They formulate a plan and take action quickly. They trade to their plan and often have good risk management skills.

Judging weaknesses. Judging traders are inflexible, often getting stopped out of what would ultimately have been winning trades because of normal noise in the market. Judging traders give advice, but they don't take it well, and they will sometimes view advice as a personal attack on their abilities. These traders often have difficulty learning new concepts, systems, and techniques. These are often some of the most difficult traders to deprogram during coaching.

Perceptive strengths. Perceptive traders are nothing if not adaptable. Changing market conditions? No problem. They are curious about learning and want to know everything. They take advice to heart and apply lessons learned. Rarely will they make the same mistake twice.

Perceptive weaknesses. Perceptive traders are in danger of conducting last-minute analysis and taking advice from people who probably aren't qualified to give it. They can be spontaneous, entering a basket of trades with little forethought or preparation, then ending up unsure of what to do with their positions. Their drive to know and understand all there is to know about trading can lead to confusion and shutdown when they receive contradictory information.

Now that you know more about yourself and how these aspects of your personality will affect you as a trader, what's the next step?

Most people would tell you to play to your strengths and avoid your weaknesses. How completely useless is that advice? Of course you're going to play to your strengths; they're making you money. Avoid your weaknesses? How? Change your personality? Get real.

Your personality is what it is. You can't change it, and you don't want to try. You've spent your whole life building it, weaving it from your background and personal experiences. Trying to change your personality is like wearing a hand-me-down suit. Yes, it covers what it needs to cover, but it looks like you've put on a gunnysack, and frankly, it doesn't fit.

The best thing to do is to stop fighting your weaknesses. Put them in a lineup, identify them, take mug shots, fingerprint them, and then release them on their own recognizance. Give them a stern warning and let them know that you'll be keeping an eye on them. The next step is to put systems in place to compensate for them. Don't give your weaknesses the opportunity to wreak havoc on your portfolio.

Jon: Typically, the weaknesses in our trading will stem from the most rudimentary driving forces of the market: greed and fear. If our discipline breaks down, it's because we either got greedy or became afraid of the trades.

About the only way to completely remove that element is to simply not care about the money. If we don't attach emotion to money, then the loss or gain of it also won't be emotional.

The problem is that this isn't simple. In fact, it's virtually impossible. I always suggest to traders that they help themselves overcome some of the fear by making their position sizes reasonable enough that even a maximum loss on a trade won't cripple them, either in terms of undercapitalizing their accounts or in terms of making future trades seem scary and formidable.

When I trade, I always look at things in terms of worst-case scenarios, and if I can handle what the outcome would be if the markets completely went against me, then I can trade without losing sleep.

We highly recommend that you find a coach to help you with this, but you need to pick the right coach. If his only advice is, "You need more discipline," fire him and don't look back. By knowing yourself, you'll come up with better systems to thwart your weaknesses than he ever could. Here are some examples.

Let's say you're an extrovert, and every time you log on to your trading platform, you feel you have to make a trade. What's the workaround? This one's simple: conduct all your analysis and trade setup outside of your broker's platform. Log in to the trading platform only when you are entering a trade. Watch the market with some other tool.

What if you're an intuitive decision maker and you find yourself looking for things that support your bias? Remove the biases. If you are relying on five, six, or seven indicators on your charts to confirm your thesis, get rid of the indicators or limit yourself to one or two. We do this as a matter of course.

What if you're a feeler and you find that your emotions are clouding your decision-making process? Calm down or look for trades opposite to your mood. If you're having a great day and you want to be long the whole market, look for short setups and enter only short positions. If you're having a bad day or you're in a bad mood, don't trade or look only for long setups.

How about the perceiving person who takes advice from anyone and everyone at the last possible minute? Stop taking advice a set time before entering the trade. Make your order execute an hour or two after you've sent it to your broker. We're not day trading here; a few pennies either way is not going to throw your game compared to getting into a bad trade because of bad advice.

Robb: When I first started trading professionally, I overtraded. If the market was open, I had to be in front of the computer screen, ready to trade. I mean, I'm at work, right? So I should be working, meaning that I should be trading. Oh, how I wish I could take back all those trades that I did just because I was sitting in front of my computer.

Finally, I told myself that this had to stop. My trading platform used to provide a secure key fob that would generate a random number that had to be entered before you could make a trade. I thought, "Great! I'll give the key to my wife Monday afternoon, after I've made my trades for the week. That way I won't be making any trades except for the ones I found over the weekend."

Well, that worked for a little while, but I always ended up standing in front of my wife and begging for the key. I had found some trade that I had to do or some position that I had to manage. I mean, here I was doing the junkie shuffle, begging for the key so that I could make a trade.

Well, that technique didn't work, because I could always talk my wife into giving me the key. It slowed me down, but it didn't stop me. I think my wife just felt sorry for me and hated to see me groveling.

I eventually overcame my desire to overtrade, but it took a couple of different techniques, and it also took time. Identify the problem and find a way to work around it.

The important thing is to know what and where your weaknesses are and then arrange things so that they don't have the opportunity to show themselves. It is much easier to put systems in place to head off your weaknesses than it is to change your weaknesses. In time, your weaknesses may get tired of not being able to wreak havoc with your portfolio, but they may also keep lurking in the shadows, waiting for the opportunity to mug your trades.

The best thing you can do as a trader is to embrace your weaknesses and your failings. Turn this into your own little Traders Anonymous meeting; stand up and proclaim to the world, "I am terrible at taking my losses when I should!" Tell your neighbors on the street that "I increase my position size after I have had a few nice winners in a row and wipe out all my gains and more ... and I'm likely to do it again! Nothing can stop me!" The point we are trying to make is that you are you, and nothing is going to change that. All the books will tell you, "Have more discipline," and, "Don't screw it up." Guess what? We are doomed to screw it up. Who hasn't cheated on a diet before and not worked out because it seemed too hard? Yet some people are able to put systems and lifestyles in place where they can achieve their goals.

Embrace your shortcomings and realize that you are doomed to make the same mistake over and over again. For the ultimate proof, look at the last time you told yourself, even screamed at yourself, not to make that mistake again. Let me guess? You did it again. Instead of fighting your personality, accept who you are and work around the problem.

Robb: I told you all the problems I had in the beginning with overtrading. No matter what I told myself, I found myself making trades out of boredom. I joke now that if the markets were open and I had buying power, I could find a great trade in less than five minutes. Pretty impressive, isn't it? There is no way to sit down and find a great trade in five minutes. A great trade takes a thorough analysis of market direction, sector selection, and finally stock selection, planning proper entry and exit points. I tried giving my key fob to my wife, but she kept giving it back to me. I finally realized that I couldn't just "be disciplined" or "sit on my hands." I had a problem bordering on a serious addiction. What I realized was that I couldn't be behind my computer most of the time. But what should I do, since I had no other job, or even a life? I made one up. I hired a personal trainer at the gym every day about 90 minutes after the market opened, where if I didn't show up, I lost $50 and looked like a jerk. I remember trying to wait until the last minute behind my system before running out the door to my appointment. After the gym, I would schedule lunch out with my wife or volunteer at my kids' school during the day. Each week I would try to fill my schedule as full as possible to keep me away from the computer. Thank goodness we didn't have mobile trading apps back then!

As you can see, the key to conquering the markets is not about the markets at all. The markets are going to do whatever they are going to do, and there is nothing you can do to change or stop them. You are the variable, and if you don't have your foundation underneath you, the market will sweep you away.

Jon: One of the issues I had to struggle with was getting out of trades too early, either taking losses prematurely or taking small gains on what turned out to be great trades, with me watching from the sidelines. I decided to limit myself to using a basket of 10 vertical spreads, leaving everything until expiration (unless there was a major break in the technicals either way), and letting my positions develop over time. I placed my vertical spreads three to four weeks out from options expiration and let them go. I was used to keeping a pretty tight leash on my trades, and watching them swing a couple of dollars for or against me was hard at first. However, I realized that when one position went down, another one of the 10 would go up, and there was no adverse effect on my account value. At the end of the expiration month, I counted up the gains, and there were a lot more than there would have been if I had been micromanaging every position. Spreading out my trades in a basket and being in spreads that can sit through a lot of volatility allowed me to see the folly of trying to micromanage every position I had and to let things work for me.

Be creative with your solutions to your weaknesses. Stop beating yourself up. You are human, and you are bound to make mistakes. Trading with a partner or in a trading group will help you a great deal with your personal trading issues. Let someone look over your shoulder and make you accountable. Professional trading firms have managers and partners looking over everyone's shoulders, monitoring their positions and accounts. They have weekly and monthly meetings where they discuss each trader's goals, current positions, and drawdowns. If a trader is struggling, the manager will team her up with a senior trader who maybe used to have the same problem or put some controls on her account until she learns how to be more consistent. We know that nobody likes Big Brother, but sometimes Big Brother is exactly what we need. Every trader needs to have someone to be accountable to and someone to knock him over the head when he is being stubborn.

We highly recommend that every trader find a firm or a trading group to join so that she has someone to be accountable with. The Internet has made it easy to reach out and find groups. Reach out and help yourself. The greatest thing about this is that you will end up helping someone else, too. When we bring traders into Maverick Trading, we let them know up front that we expect them to help other traders' profitability and to do what they can to help promote the prosperity of the entire firm. We have some people who are natural teachers who step in and teach trading courses, and some of our traders are great programmers who write trading programs for the firm. Being part of a group can be a great way to get the accountability we all need and give you a chance to help out your fellow traders.

But in the end, this method is work, and there is no quick fix. You may have to try several different systems before you come up with one that eliminates the opportunity for your weaknesses to show themselves. But the rewards are worth the work.

This method causes less stress than trading against your personality. The stress caused by trading against your personality will cause just as many trading problems as your natural weaknesses and will have the added effect of influencing your health and happiness.

CHAPTER

YOU VERSUS THE WORLD

We mentioned in the introduction that trading as a profession can be a rewarding and a personally and financially liberating endeavor. It can.

It can also contain a wide variety of maddening events. Each of us has had perfect setups trigger and then either immediately move against us for a loss or languish, doing absolutely nothing and just tying up capital. Each of us has sat in front of our computer and asked, "Why is this happening?" Our computers have never answered us.

Sometimes it feels as if the world is arrayed against you and everyone is conspiring to ruin your personal trades. You start checking your house for bugs and other surveillance gear, convinced that the black helicopters are getting ready to descend on your home. Hey, even paranoids have enemies.

Fortunately, few of us have enough capital in the market to warrant these delusions. Hedge funds will routinely attack another troubled fund. They are in tune with the workings of other funds and know when one is in trouble; they can smell the blood in the water. If you get hurt in the market, it's just considered collateral damage. None of the big players, the institutions, will celebrate either your success or your demise. The only people who will be engaging in some private schadenfreude are the mutual fund managers, who will smile wryly, shake their heads in a knowing way of false commiseration, and subtly say, "I told you so. Now, why don't you let us invest for you?"

If we haven't scared you off yet and you still want to become a professional trader, you have some decisions to make with regard to how you will execute your plan.

ARE YOU SUPERMAN? GOING SOLO

The financial industry attracts some flamboyant personalities. There is a core of rugged individualism in every trader—a need to stand up and be counted, take your rightful place in the world, and climb that mountain until you successfully emerge above the morass of mere mortals.

There is personal satisfaction when your portfolio has made a gain on a down day in the market or when a 2 percent move up in the market nets you a 4 percent gain. The endorphins are flowing freely. You feel unstoppable.

And then there can be moments of utter despair and feelings of ruin. This is especially true when you're first starting out.

The pressure to perform puts stress on you and stress on your family. This is magnified when you've had a bad day or a bad week.

If you want to trade as a profession, you are eventually going to have to make a choice: go it alone, or trade with some support.

If you are wearing pajamas and a cape under your street clothes and you fight crime in your off-hours, by all means, go it alone. Either you are a superhero and can handle all the decisions that need to be made with no outside assistance, or you're too weird for anyone to want to trade with anyway.

There are thousands of traders who make a good living trading alone, but they are fewer than you would imagine. With no one to provide a critiquing counterpoint, they have to gauge the market direction; conduct analysis of each sector; identify outperforming and underperforming stocks; set entry points, stop losses, and price targets; choose strategies; manage risk; execute the trade; book profits; and do it all again the next day.

Self-doubt and overconfidence burden these people continually. Their institutional experience is nonexistent beyond what they remember and put in their trading journals.

The trader who is trying to become a superhero often insulates himself and actually avoids critiques from dispassionate observers. With no one to provide a counterpoint to an investment thesis, such a trader often loses objectivity and looks for any scrap of data, no matter how insignificant or esoteric, to support his thesis.

Any questions from friends and family about how his trading is going are seen as an attack on or inquisition regarding his moral worth. This is reflected in his moods and emotions. If he is up in the market, then he views himself as a person of moral and societal value, sometimes to the point of being insufferable. If he is down in the market, he views himself as having no worth and being a drag on his family, his friends, and society as a whole.

These traders are shouldering the benefits of success and the burdens of failure completely on their own.

Now, none of us are psychologists; we aren't licensed to ask, "And how does that make you feel?" But even a layman knows that wild mood swings are not a healthy sign. You'll see it, too.

Mothers caution children, "Don't ask Daddy about the market today."

or

"Hey, Bob, where'd your iPhone go?"

"Oh, yeah . . . that. Peggy was long Apple, and it dropped 10 points. End of iPhone."

Robb: I remember that in my first year of trading, my mood was tremendously tied to my account balance. When I came home on a Friday after a great week of trading, I would say crazy things to my wife like, "Let's go shopping!" Of course, she thought this was great until the next weekend, when she was ready to go shopping again and I told her that we had to stay home eating ramen noodles and putting things up for sale on eBay. I felt either rich or poor based on my trading results. Over time, I began to see that everything evened out over weeks and months of time, and that even if I had a great week, I could still have a subpar month. And even if I started with some losses early in the month, it could easily turn into my best month ever. My emotions were no longer tied to my account value at the moment, and trading as a long-term profession became much easier. I also stopped saying crazy stuff like, "Let's go shopping!"

For traders who go the superhero route and succeed, the benefits in personal gratification are immense. They have soloed a treacherous mountain that has been climbed by very few. They are, and should be, justifiably proud. But their success often comes at a high cost in time, family, and social relationships.

The question then becomes how to achieve success on your own while maintaining your sanity and your relationships.

EVEN PROFESSIONALS HAVE COACHES

One way to maintain your sanity and still achieve success as a trader is to get a trading coach.

Now, you shouldn't read this book, open a trading account, and immediately get a trading coach. You'll do nothing but put money in the coach's pocket that would be better served going back into your trading account.

The reason is that you probably haven't developed enough of a record to determine what your good habits are, what your bad habits are, where your trading strengths are, and where your trading weaknesses are. A trading coach is going to be helpful only when you've achieved a certain level of success, but your performance has reached a plateau.

Jon: Whenever I ask people about golf and they tell me that they would like to be a better player, I ask them who they think the best coach would be. Without thinking, they always say Tiger Woods. I quickly tell them that while Tiger is surely a great player, he might not be the best coach. Once they think about it, they always come to the realization that they want the person who coaches the best player in the world.

When you are at a point where you feel that a trading coach would be beneficial, there are several things that you need to keep in mind.

Coaches are often married to particular trading systems. Getting a coach who is not a trader or who is not trading with the same trading system that you are using is counterproductive. You'll immediately be at odds with the coach, and you would achieve better results by flushing $100 bills down the toilet. At least when you flush the money, you'll have some idea where it went.

We can't stress enough that your coach should be intimately familiar with what you are doing. If you're a trader and your coach is geared more toward medium- to long-term investments, you'll butt heads from day one. Your coach won't necessarily care, as he's still getting paid, but you'll be trying to apply his advice to a style of trading that it's not suited for.

Likewise, if your coach made his bones as a day trader and you're a position and swing trader, you'll find yourself trying to apply advice that's counter to your style. You'll lose money that way, too.

If you've got your trading style and system identified, make sure that your coach has achieved some success with those criteria. We're talking real success over a period of years. Too many times, we've seen one-shot wonders put themselves forward as coaches, then promptly start giving bad advice.

If the coach is with a firm, you're a little safer than if she's established herself on her own, in that the firm should have, and probably has, conducted due diligence on her track record before bringing her on board. However, there are many coaches who have established themselves independently and have excellent track records, not only personally, but with the people they have coached.

If the coach is independent, ask to see the most recent three-year track record of his personal trading. Compare it to market performance. When someone is putting himself out in the marketplace as an expert, you should see significant outperformance compared to the market. Get net performance, after deducting commissions and costs, as well.

With independent coaches, ask for at least two references that you can call and speak with. This may be an issue for new coaches, but there are plenty of people out there who won't bother to conduct the necessary due diligence prior to hiring a coach. Let them be the guinea pigs, and possibly take another look at the coach once he's established a record of success with his students.

When you've found a few coaches that you think you might be interested in, you need to have some idea exactly what it is you want to accomplish with a coach. You could very well contact a coach and say, "I want you to help me trade better."

That coach's eyes will roll back with dollar signs. That's the easiest money she can make. To her, it's a quick conversation, maybe watching you trade for a little bit, making some very simple suggestions, and then sending you the bill.

This is part of the reason we recommend that people have been trading for a while and have achieved a modicum of success before they think about engaging a coach. By this point, you will have become proficient in whatever system you are using, and to some extent, you can self-diagnose some aspects of your trading that are holding you back.

Some examples would be: "Lately, more than half my trades are getting stopped out for small losses. Am I putting my stops too close to my entry points, or am I misreading the setups?" Or, "I've noticed in my vertical spreads that after the stock hits my target and I exit the position, the stock continues on well past my target. Are these flukes, or do I need to adjust the way I am calculating my price targets?"

We hope you realize the difference between, "I want you to help me trade better," and the two examples we used. The first statement is amorphous; the second two ask for specific help on discrete aspects of a trader's technique. The more specific you can be concerning the traits that you want your coach to help you with, the easier it will be for your coach to help you, and the more impact his help will have.

In addition, when you give your coach a baseline for what you want help with, the coach can begin looking at the perceived problem from your point of view. This may actually show the coach that the problem is not what you thought it was, but something else that you hadn't thought of.

Finally, when choosing a coach, keep in mind that you get what you pay for. This is a reinforcing reason to wait until you've achieved some success before you decide to get a coach. When you first start trading as a professional, you may feel that you need a coach, but you may also feel that you can't afford one who meets all your criteria.

The bad advice that you'll get from an untested, unqualified coach who is charging you only $20 an hour, which you thought you could afford, may actually be detrimental to your portfolio and your long-term success as a trader. Conversely, waiting until you can afford the $100 an hour coach with a proven track record and list of successful traders may allow you to identify and resolve problems much faster, speeding your journey to success.

Jon: The true sign of a professional is not only that she has made some money in the markets, but also that she is humble enough to recognize the fact that no individual is so smart or so determined that the market won't beat her up from time to time. The market will chew up and spit out know-it-alls and dice rollers. Having a good coach who can keep you in tune with the markets and assist you in crossing the t's and dotting the i's of your trading is imperative.

The idea of mentors is a time-tested and proven method of achieving proficiency and even excellence. Your single set of eyeballs on the market can't compete with someone who has access to shared ideas, confirmation, and careful scrutiny of his methods.

At Maverick, in our daily operations, our community of traders allows for this paramount advantage over the individual retail trader. In addition to our community of traders, each trader has access to one-on-one coaching with one of the firm's most successful and experienced traders. In these sessions, the trader and the coach can work together on weaknesses, specific trades, or clarification of ideas.

PROPRIETARY TRADING FIRMS: THE GOOD, THE BAD, AND THE UGLY

Time for another period of full disclosure: Maverick Trading makes the vast majority of its revenue as a proprietary trading firm. Yes, we have a vested interest in a minuscule percentage of the people who read this book coming to our firm to trade with us. That being said, you can view this next section as either a bit of blatant self-promotion or a genuine description of the different practices that we've seen in the industry.

So, when you read this section, take everything we say with a grain of salt. If, after reading it, you see the benefits of trading with a reputable firm, all we ask is that you conduct your due diligence. We expect it from all the traders who express an interest in joining Maverick, and frankly, we are a little leery of traders who don't conduct due diligence on us.

First of all, what is a proprietary trading firm? Most retail traders have never even heard the term, nor do they realize that such firms exist.

What is proprietary trading? It is trading done by a firm for its own accounts. In this type of trading, the firm is interested solely in the gains it can achieve in the market rather than in the commissions that its traders generate.

A proprietary trading firm, or prop trading firm, is a firm that is designed to enable traders to join it, get advice from it, greatly increase their available trading leverage, receive training, develop themselves as traders, and be more successful trading in a group than they would be on their own. In return for providing these services, prop firms receive a percentage of traders' booked gains. The theory is that even after the profit split, the trader is still more successful (profitable) with the firm than he would be on his own.

To begin to recognize the different types of prop firms that are available, it's important to understand that firms are usually centered around a particular trading style. The vast majority of prop firms are geared toward day trading, for reasons that we'll see shortly. A far smaller percentage are geared toward swing and position trading, as Maverick is.

Very few prop firms, if any, are geared toward medium-term to long-term investing. The reason is that the capital turnover in this style of investing is so slow that it takes a substantial base of assets in order to turn a respectable profit. Additionally, with this type of investing, the firm begins incurring costs for bottom-up research, further biting into its profits.

When you are researching prop firms, you have to narrow down the list to firms that resonate with your style of trading. If you are a position or swing trader by inclination, affiliating with a prop firm that is focused on day trading will be a money-losing endeavor. You'll be trading against type.

If you are a day trader, (1) we applaud you for getting this far in a book that really has no bearing on the way you trade, (2) your choice of prop firms focused on day trading is much more extensive, and (3) trading with a firm that focuses on position and swing trading would probably be a money-losing endeavor for you. You need to pick a firm whose trading style resonates with your personality, risk tolerance, and psychological makeup.

After you have found out the trading style of a prop firm, you're pretty much headed directly into conducting due diligence. There are many factors that need to be addressed when you're choosing a prop firm to affiliate with. We'll try to hit the high points, but you're dealing with your money and your financial future. You should exercise skepticism until you've gotten a good feel for the firm and the people associated with it.

One of the first things that will come up is whether the firm offers training or just offers a venue where traders can trade with the greater leverage offered through an institutional-grade account.

If the firm doesn't offer training, this should be a flashing yellow light on your list of topics. In general, it means that the firm isn't particularly concerned about whether or not its traders are successful. Its revenue model is geared toward making money from its traders in other ways than through profit splits.

If the firm does offer training, you need to look a little more closely. Is the training based on a proprietary program in which the firm has invested time and capital to ensure that the program works, or is it an off-the-shelf, buy-low, sell-high system that your five-year-old could come up with? No one firm has a lock on good ideas, but some firms are more equal than others when it comes to trading philosophies.

When evaluating the training and the system together, ask for the last three years' returns. It's doubtful that you'll get the firm's trading financials, but you should at least be able to get year-end portfolio return statements. If the system works as advertised, the firm's management will be happy to show these returns to people who are serious about trading with the firm. Just don't ask for them if you're still tire-kicking firms. This type of information should be requested only right before you pull the trigger to sign up with the firm.

If the firm has a proprietary system that has performed well and offers training, how is the training conducted? Don't be put off by remote training, as long as the classes are conducted live and have actual instructors who are traders with the firm. When are the classes given? If you're intending to make the transition to trading part-time at first, keeping your day job, you'll want to ensure that the classes are recorded and are accessible when you have time to view them. In addition, make sure that you can e-mail the instructors if you have questions pertaining to the class.

How long does the training last? Some firms will have a prescribed 30-day training period, and then you're live. There's the deep end of the pool . . . now jump. If you're not able to take the classes at your own pace and fully understand what's going on, from our point of view, it looks as if the firm is trying to get you trading as soon as possible rather than working with you to make you the best trader possible before you begin risking your capital and the firm's.

At Maverick, the minimum time period to complete the firm's training program is two months. We simply won't let people trade live with the firm before that. There's too much information to understand, and we often have to break traders of bad habits that they've developed on their own or with other firms. Likewise, we don't mind if a trader takes six months to complete her training. We know that this particular trader is taking things very seriously and learning our methodology in great detail. Our goal is not to get someone trading quickly; our goal is to make her the best professional trader possible so that she can succeed over the long run.

Don't be put off if most of the firm's traders trade remotely. Technology solutions have reached the point where remote affiliation not only saves the firm operating capital, but offers the trader a more comfortable trading environment. Firms that require relocation to a specific site generally do so for one or more of three reasons: (1) they haven't joined the twenty-first century yet, (2) they are looking for an excuse to charge their traders a "desk fee," or (3) they want direct supervision of their traders to ensure that they are trading only those stocks where they get a rebate on commissions.

Look specifically for access to the firm's instructors during your training period. There's a pretty wide line between allowing you to ask questions to ensure that you understand the material in the training program and individual coaching. Some firms treat access outside of classes as personal coaching and require that you buy a coaching package.

Are there fees for training programs? We'll be honest; we get some pushback from traders seeking to join the firm who balk at a training fee. That's fine. Skepticism is good. The reason we charge a fee for our training program is that it's taken us more than 14 years to develop, test, and refine it. We value our time, we value the time of each of our instructors (who are also traders with the firm), and we expect traders who want to join the firm to value their time as well. We suppose you could say that it's a philosophical issue: if you've ponied up good money for a program that has proved to be successful over an extended period of time, we know that we have your undivided attention when it comes to learning the material.

We can guarantee that each of us, individually, has incurred losses greater than what the firm charges for the training program. Looking back, if someone had offered each of us the same training program and showed us how we would have more than recouped our initial investment in terms of bad trades not taken, we would have jumped at the opportunity. This doesn't even take into account the gains that we would have made if we had started our careers with Maverick's system.

Based on what we've each seen in the industry, it is not a matter of whether a firm charges for instruction in its trading methodologies, but of what you're getting in return. If you get a load of materials dumped in your lap and some nameless person at the firm tells you to go forth and study on your own, that would be a cause for concern.

You also have to inquire as to who the instructors are. Are they members of the firm who also trade on a daily basis (good); are they people who are employed by the firm solely to instruct, but who do not trade (questionable); or, does the firm outsource its instruction to a third-party firm whose sole job is product fulfillment (not good)?

If a firm is serious about its training program, it will have two additional aspects besides classes. There will be an objective testing system that relates directly to the material covered, and there will also be a subjective portion based on returns from paper trading.

The testing portion of the training program shows that the firm wants to be sure that you understand the quantifiable basics of its system. This helps the instructors to identify concepts that a new trader is having problems grasping and allows them to answer specific questions and provide additional instruction to help the student understand key concepts. If the firm doesn't care about the long-term success of its traders, it will let its new traders jump into the markets with just a patina of training.

The subjective portion of a good training program, the requirement for paper trading, further shows that the firm is interested in its new traders being successful when they step out of the gate and into live trading. Reputable firms fully expect that their new traders, while going through training, will make mistakes. Paper trading lets the traders make these mistakes without losing precious capital. It also has the added benefit of identifying some bad habits that the trader may have picked up previously.

The next factor that you'll want to look at when you're evaluating a prop firm is fees. The mere existence of fees shouldn't raise a red flag, but you need to understand what the fees are and whether they're being charged to defray the cost to the firm or marked up as a revenue-generating aspect of the firm's business model. At Maverick, the firm does not mark up the fees its traders pay for data feeds and commissions, nor does it receive rebates on these fees. The firm has used its size to negotiate the lowest commissions and fees possible and passes these directly to its traders.

You should become wary if data feed charges or commissions are marked up, or if the firm receives rebates on either charge. The best way to find out whether the firm is marking up its data feed charges or commissions is to ask for a list of fees and then ask the firm directly whether the listed charges are what the firm pays and whether they've been marked up. The answer should be a clear and concise no.

Commission rebates to the firm are a little harder to determine, as their existence is usually considered closely held information by firm management. Here's a little secret: if the firm is a registered broker-dealer, chances are that it is getting commission rebates from the exchanges. Ask someone in management whether the commission rebates are passed on to the traders at the end of the month or whether the firm is pocketing the rebates.

Commission markups and rebates from exchanges are two reasons why some prop firms, especially those that are centered on day trading, force their traders to trade only from a list of "approved" stocks and mandate that their traders have a minimum daily churn, or number of shares traded. In such cases, whether the trader is profitable or not, the firm is making money on her each and every day. We consider this to be unsavory at best and a clear conflict of interests between the firm and the trader, regardless of the trader's profitability.

This leads us directly to licensing requirements. Those prop firms that are FINRA-registered broker-dealers use this registration as a marketing tool: "Hey, look at us. We're registered. We're professional. Doesn't that make you feel good?"

While some of these firms have side businesses as securities dealers to the public, and therefore need to be registered with FINRA, FINRA registration of a prop firm is wholly unnecessary and serves two separate purposes, neither of which is to the benefit of the prop trader.

The first benefit is the ability to receive commission rebates from the exchanges, which we've already covered.

The second benefit to the firm is that this allows the firm to require its traders to take the Series 7 and Series 63/65 tests and receive their licenses. The purpose of this generally isn't to allow the trader to sell securities to the public; instead, it is a safety measure for the firm that takes the place of competent training and mentorship.

If the firm has required its traders to get the Series 7 and Series 63/65 licenses, the traders are now considered to be "professionals" and basically have no recourse to the firm if they implode their accounts.

Many of the topics we've looked at in this chapter deal with hurdles that the trader faces mostly prior to live trading. To get a feel for the success of the firm once the traders are trading real capital, take a look at the turnover rate. How long do most traders last at the firm? How many move on within a year? How many are still there after three years?

We really can't give you metrics on what a high turnover rate is among prop firms. Maverick's turnover rate runs about 2 percent annually; when traders join the firm, they stay for the long run (and profits). However, you're probably looking at a decent prop firm if the one-year retention rate is north of 90 percent and the three-year retention rate is north of 80 percent.

Once you get down to the final stages before joining a firm, a good firm should be able to provide you with a few references from people who have been trading at the firm. A good mix would be someone in the firm's training program (if it has one), someone who's been at the firm and trading live for six months to a year, and someone who's been at the firm for one to two years or more. These references will probably all have glowing things to say about the firm (firms aren't usually so stupid as to give you a reference that will slag them), but at least it has some traders who are appreciative enough of the firm to give it a seal of approval.

Regardless of what prop firms you are evaluating, you should always expect a requirement that you post some risk capital. The minimum amount of risk capital that you should expect to have to post with the firm is $5,000. You should expect greater leverage with a prop firm than you could get with a retail margin account; you're leveraging the firm's capital and institutional account to your personal account. At Maverick, we start new traders off with 5 times leverage, which we may increase as the traders demonstrate mastery of risk mitigation and Maverick's investment system.

With greater leverage comes potentially increased risk. If the firm is committed to the long-term success of its traders, it will have automatically enforced loss limits. If you lose too much in a single trade, the firm will liquidate the trade. A firm that views its traders as a perishable commodity will let them continue to trade until they've burned through their risk capital, then shut them off.

Finally, we need to address profit splits and how they are paid to the traders. Only you can put a value on trading in a firm with an established system and a track record of outperformance. The simple method of finding out whether the firm is worth trading with is to take its gross returns and multiply them by the percentage of the profit split that you would get. Whatever that number is should be several points in excess of both market returns and what your past performance has been. If it's not, find another firm.

The majority of prop firms have profit splits in which between 25 and 50 percent of profits go to the firm. At Maverick, our beginning traders receive 70 percent of profits, and as they progress, their profit split increases to 75 percent and finally to 80 percent.

Please, please check to see how the profit split is paid out. If you encounter the term *vesting* or *bank*, run, do not walk, away from the firm. Set your Internet firewall to forbid access to the firm's site, and have your e-mail auto-delete messages from the firm. Shred hard copies of any information you have, and don't look back. Finally, wash your hands.

What these firms are doing is locking up the profits that you generated. We have seen profit vesting occur after periods ranging from six months to a graduated vesting scheme with full vesting coming after three years. Regardless, if you can't get to the profits you generated as soon as is reasonably possible, it should be a very red flag.

Not only are the firms getting the benefit of the float on the funds, but when you get fed up with the system and quit, the firm keeps all the gains that you have made, but that haven't yet vested to you. We've discussed this practice among ourselves, and the most polite and printable word that we've come up with to describe the scheme is "unsavory."

The sad thing is that this is all done legally and is spelled out in the affiliation agreements between these firms and their traders. It can put the traders at these firms in a real bind. They start trading and have to live off their savings until they become vested in the gains that they've made, and then they end up being chained to the firm that is bleeding them dry because they don't want to forgo the gains that they've made. It's self-imposed indentured servitude.

At Maverick, after options Expiration Friday, traders who want access to their profits, or a portion of their profits, for the month contact management. We cut checks for the specified amounts or make the transfers by wire by the fifth of the next month. There's no discussion; we don't ask why you want the money—it's none of our business. We just cut the check. The money's in your subaccount; you've generated the gains; there's no reason for you not to have access to it when you need or want it.

Most traders roll their gains so that they have more capital to trade the next month and then take a partial distribution on a quarterly basis. This both provides them with an income and allows them to steadily grow their portfolios.

Maverick takes aligning its interests with its traders a step further. Each trader is a member of the LLC that is managing the firm. At the end of the year, a portion of the firm's profits is distributed proportionally to Maverick's member traders. The traders benefit from both their personal success and the success of the firm as a whole. If there's a better compensation structure out there, we haven't found it.

One aspect of Maverick that might seem odd to you at first is that we don't allow our traders to hold their subaccounts in their own names as sole proprietorships. We require our traders to trade through an LLC or a corporation. For most of our traders, this is the first time that they've had to create a separate business entity. Twice a year, the firm hosts a special presentation on trading as a corporation and invites Maverick's accounting firm to present the benefits to new traders in Maverick's training program.

We're not accountants, so we're not going to go into detail about the benefits. It should suffice to say that Maverick has had no pushback from its traders about this requirement, and that several of the more experienced traders asked why the firm hadn't mandated this practice earlier. We'll have to limit our commentary on this practice to stating that the benefits to both Maverick's traders and the firm as a whole are recognizable and substantial.

To sum up what to look for in a prop firm, it really comes down to determining whether there is an alignment of interests between the traders and the firm. You need to assemble the information and determine whether the firm and you have the same goal: to make profitable trades. Is the firm succeeding only when you succeed, and therefore viewing you as a long-term investment, or is the firm bleeding you dry at every turn and turning a profit whether you are successful or not, and therefore viewing you as a perishable commodity?

At Maverick, we view our traders as our greatest asset. We invest considerable time and resources into each trader prior to his trading live. Yes, we're in business to make money, and we would like to see a return on that investment, but we've determined that the best way to do that is to prepare our traders to the greatest extent possible so that they are profitable in their accounts as soon as possible. We're looking for a long-term relationship with each of our traders, and the best way to do that is to make sure that our traders are profitable.

CHAPTER

THE END OF THE BEGINNING

First of all, take a minute to pat yourself on the back. In a world in which people get most of their information 140 characters at a time, you've managed to make it through a nearly 300-page book.

Congratulate yourself again, because you've also put yourself in the top quartile of retail investors and traders: you've actually invested time in learning about the markets and finding a system that you can use to make money.

We would like to tell you that after reading this book, you know everything you need to know in order to retire next quarter. We'd like to tell you that, but we can't. And please don't try; you'll just hurt your mouse finger and your portfolio.

Maverick's in-house training program for its new traders distills 14 years of research, trial, and error into almost 50 hours of core instruction, with another 100 hours of classes on specific topics or live market trading that takes at least two months to complete. We've taken that training program and distilled it even further to produce this book. We're happy with what we've been able to share with you, but we didn't have the space to put in everything we wanted. We would have ended up with a tome rivaling *War and Peace*, and books that size rarely get read and usually end up as doorstops.

What you have read is a basic primer on the system that Maverick and its traders use to consistently produce gains in excess of market returns. If you follow this system and use it correctly, with proper risk management, you should be able to see recognizable gains in your portfolio.

Maverick's system is not a get-rich-quick scheme. If that's what you're looking for, you'd be better off answering that e-mail in your junk folder from the nice young man in Nigeria.

Maverick's system describes a long-term methodology for creating generational wealth. We wholeheartedly encourage you to read the lessons and techniques in this book and apply them to your own trading accounts, your retirement accounts, and your children's educational funds. More important, pass these lessons on to your children and your nieces and nephews. The sooner they learn, the more they can earn. We were serious when we said in the introduction that a fifth-grader would probably be able to take this system and run with it.

Right now, you're in a position that is potentially dangerous: you know and understand a little information. Granted, it's more information than three-quarters of retail traders bother to learn, but it is just a beginning.

There are a few things that we've noticed about our traders as we've watched them progress through Maverick's training program and then move on in their progression as professional traders.

Despite all the focused instruction that we provide, it takes new traders about six months of live trading with real capital before they can say with confidence that they fully understand the ins and outs of Maverick's system. During the training period, our traders fully embrace the basics of the system. It's proven itself to be profitable, it resonates with the traders on a primal level, and the support structure provided by the firm's mentors and the weekly Trading Room allows traders to explore the bounds of their understanding in an encouraging environment.

After six months of trading with the firm, a new trader's performance continues to improve, but at a slower pace. The period between six months and three years of trading is very much like an apprenticeship. Gradually the trader learns what tangential information he needs to seek and incorporate into his market outlook. Personal experience begins to meld with the institutional memory provided by the firm and the other traders. Then, one day, he finds that he is subconsciously making decisions and evaluating the market, sectors, and individual stocks much faster and more accurately than he did at the beginning.

Add this to the growth in his portfolio, and this is usually the point where the trader can give up his other job and fully enjoy the benefits and freedom of being a full-time professional trader.

WHAT NOW? NEXT STEPS AS A PROFESSIONAL

By this point, you should have the blueprints to build your own house of wealth through becoming a professional trader. As with construction in the real world, the next step is to lay in the utilities and build the foundation. Plumbing for utilities is relatively easy; find a good broker or firm that supports what you want to do. This will give you access (water, gas, and electricity).

The foundation will take some more time and care. You want it strong and deep. It is what the rest of the house is anchored to, and it needs to be able to withstand the occasional earthquake and mudslide that will hit you over the course of your career as a trader. Be methodical and dig deep. Make sure you understand the concepts we've explained in this book. Make sure that the concrete is well mixed—that you understand how each concept is related to the others and what the impact of one step is on the next.

Even if you don't feel confident about beginning trading right away, start analyzing the markets on a daily basis. Use the

Top-Down Approach to identify trends in the broad markets. Is the market bullish, bearish, stagnant, or reversing?

Conduct your sector analysis. Which sectors have shown strength, and which have shown weakness? Compare time frames: daily, weekly, monthly, and for the past two months. This will tell you where the money is flowing in a particular market. Are the institutions seeking returns through emerging growth stocks, or are they hunkering down and putting money into historical safe havens like consumer staples? Identify the top two and bottom two sectors and see what's been happening in each of them.

Start identifying chart setups for stocks in the sectors that you've researched. Which stocks are forming identifiable chart patterns? Which ones are trending? Which ones are overextended? All this will come to you with practice.

Once you've developed some faith in your own abilities, take a shot at paper trading. Start applying your SET procedures: where is the entry or trigger for a trade, where will you put your stop, and what is your target price? Keep a trading journal and track both your batting average (win-loss ratio) and your reward-risk ratio.

Start to experiment with the different strategies we've shown. If you're paper trading, there's nothing wrong with trying two different strategies on the same setup. One strategy may have a higher percentage chance of being successful, while another strategy may have a higher reward-risk ratio. Feel out where you have the most comfort in balancing your win-loss ratio with your reward-risk ratio.

The best way to become proficient and profitable is to practice every day. You don't need to spend eight hours a day conducting research and analysis, but investing an hour or two each day will keep your hand in the market and build your faith in the system and your confidence in your own abilities.

When you do start trading with live capital, start small. It's much easier to ramp up your risk once you've confirmed that you're tuned in with what you're doing than it is to humbly dial your risk back down because you were guilty of ready, fire, aim.

Be sure to track your progress, your win-loss ratio, and your reward-risk ratio. There's no way to know whether you're improving or by how much if you don't keep records. Having identifiable metrics for your performance will show you where you have room for improvement.

Get to know yourself, your strengths, and your weaknesses. You will naturally play to your strengths. Look for ways to avoid your weaknesses. Don't try to trade against type; you'll just cause yourself stress and losses.

Once you've achieved some success, associate with others who share your trading style. Consider engaging a coach. Just pick a good one.

You've taken the first step toward becoming a professional trader. The only thing left to do is to keep putting one foot in front of the other.

HONING THE EDGE: PROFESSIONAL DEVELOPMENT

At the risk of sounding trite, never stop learning. Just the act of seeking knowledge keeps you sharp and helps to prevent you from falling into the rut of comfortable habit.

We had many spirited debates among ourselves regarding the scope of this book: what should we put in, and what should we leave out? In the end, we came to agree that the techniques we included in this book would set up new traders with the tools they would need to achieve success in a variety of market conditions.

The strategies that we've covered are by no means completely comprehensive. There is a world of other techniques available to traders. In our discussions, we further agreed that these techniques would be best covered in structured training, as we do with new traders at Maverick, or in a different work. Their use is more specialized and requires more detailed instruction regarding their applicability and implementation.

Once you understand the situations and techniques that we've described and are able to capitalize on them, you should increase your breadth and depth of knowledge by starting to seek out some of these other techniques and learning how to use them.

As time and experience has developed each of us as traders, we have found that we have become more discerning, critical, and selective as to what information we pay attention to, whose opinions we value, and what other systems we put credence in. We're extremely pleased with Maverick's system, but we're not so conceited as to think that we have a monopoly on good ideas.

This is not to say that the world is full of good ideas and you should grab hold of every one that comes down the pike. There's an attitude that's become a running joke during the firm's weekly Trading Room when we discuss what some of the talking heads that appear on the major financial networks say during their 60-second sound bites. You can't go a day watching these networks without hearing someone say with the utmost gravitas that he is "long-term bullish, but short-term cautious." That's just another way of saying, "Please don't redeem your funds if we lose money for you in the next year. We'll make it up over the next 10 years. We promise."

As you develop and grow as a trader, your immediate reaction upon hearing anyone's opinion will be skepticism. By comparing the statements and outlooks of the people identified as experts with the actual performance of the market, you'll soon be able to determine which experts are really in touch with the market and which are, frankly, oxygen thieves.

Occasionally, you will come across a piece of information, a view of the market, or an interview that your now-skeptical mind wants to dismiss out of hand, but something will stop you and make you start thinking. Keep thinking. This alone will separate you from the sea of fools who glom on to every piece of advice they are spoon-fed.

As you master trading, your research and your interest in the market will begin to influence your worldview. You'll begin to see the markets not as discrete nuclei in which certain instruments are traded, but as part of an interconnected web, where a tug on one strand of the web can have far-reaching effects, across markets, asset classes, and economies.

Some readers are currently thinking, "Well, of course the markets are interconnected. That's a given." This concept is easy to parrot at face value, but until you find yourself constantly adjusting your longer-term views of the market, synthesizing information in a conscious and then a subconscious manner, you don't gain the full effect of this understanding.

Current political administrations notwithstanding, the interconnected nature of the markets cannot be studied exclusively in theory. The best way to understand these relationships is to actually be trading the markets. Once you've achieved some success and have seen your performance plateau, start following other markets: foreign exchange, futures and commodities, and possibly even fixed income. We're not necessarily recommending that you actively trade these markets, but knowing the trends in each of them and the activity of the more influential instruments will help to inform your worldview and your longer-term view of the market.

Price and volume will always influence the short- and medium-term market, but having a long-term view of the market will help to keep you from becoming overextended at market tops and bottoms.

We hope you've enjoyed reading this book as much as we enjoyed writing it. Our intent in writing this book was to give retail traders the opportunity to understand the market from the point of view of the major players, the institutions, and to show these traders ways in which they can profit from identifiable patterns in the market, and do so safely with clearly identified and manageable risk parameters.

Each of us hopes that you will take this information and trade the market within the guidelines that we've given so that you can enjoy the profits from your work. Becoming a professional trader is a serious undertaking, requiring commitment and an investment of time on your part, but the rewards of success are well worth the effort.

Properly applied, Maverick's system can assist you in creating generational wealth. To that end, if you have children, grandchildren, nieces, or nephews, we encourage you to let them read this book. Break the cycle of ignorance perpetuated by the government and the financial industry. Remove the mystique of the markets. Free your children from the drudgery of being wage slaves whose financial success is predicated on the whims of others. Don't sentence them to a lifetime of being cubicle prisoners.

Most people work very hard, and we respect that. We also know that many people work too hard and at occupations and in conditions that they don't like. Our outlook, and one of the goals with this book, is to allow people to work at something they love and to have the freedom to enjoy life and the benefits of financial freedom.

Achieving success as a professional trader is not a short journey. For those who are able to achieve success, the freedom, security, and personal fulfillment are well worth the investment in time and effort.

Good luck!

INDEX

Note: page numbers followed by f indicate figures

typical trade distribution, gains
  and losses, 11, 11f
what can you control?, 7–8
worry and position size, 15

S

Scholes, Myron, 124
Screening criteria:
  bearish patterns, 94, 98,
    101, 105
  bullish patterns, 83, 85, 89, 90
Sectors:
  identifying strengths and
    weaknesses, 31–34, 32f
  market direction escalators,
    22f–27f, 23–27
Sensing and decision making,
  234, 238
Series 7 exam, 263
Series 63/65 exam, 263
SET:
  bullish techniques, 147, 176,
    177, 178
  stagnation techniques, 185
  volatility techniques, 194, 195,
    196
Setups (See Trade setups)
Shooting star pattern, 58–59, 59f
Short positions:
  bearish patterns, 96–97
  bullish patterns, 84, 87, 88
  market direction, 17–18
  short call, 114, 182–183
  short stock, 172–175, 173f
Shortable position selection,
  35–36
Sideways chart patterns, 106–108
Simple Moving Average (SMA):
  bearish patterns, 95, 99, 101, 102,
    105, 107
  bullish patterns, 78, 79, 83,
    87, 91

candlestick patterns, 68, 78, 79,
  83, 87, 91, 95, 99, 101, 102,
  105, 107
candlesticks, 67–70, 70f, 79, 83,
  87, 91, 95, 99
  protective stops, 142
  use of, 40
Sketch it out, live trading,
  225–226
Skills, live trading, 222–223
SMA (See Simple Moving Average)
Solo practice of professional
  trading, 250–252
Speculation, 116, 118
Spreads:
  bear put spread, 177–179, 179f
  bull call spread, 152–155, 155f
  diagonal call calendar spread,
    155–159, 157f
  diagonal put calendar spread,
    179–182, 181f
  horizontal calendar spread,
    184–188, 186f, 187f
  vertical spreads, 152–155, 158,
    177, 178
Spreadsheet tracking results, paper
  trading, 215–217
SPY ETF, 150–151
Stagnation chart patterns,
  106–108
Stagnation techniques:
  butterflies, 188–191, 191f
  call butterfly, 189, 190–191,
    191f
  call condor, 190
  condors, 188–193, 191f, 192f,
    193f
  horizontal calendar spread,
    184–188, 186f, 187f
  iron condor, 188–193, 193f
  put butterfly, 190, 193
  put condor, 189, 190, 191–192,
    192f